Mexican
Postcards

V

Critical Studies in Latin American and Iberian Cultures

SERIES EDITORS:
James Dunkerley
John King

This major series – the first of its kind to appear in English – is designed to map the field of contemporary Latin American culture, which has enjoyed increasing popularity in Britain and the United States in recent years.

The series aims to broaden the scope of criticism of Latin American culture, which tends still to extol the virtues of a few established 'master' works and to examine cultural production within the context of twentieth-century history. These clear, accessible studies are aimed at those who wish to know more about some of the most important and influential cultural works and movements of our time.

Mexican Postcards

CARLOS MONSIVÁIS

Edited, translated and introduced by

JOHN KRANIAUSKAS

VERSO

London • New York

First published by Verso 1997
Reprinted 2000

© Carlos Monsiváis 1997
Translation and Introduction © John Kraniauskas 1997

Verso
UK: 6 Meard Street, London W1F 0EG
USA: 180 Varick Street, New York NY 10014-4606

Verso is the imprint of New Left Books

ISBN 0-86091-454-2
ISBN 0-86091-604-9 (pbk)

British Library Cataloguing in Publication Data
A catalogue record for this book is available from the British Library

Library of Congress Cataloging-in-Publication Data
Monsiváis, Carlos, 1938–
    Mexican postcards / Carlos Monsiváis : edited, translated and
introduced by John Kraniauskas.
        p. cm. — (Critical studies in Latin American and Iberian
cultures)
    ISBN 0-86091-454-2 (hb). — ISBN 0-86091-604-9 (pb)
    1. Mexico—Civilization—20th century. I. Kraniauskas, John.
II. Title. III. Series.
F1234.M779 1997
972.08´2—dc21   96-52425
                                                        CIP

Typeset by M Rules
Printed and bound in Great Britain by Biddles Ltd, *www.biddles.co.uk*

To Harry

Contents

INTRODUCTION

Critical Closeness: The Chronicle-Essays of Carlos Monsiváis

Open letters

Carlos Monsiváis is probably Mexico's most influential and prolific writer. He writes about and documents cultural and political change, and he does so constantly, refocusing his attention to suit his object and public in newspapers, magazines and journals, inside the academy and, most importantly, outside. He makes his living from writing, but it is also possible to detect in his many texts – and their extraordinary range – a basic need to communicate. Indeed, his presence is so pervasive that his work has become indispensable to any approximation to Mexican culture, and this is not only because he describes it so well, but also because his work has become one of its paradigmatic voices.[1]

In what many might think his most idiosyncratic book, *El género epistolar: un homenaje a manera de carta abierta* ['The Epistolary Genre: A Homage in the Form of An Open Letter', 1991] – a history of letter-writing commissioned by the Mexican Post Office – he remarks that 'the postal system [was] a cultural institution of great importance that encouraged writing, linked people and communities, inspiring and keeping the hope of change alive'. Letters, he continues, 'may be described as "the bottle which the shipwrecked receive and send on" . . . they make their journeys there, towards the illumination of the addressee, by foot and by horse, by stagecoach and by train, braving misadventure: abandonment, loss, theft and surveillance. . . .'[2] Although he is referring to the turn-of-the-century dictatorship of Porfirio Díaz (1876–1911), it is clear that his reflections on letter-writing and the barriers to communication in the past have contemporary resonances for the authoritarian political culture of Mexico. Monsiváis writes in order to maintain his own presence in overlapping public spheres and counter-public spheres structured by the logics of the state, private enterprise, popular organizations and intellectuals (the concept of 'bourgeois and proletarian' spheres is too simple here, although hardly irrelevant), and he writes to keep 'the hope of change alive', for himself and for his readers.

Writing contains a kind of utopian impulse that feeds Monsiváis's fascination with cultural process, which then circulates in a caudillesque intellectual domain – the shifting shape of a hybridized and fragmented 'public' sphere in which ties of loyalty and dependence prevail over critical inquiry – and back again. This open loop describes the space of Monsiváis's work, positioning him, despite his own strongly held views in this regard, as both rebel *and* wielder of cultural status and power (two other important figures of this kind – although hardly rebels – are the poet and essayist Octavio Paz, a veritable hegemonic machine, and the historian and novelist Héctor Aguilar Camín – editors, respectively, of the two most important cultural magazines in Mexico, *Vuelta* and *Nexos*[3]). Monsiváis is, of course, very aware of the Mexican state's (that is, the ruling Institutional Revolutionary Party's [PRI]) *brutal hegemony*, which combines violent repression (for example, the 1968 Tlatelolco Massacre) with a technocratic ability, at both national and regional levels, to negotiate and manage its rule through corruption (the illegal re-privatization of public – state – resources), the fabrication of consent (the strategic satisfaction of needs) and 'transformism' (the state's power over intellectuals like himself).[4] In his work he addresses this context punctually, responding to foci of possible resistance and protest, alternative moralities and just plain tactics of survival. In 'Millenarianisms in Mexico: From Cabora to Chiapas' (Chapter 10 in this volume), for example, Monsiváis looks to what he conceives as the secular utopian gestures of feminist, ecological, human rights and AIDS activists as well as – more fundamentally in his work as a whole – to the creativity found in popular culture in contexts of rapid urbanization and economic deprivation.

If letter-writing could be thought of in utopian terms at the turn of the last century, it is its waning with the rise of the telephone and fax that Monsiváis describes in *El género epistolar*. Five years later, however, he revises his prognosis: responding in January 1996 to a letter from Subcommander Marcos of the EZLN (Zapatista Army of National Liberation) – who reveals that he has just finished reading Monsiváis's most recent collection of chronicles, *Los rituales del caos* ['The Rituals of Chaos', 1995] – he acknowledges: '[t]o you . . . is owed the reactivation of the tradition of sending letters. . . .'[5] Indeed, Marcos is well known for the e-mail correspondence he has initiated with regard to the neo-Zapatistas' rebellion (with John Berger and Régis Debray, for example) – so much so that the rebellion has been very much defined by its use of the media: 'the postmodern insurrection'! So today in Mexico, towards the end of another century (and the millennium), the connection between utopian movement and letter-writing is re-established. Indeed, this may be one reason why he wanted to call this collection of his work *Mexican Postcards*. But Monsiváis's writings are not written as private correspondence, and do not take the form of letters; or if they do, such texts are 'open', addressed to the 'public' and, like Marcos's own letter and his response to it, intended for interpretation and discussion beyond their immediate addressee. In this sense – like all private correspondence intended for posthumous publication – they tend towards the essay in form.[6]

Of essays and chronicles

This brings me to another important point about the literary characteristics of Monsiváis's work: much of it belongs to two very important 'in-between' genres in the history of Latin American writing: the essay (between science and litera-ture) and the chronicle (between historical and fictional narrative). And it is Monsiváis's radicalization of both, through their combination and mixture, that makes him not only one of Mexico's most important cultural critics, but also one of its foremost contemporary literary figures – alongside Octavio Paz, Elena Poniatowska, Carlos Fuentes, José Emilio Pacheco, Margo Glantz, Sergio Pitol and José Agustín (to name but the most well known).[7] Refusing the monu-mentalism of the murals, one might nevertheless say that Monsiváis's art – the chronicle-essay – is a public one: in the artistic division of labour, his writing is closer to a kind of counter or alternative urban design than to poetry.

How does Monsiváis's writing work? As the texts in this volume show, he nar-rativizes his essays. They all tell histories, but they do so in order to focus all the better on issues of contemporary concern. Essayistic relevance is thus central to all his chronicles. Most importantly, however, Monsiváis does not turn to the resources of historiographical narrative or to the apparatus of scientific or acad-emic articles, as might be expected, to legitimize his work as chronicler and essayist, but to the resources of literature, so as to dramatize it. He incorporates into his texts the heteroglossia which, Bakhtin suggested, defines the novel as a cultural form (and which he associated with the experience of urban living), creating a dialogized environment (a city) of voices and sociolects, whose effect includes the vernacularization of his own voice. Such a technique serves to high-light the cultural and political conflicts addressed in the text, as well as engaging with other points of view on the matter at hand. Monsiváis quotes, not merely in order to legitimize his portrayal, but to provide the reader with alternative centres of narrative authority. While he recognizes the power of the Mexican state, through parody, he simultaneously evokes and rearticulates the mocking humour of the masses. Fiction (or its 'reality effects') also has its place in his narration of real events: a 'character' – for example, the 'naco' in 'The Funky Dive' (Chapter 4 in this volume) – may 'speak' so as to underline a point being made, endowing it with psychological depth, or to foreground aspects of popular language and humour. Monsiváis thus records those he is talking about, endowing them with a textual agency they are usually denied, while also democratizing conventional literary language and the language of journalism. In this case, the 'nacos' – 'the mass presence that now defines Mexico City' – rebel against racist stereotypification (their naming) while exhibiting their desires, dancing and sweating, enjoying the rock music in clubs in northern Mexico City. This is definitely 'not Anthropology', as Monsiváis says in his chronicle on the celebration of the Virgin of Guadalupe ('Tradition Hour': Chapter 3), neither is it a simple question of representing those who supposedly cannot represent themselves.

In particular, the use of free indirect discourse – in which the distance between the author's organizing voice and those of his various 'characters' is blurred – defines the textuality of Monsiváis's inventions, and is central to this process of socialization to which he submits the chronicle-essay. It is also another example of his use of the resources of the history of the novel: suddenly, without the warning of diacritical marks, usurping the writer's own privileged textual space, a voice emerges in mid-paragraph to speak the words of the ideology or cultural form being analysed, performing it in discursive action. Again, the racism that 'names' the 'naco' is a case in point (in 'The Funky Dive' below). Another may be the 'porfiristas' welcoming us and another fictional 'character', the photographer, into their aristocratic home (in 'Mexico 1890–1976: High Contrast, Still Life': Chapter 1), or the assertion of the sensationalist magazine editor: 'We are talking about real crimes here, not just the stabbing of an unfaithful wife' (in '"Red News": The Crime Pages in Mexico': Chapter 11) – all adoptions of the voice of power. In 'Bolero: A History' (Chapter 12), he even momentarily takes on the genre's own codes and rhythms to narrate its history: 'believ[ing] themselves to have wrought in words and melody what they sought in love and found in melancholy'.

In literary terms, Monsiváis 'shows' rather than 'tells', and in so doing he moves across and through the experiences and ideological positions of the cultural field under investigation. His socialized chronicle-essays are thus polycentric and performative, activating ideologies in conflict and celebrating small victories wherever they may be found – hardly the defining points of either the conventional essay or the chronicle.

Critical closeness

Marx's observation that '[r]eligion is the general theory of this world, its ency-clopedic compendium, its logic in popular form . . .'[8] is nowhere better dramatized than in the work of Juan Rulfo, the subject of one of Monsiváis's por-traits included in this volume (Chapter 5). It is exhibited, too, in the history of the faith healer Boy Fidencio, in the celebrations of the Virgin of Guadalupe and, of course, in the history of conservative utopian movements in Mexico. At the organizing centre of Monsiváis's texts, however, there is no simple critique of the false consciousness of those in thrall to such practices, which would only serve to celebrate the post-colonial ideology of progress, the myth of the Mexican Revolution, and the devastation they have produced (particularly for the Indian and peasant populations of the country). What may be detected instead is a con-stant and steady sympathy and solidarity for the poorest and most marginalized sectors of Mexican society, and a huge appreciation for their strategies of survival. These include the rearticulation of a historically imposed Christianity according to a variety of local cultural scripts and economic needs, so well captured in all its desperation in Rulfo's extraordinary novel *Pedro Páramo*, and in Monsiváis's reading of it. They also include humour and fun, particularly in the form of what in Mexico is known as 'relajo' – exemplified in this volume by the very dif-ferent figures of comic actors Tin Tan and Cantinflas (Chapters 7, 8).

I have rendered the term 'relajo' as 'fun' here, which is not quite exact, for it also hints at a dimension of mockery (as in 'making fun') and transgression, and refers to an attitude towards dominant values – which 'relajo' refuses to take seri-ously, 'cancelling', says the philosopher Jorge Portilla, 'the normal response to value, and removing itself from any obligation to realize it'[9] – rather than the merely comic. For many writers, 'relajo', having originally represented a form of popular self-defence and defiance, has now become instead part of what Roger Bartra has called the 'metadiscourse' of the national in Mexico – 'an intricate net-work of points of reference to which many Mexicans (and some foreigners) turn to explain national identity . . . it is the place from which come the myths which not only give *unity* to the nation, but also make it different from any other'[10] – or, more specifically, an ideologized sign of the cultural experience of modern (which in this context means post-Revolutionary) *urbanization*.

While the latter has arguably always been Monsiváis's principal interest, he has resisted contributing to the establishment of any kind of national identity – by way of 'relajo' (fun), or any other supposed national trait. 'Relajo' is, rather, set to work in his own writing, creating in his texts an ironic distance filled with humour, and in such a way that – paradoxically – his critical distance becomes a kind of critical closeness.

Closeness to what? To cultural process. Monsiváis's writing – inflected by the humour of irony and 'relajo', and the narrativity of the chronicle – facilitates the kind of perspective articulated, for example, by Raymond Williams in a critique of the concept of *mass culture*:

> the real institutions of mass culture in any central sense predate the modern media. I mean, the mass cultural institutions are the mass meeting and the mass demonstration, where people are physically assembled in large crowds and where certain modes of communication – the display of banners, certain shouts, and so on – are wholly appropriate to that kind of physical assembly.[11]

It is precisely such cultural and political sensitivity, which is able to historicize against the grain of critical common sense, that is evident in Monsiváis's first collection of chronicle-essays, *Días de guardar* ('Days of Observance', 1970), centred on the student movement of 1968, which is clearly influenced not only by the writers and attitudes of the US counter-culture of the 1960s (of which Monsiváis has always been a great fan) but also by the banners and slogans of the mass street demonstrations in Mexico City that are intercalated into his texts as direct quotations of the demands, needs and humour of the movement.

And, as I have suggested, Monsiváis has continued to develop this 'stance of extreme closeness' ever since. His chronicle of the aftermath of the 1985 earthquake in Mexico City – when the population itself takes charge of the initial effort at rescue and rebuilding in the face of government inertia – is an extraordinary case in point.[12] These chronicles of 1968 and the earthquake are not, however, included in this volume, for it seems to me that they constitute key moments of a political history which is still being played out now in Chiapas, since the uprising of 1994 – and throughout the rest of the country, too, which, since the earthquake, has seen a remarkable proliferation of independent social movements that are radically changing the parameters of politics in Mexico and the relation between the state and civil society. They await, therefore, inclusion in another possible future volume of Monsiváis's chronicles in English which would focus on these newly emerging political formations.

This narrative position of proximity is also present in Monsiváis's writing about history and culture. Throughout his texts – as is evident, for example, in

'"Red News": The Crime Pages in Mexico' – Monsiváis writes about the past as a continuous present, politicizing history, making it a contemporary experience for his readers. The effect is to narrate the origins of the present, making connections – for example, between crime and the post-Revolutionary state – which in fact constitute structural continuities and demand a political response. In choosing to narrativize his essays through recourse to the chronicle, Monsiváis deliberately shuns the juridico-moral stability and perspective on the present characteristic of what Hayden White calls 'history proper' – which incorporates the end into a coherent narrative order, unlike the chronicle, which 'is marked by a failure to achieve narrative closure . . . start[ing] out to tell a story . . . [it] . . . breaks off . . . in the chronicler's own present; it leaves things unresolved' – preferring the openness of a shifting proximity over a centred critical distance. In this sense, Monsiváis's writing is cinematic, his point of view a camera eye.[13] Such a refusal of closure, it seems, also represents an openness to change and transformation, as well as a basic (empiricist) materialism – one of whose effects on the subject of enunciation is *awe* – that may constitute the 'truth' of the chronicle as a cultural form.[14] To criticize Monsiváis for merely having 'occurrences rather than ideas', as Octavio Paz has done, is, therefore, entirely to miss the literary and political point:[15] the ideas produced in Monsiváis's essays are emplotted back into the lives and dramas he is writing about.

According to Adorno, the essay is a form that borrows from scientific and literary genres, but is reducible to neither. On the one hand, it shares the subjective freedom of literature to invent without sharing its purely 'fictional' character; while on the other, it refuses to relinquish the will to knowledge and truth shared by the human and natural sciences. Essays do attempt to convince, but without the conceptual elaboration or burden of proof characteristic of the sciences.[16] From this point of view, we might say that Monsiváis's essays narrate real events, like history, but without its scientific apparatus; preferring to remain – ambiguously, from the generic point of view, but coherently, from the political point of view – anchored in the present and in the realm of literature. In sum, what I am referring to as 'critical closeness' here is a politics, an epistemology and a practice of writing.

Melodrama and modernity

Carlos Monsiváis was born in Mexico City in 1938, and brought up in a Protestant family. Already from early childhood, then, his relationship to dominant Mexican society and culture – and I am thinking here of institutional

Catholicism – was oblique; providing, perhaps, a biographical reason for his subsequent slightly off-centre standpoint of critical closeness (in this context, see his concluding remarks to 'Tradition Hour', Chapter 3 below). It may also go some way in explaining his own particular attraction to Anglo-American culture, from cinema and new journalism to rock music. The influences of the radical sensibilities of the counter-cultures in the USA, Europe and Mexico, as well as their literatures, are all crucial to his work. Monsiváis seems always to have been of the libertarian Left – particularly close, in the period of the student movement of 1968, to the heterodox Marxism of the novelist José Revueltas. Indeed, he saves some of his most ferocious remarks for the debilitating conventionality and sexism of the orthodox Left and the textbook Marxism of the universities. He was also born into a nation with a fairly new, consolidated, post-Revolutionary state with enormous power and resources at its disposal, and its eyes – now turned away from the redistribution of the national cake (in the form of land and myths) – set on rapid modernization.

Education was always important to the post-Revolutionary hegemonic bloc as the population was instructed – through new public forms like the murals – into the new ways of a newly configured nation. The turn to modernization in the 1940s, however, also saw the beginnings of a massive growth in higher education to satisfy the demands of a new middle class emerging from rapid capitalist development and seeking education and professionalization. Carlos Monsiváis was thus only one of thousands of young men and women who began to flood the UNAM (National Autonomous University of Mexico) and other new universities in the 1950s and 1960s looking for training, culture and politics – to be 'modern' according to the newest of codes – and he found much of what he was looking for. The influence of the US-dominated culture industries on the youth of rapidly growing cities was also great, especially in the fields of film, music and television. New ways of writing, speaking and being emerged from such processes, as well as new political desires: democracy. The ruling party's rhetoric of 'development' and 'progress' thus paradoxically furnished the framework for the cultural and political demands of the Mexican counter-culture it would later, in 1968, so ferociously repress. The conditions for the production and reception of Monsiváis's work – in other words, Monsiváis the author, his texts and his readers – emerge from such a context, characterized, furthermore, by the growing influence of the culture industries – perceived as Americanization – on the youth cultures of rapidly growing cities, and intense social conflict. As I have suggested, Monsiváis has written micrological histories of this (as it turns out) deeply uneven process – 'In the last twenty years,

Mexican society has contracted new habits, seen the abyss of inequality and injustice deepen, renounced many of its more nationalistic expressions, is "Americanized" and simultaneously "de-Americanized" . . . it wants to be modern and fails, wants to hang on to tradition but is unable'[17] – by resorting to the very popular languages and urban attitudes generated by this process of modernization, and from this point of view, he has targeted the racism and class chauvinism that produced the discourses of the 'naco', the 'pelado' and 'peladito' as Mexico City was invaded and remade by mass migration from the countryside (see 'Cantinflas: That's the Point!' [Chapter 7]). Following in the footsteps of the poet and chronicler of Mexico City Salvador Novo (1904–74), whom he quotes often, Monsiváis has served an almost avant-gardist function in transforming conventional conceptions of journalism, literature and culture (and the relations between them) in Mexico by opening up these fields to new – perhaps more 'ordinary' – objects, desires and concerns and, like the most genuine of avant-gardes, risking cultural populism without being entrapped by it.[18]

'What the bourgeoisie and proletariat, middle class and lumpenproletariat look for throughout the length and breadth of the culture industry, and find without knowing it, is a systematic understanding of society unified and trans-figured by melodrama.' This brief passage from 'Mexico 1890–1976: High Contrast, Still Life' (Chapter 1), the earliest of Monsiváis's texts included here, expresses what may in fact be interpreted as his major theme. Much of Monsiváis's work may be thought of as investigating melodrama – not just as a genre, but as the product of an uneven and transcultural modernity in Mexico – as if it were something like what Raymond Williams has called a 'structure of feeling' (as formulated in *Marxism and Literature*):

> We are talking about characteristic elements of impulse, restraint, and tone; specifically affective elements of consciousness and relationships: not feeling against thought, but thought as felt and feeling as thought: practical con-sciousness of a present kind, in a living and inter-relating continuity. We are then defining these elements as a 'structure': as a set, with specific internal rela-tions, at once interlocking and in tension. Yet we are also defining a social experience which is still *in process*, often indeed not yet recognized as social but taken to be private, idiosyncratic, and even isolating, but which in analysis (though rarely otherwise) has its emergent, connecting, and dominant char-acteristics, indeed its specific hierarchies.[19]

The domain of cultural experience outlined here is precisely where the otherwise very different works of Williams and Monsiváis meet: in the case of the former, in his struggle to think about culture as both lived 'ordinary' experience and historical formation; in the case of the latter, through the critical closeness to cultural practices that the chronicle-essay permits. Melodrama in Monsiváis's account is a question of 'impulse' and 'restraint'; it is 'specifically affective'; it concerns the production and education of 'feeling'; it is a 'structure' and a 'process' – that is, a cultural formation with a history – and as such, of course, thoroughly ideological. It does not, therefore, constitute an identity but, rather, a power-knowledge.

The cultural experience that particularly interests Monsiváis is the impact on everyday life of the culture industries and the state apparatus, providing pedagogies of, and into, modernity and nationhood, in a context of rapid urbanization. Melodrama, in Mexico, is a peculiar form of such cultural modernization. It elicits passion and romance so as to educate and steer them – by way of sacrifice if need be – past forbidden alliances and into nuclear family life. Indeed, Monsiváis suggests that the power of melodrama in Mexico 'depends on . . . the partial transference into private life of religious sentiment'; and, furthermore, that it became a secular form of catechism: modernity condensed, made consumable and simple.[20] From this point of view, romantic song, for example, is a kind of mysticism of the heart, providing its listeners with the changing ways and means of falling in and out of love. Monsiváis traces its history and cultural significance in Mexico – from the Porfiriato until now – in 'Bolero: A History' (Chapter 12). The melodramatic sensibility, however, does not stay put, and what may be ultimately conservative and disciplinary in one domain may, in another, become hilariously subversive. Love of the nation, for example, becomes a kind of state sentimentalism when it is evoked in romantic song by a brave cowboy, and the masculinist discourse of nationalism, subverted and feminized. In so far as it is a genre that mobilizes emotion, melodrama is always potentially subversive, refusing containment. This, I think, is its fascination for Monsiváis. And as the texts collected here show, it is Monsiváis's ability to relate questions such as those of the heart to broader historical and political issues that makes his work as a cultural critic exemplary both inside and beyond Mexico.

The texts included in this volume are as follows:
Chapter 1, 'Mexico 1890–1976: High Contrast, Still Life' is taken from *Amor Perdido* (1977), Ediciones Era, Mexico City, 1984; Chapters 2, 3 and 9 – 'Identity Hour', 'Tradition Hour' and 'The Boy Fidencio and the Roads to Ecstasy' – from *Los rituales del caos*, Ediciones Era, Mexico City 1995; Chapters 4, 6 and 7 – 'Dancing: The Funky Dive', 'Dolores del Río: The Face as

Institution' and 'Cantinflas: That's the Point!' – from *Escenas de pudor y liviandad*, Editorial Grijalbo, Mexico City 1988; Chapter 5, 'Yes, Nor Do the Dead Speak, Unfortunately: Juan Rulfo' (1980) from Juan Rulfo, *Toda la obra* (Critical Edition co-ordinated by Claude Fell), Colección Archivos, Nanterre 1992; Chapter 8, 'Tin Tan: The Pachuco', from *Intermedios* no. 4, October 1992; Chapter 10, 'Millenarianisms in Mexico: From Cabora to Chiapas', from Josefina Ludmer (compiler), *Las culturas de fin de siglo en América Latina*, Beatriz Viterbo Editora, Rosario 1994; Chapter 11, '"Red News": The Crime Pages in Mexico', from *Nexos* no. 176, August 1992; Chapter 12, 'Bolero: A History', is as yet unpublished in the Spanish language; and the Epilogue, 'A New Catechism for Reluctant Indians', from *Nuevo catecismo para indios remisos* (1982), Lecturas Mexicanas 61, CONACULTA, Mexico City 1994.

I would like to thank Carlos Monsiváis, Tim Girven, Rob Kennedy, María Eugenia Mudrovcic, Guillermo Zermeño and the Research Committee of the Department of Spanish, Birkbeck College, for their assistance in putting this volume together. Without the help and patience of Carol Watts it would never have seen the light of day.

Notes

1. See Sara Sefchovich, *México: país de ideas, país de novelas*, Grijalbo, Mexico City 1987, p. 203:

> With wisdom and ingenuity, irony and lucidity, Monsiváis listens to the romantic songs of Juan Gabriel, supports popular causes, is the ally of minorities and the marginalized, writes all the time and mocks everyone. 'He opens doors, points and creates awareness,' says Elena Poniatowska of this chronicler of our delights and misfortunes, translator and journalist, questioner, cartographer and definer of Mexican culture . . .

Christopher Domínguez Michael, a very different kind of literary critic, nevertheless agrees with Sefchovich on this point:

> An indispensable writer when it comes to understanding the last twenty-five years of Mexican culture, an archeologist and inventor of myths, well-known incognito to be seen on the arm of María Félix as well as in left-wing meetings at the University, he is a stupendous narrator . . .

See Christopher Domínguez Michael, 'Introducción' to Book Four of his *Antología de la narrativa mexicana del siglo XX*, vol. 2, Fondo de Cultura Económica, Mexico City 1991, p. 68.

2. Carlos Monsiváis, *El género epistolar: un homenaje a manera de carta abierta*, Miguel Ángel Porrúa, Mexico City 1991, p. 28.

3. See Antonio Gramsci on Benedetto Croce for a possible approximation to the significance of Paz in Mexico: 'a kind of lay pope and an extremely efficient instrument of hegemony – even if at times he may find himself in disagreement with one government or other . . .', in *Selections from the Prison Notebooks* (ed. and trans. Quintin Hoare and Geoffrey Nowell Smith), Lawrence & Wishart, London 1971, p. 56 n.5. Monsiváis himself has been associated with two cultural magazines of considerable power and weight: *La cultura en México*, cultural supplement of the weekly *Siempre*, during the 1970s; and *Nexos* during the 1980s. These are now 'semi-official' organs, and Monsiváis has little to do with either. See the novelist José Agustín's *Tragicomedia Mexicana 2*, Editorial Planeta, Mexico City 1992, pp. 210–15. For the changing relationship between Monsiváis and Paz from the 1960s on, see María Eugenia Mudrovcic's excellent 'Carlos Monsiváis, un intelectual post-68', paper presented at the XXX Congress of the Instituto Internacional de Literatura Iberoamericana, University of Pittsburgh, Pennsylvania, 12–16 June 1994. Since the mid 1970s it has been possible to read Monsiváis as a kind of 'counter-Paz' – that is, in so far as the latter, from his own position of power, has articulated positions associated today, both politically and culturally, with neo-liberalism (which Monsiváis refers to as 'savage capitalism').

4. For a recent satirical attack on the politics of intellectual life in Mexico – which even includes a character known as the 'narco-poet' – see Enrique Serna's very funny thriller *El miedo a los animales*, Editorial Joaquín Mortiz, Mexico City 1995 (Monsiváis is one of the many names dropped by its pathetic and unlucky narrator, a journalist turned corrupt policeman who wants to make good! See p. 180: 'Mexico was a country without memory, Monsiváis has said as much.') I would like to thank Guillermo Zermeño for bringing this novel to my attention.

5. Carlos Monsiváis, 'Fábula del país de Nopasanada (Carta dirigida al Subcomandante Marcos, en donde se encuentre, para notificarle acuerdos, discrepancias y modestas reflexiones)', *La Jornada Semanal*, 14 January 1996. Monsiváis debates with the Zapatistas, shares ideas, disagrees and agrees. Here he notes, for example, the power of the state on intellectuals, 'transforming' once critical voices over to its side. And of the many beneficial effects of the neo-Zapatista uprising, he believes the most important has been the emergence of independent Indian movements that are national in scope: 'Those who discuss Indian questions today are mainly the Tojobales, Tzotziles, Tzeltales, Nahuas, Mixtecos, Zapotecos, and so on, to include all the 56 ethnic groups.' See also Subcomandante insurgente Marcos, 'De árboles, transgresores y odontología', ibid. Three texts from *Los rituales del caos* are included in this volume: 'Identity Hour', 'Tradition Hour' and 'The Boy Fidencio and the Roads to Ecstasy'.

6. Perhaps the most famous letter-essay of this kind, written on the eve of Latin American independence, is Simón Bolívar's 'Carta de Jamaica' (1815), originally written in exile in Kingston, Jamaica, to Henry Cullen, 'a gentleman of this island'. In John Lynch's words, it is 'a mordant attack on the Spanish colonial system, a criticism of the revolution's failure, and an expression of hope in the future', *The Spanish-American Revolutions 1808–1826* (2nd edn), Norton, New York 1986, p. 210. For the 'letter', see Simón Bolívar, *Escritos políticos*, Alianza, Madrid 1981.

7. For the chronicle as a form of narrative, see Hayden White, 'The Value of Narrativity in the Representation of Reality', in *The Content of the Form*, Johns Hopkins University Press, Baltimore, MD and London 1987, pp. 1–25. For the essay, see T.W. Adorno, 'The Essay as Form', in *Notes to Literature* (vol. 1), trans. Sherry Weber Nicholsen, Columbia University Press, New York 1991, pp. 3–23. Despite his comments on Monsiváis's abilities as a narrator, Domínguez Michael nevertheless states that the 'Introducción' to his *Antología de la narrativa mexicana del siglo XX* is 'not the place to discuss Carlos Monsiváis as a public figure, chronicler of urban life . . .' (p. 68). The point is, of course, that he is a public figure only in so far as he is a narrator, and vice versa!

8. Karl Marx, 'A Contribution to the Critique of Hegel's Philosophy of Right. Introduction' (1844), in *Early Writings* (Introduced by Lucio Colletti), Penguin, Harmondsworth 1977, p. 244.

9. See Jorge Portilla, *Fenomenología del relajo* (1966). Fondo de Cultura Económica, Mexico City 1992, p. 19. Although it is popular, 'relajo' is not quite 'carnivalesque' in the more festive Bakhtinian sense of the word. What is attractive about Portilla's essay, and what perhaps appeals to Monsiváis about it – for this is a conjecture – is its open affirmation that the streets are the proper place for philosophy.

10. Roger Bartra, *La jaula de la melancolía: identidad y metamorfosis del mexicano*, Grijalbo, Mexico City 1987, pp. 17, 194–8.

11. See Stephen Heath and Gillian Skirrow, 'Interview with Raymond Williams', in Christopher Prendergast (ed.) *Cultural Materialism: On Raymond Williams*, University of Minnesota Press, Minneapolis and London 1995, p. 360.

12. The quotation, and the idea of 'critical closeness', are taken from Peter Sloterdijk, *Critique of Cynical Reason*, trans. Michael Eldred, Verso, London 1988, p. xxxiii; he, in turn, has taken it from Walter Benjamin. For the events of 1968, see Carlos Monsiváis, *Días de guardar*, Ediciones Era, Mexico City 1970; for the Mexican earthquake, see Carlos Monsiváis, 'Los días del temblor', in *Entrada libre: crónicas de la sociedad que se organiza*, Ediciones Era, Mexico City 1987.

13. See Walter Benjamin, *One-Way Street* (trans. E. Jephcott and K. Shorter), New Left Books, London 1979, p. 89. Monsiváis is a well-known cinephile.

During the 1960s he hosted a weekly radio programme on cinema for *Radio Universidad*. See, in particular, 'Dolores del Río: The Face as Institution', Chapter 6 in this volume, as well as his contributions to A. Paranagua, ed., *Mexican Cinema*, British Film Institute, London 1996.

14. Hayden White, 'The Value of Narrativity', p. 5. Monsiváis has, of course, written a history of the chronicle in Mexico. See 'Y yo preguntaba y anotaba, y el caudillo no se dio por enterado', his introduction to Carlos Monsiváis (ed.) *A ustedes les consta: Antología de la crónica en México*, Ediciones Era, Mexico City 1980, pp. 17–76.

15. Octavio Paz, 'Aclaraciones y reiteraciones', *Proceso* 61, 2 January, 1978, quoted in María Eugenia Mudrovcic, 'Carlos Monsiváis'.

16. 'While the essay coordinates concepts with one another by means of their function in the parallelogram of forces in its objects, it shrinks from any over-arching concept to which they could all be subordinated. What such concepts give the illusion of achieving, their method knows to be impossible and yet tries to accomplish.' (T.W. Adorno, 'The Essay as Form', p. 16) An excellent comparison of the standpoints adopted by Monsiváis and Paz may be found in their respective texts on the events of 1968 in Mexico. See Octavio Paz, 'Critique of the Pyramid', in *The Labyrinth of Solitude* (enlarged edn), Penguin, Harmondsworth 1990.

17. Carlos Monsiváis, 'Para un cuadro de costumbres. De cultura y vida cotideana en los ochentas', *Cuadernos Políticos* 57, May–June 1989, p. 84.

18. For the chronicles of Salvador Novo, see his *La vida en México en el período presidencial de Lázaro Cárdenas* (compiled by José Emilio Pacheco), CONACULTA and INAH, Mexico City 1994. This is the first of three volumes of Novo's weekly chronicles published in the weekly *Hoy*. The other two volumes cover the governments of Manuel Ávila Camacho and Miguel Alemán.

19. Raymond Williams, *Marxism and Literature*, Oxford University Press, Oxford 1977, p. 132.

20. Carlos Monsiváis, 'Se sufre, pero se aprende (el melodrama y las reglas de la falta de límites)', in Carlos Monsiváis and Carlos Bonfil, *A través del espejo: el cine mexicano y su público*, Ediciones El Milagro, IMCINE (Instituto Mexicano de Cinematografia), 1994, p. 100. See also María Eugenia Mudrovcic, 'Entre el Camp y el Kitsch: Carlos Monsiváis ante la sociedad de masas', paper presented at the XIX Congress of the Latin American Studies Association, Washington, DC, 28–30 September 1995.

Mexico 1890–1976:
High Contrast, Still Life

I   Nature should be imitated, not corrected

Like memory, light organizes. It gathers and separates, placing each and every one of those gathered here in their appropriate groups. . . . And you in the middle, please, and you to the side, as if you had just strolled by. That's it, good. . . . The light is perfect – the perfection of a banquet in honour of His Excellency the President of the Republic – producing a whole in which even the smallest detail has been the object of long and arduous meditation. *Harmony in White*: gloves, belts, parasols, roses and folding chairs. Everything has been inscribed into a pause, a parenthesis in this bright and hazy light. Such gallantry, presence and poise must be thought of as 'refined'; if not, they become suspended in midair, like the smile of the Cheshire Cat. Time for more time: the ladies in white smile, discreetly, certain that even the slightest titter would destroy the bucolic charm. Oh, Divine Pleiade!

How do we approach such a scene? Should these figures be placed within the moral domain of a Henry James novel, would they fit into a scene of melancholic happiness as it suddenly appears in a Katherine Mansfield story, or do they deserve the historical treatment of a Luchino Visconti or a Joseph Losey? This might indeed be the case. We find ourselves – the intense midday light tells us so – in a world that is dominated by and lived through purely external sensation: social pride, social discretion, controlled and administered happiness, social disdain. Individual feelings do not matter very much. If they do not serve either to announce a great passion, or methodically to arrange an 'interior life', they are inadmissible luxuries. There is no introspection, because the people gathered here are *porfiristas*, a handful of Mexicans who have taken control of the turn of the century, a courtly society in a colonial country. They spread, embody and preserve tradition, as in a carnival dance where everyone has turned up dressed for a coronation, but the watchword is to allow no noise at all.

The image in the mirror: the arrogant individuality of one *porfirista* is identical to the unique character of his neighbour (your loyal servant and God's). It is not only our historical perspective that equalizes them, but their own docile cooperation in attempting – amid homages to President Juarez – to create a Mexican Aristocracy. *Good manners*: hold your parasol with care, twist and turn it, breathe in, let neither jealousy nor eagerness show, direct an understanding glance at your partner. *Servants in uniform*: a residence is, always, an educational and erotic commitment, everything in its proper place: cameos, the walnut wardrobes, Turkish stools, mother-of-pearl marquetry, gold-framed mirrors, porcelain and glass flowerpots – and, in the garden, port and cognac. *Impeccable morality*: honour is your prime gift, my daughter; honour is your shield and your fortress, your relief, your *raison d'être* and your plenitude. *Ancestors*: we are gathered here to pose for this photograph which shows that we have been in existence from time immemorial, and if my father did in fact invent a great-grandparent or two, it was to spare us feeling like orphans. By the way, have you seen our coat of arms?

Pitiless light: the portrait of the President of the Republic, Don Porfirio Díaz, centres and organizes the gaze. Around him are arranged a family life, a living room, recently acquired wealth, and the need for protection. *Porfiristas* gather in (naturally shady) salons to accumulate and distribute respect among the statuettes, flowing curtains, candelabra, Persian carpets, fans (painted with Versaillesesque scenes), tiger skins, porcelain vases and landscape paintings that will never become famous because of the sad lack of colour rotogravure.

Generous, the *porfiristas* donate mountains of cake. Charity – both yesterday and today – is first of all a spectacle, then a concession in which money, moral superiority, and the (periodic) decision to alleviate suffering are all theatricalized. To be rich is to be born again with elegance. The Distinguished Families: a group of extras in a film with just one speaking part.

For thirty years of decreed and concentrated harmony, the multifaceted Republic of Mexico knew (formally) only one style: *porfirismo*. Don Porfirio Díaz, elected and elected again caudillo and Prince of Peace – a synthesis of Mexico, a blow-up version of our very own personality cult – gave his name to a period of history, injecting it with his own gifts of perseverance and transcendence. The Porfirian period aspired to self-sufficiency, concealing or eliminating those contradictions that revealed a dialectics at play and proved to be unnecessarily bothersome. It was successful, to an extent, since in that unknowable entity known today as the 'collective memory' (an abstraction welded in the cinema and concentrated by television), the Porfirian period appears as a closed, monolithic universe without fissures. Who can think of more Porfirian adjectives for *porfirismo*? Here we go: imposing, serene, severe, classic, immutable, forthright.

What is *porfirismo*? The statistics of Mexico City in 1900: 368,898 inhabitants; 500,000 litres of *pulque* a day; 6,000 bicycles in circulation. A procession that starts from the Municipal Building to offer two cinerary urns at the Rotunda of Illustrious Men. A syndicate of surnames: Romero Rubio, Escandón, Redo, Lancaster Jones, Corcuera, Martínez del Río, Romero de Terreros, Rincón Gallardo, Algara, Braniff, Sánchez Navarro, Casasús, Cortina, Elízaga, Goribar, García Pimentel, Ituarte, Mier, Prida, Terrazas, Lascuráin, Paz, Landa, Limantour, Iturbe, Santacilia. A mass of carriages: landaus, brakes, mail coaches, berlins, coupés and *vis-à-vis*. The truth is social, and the social is true: the dictatorship demands to see itself reflected everywhere: in the El Globo cake shop, saint's-day celebrations, charity balls, official balls, inaugurations and cutting ribbons, and more inaugurations; and in the Bishops' blessing, the triumphal arches, the receptions and garden parties celebrating Doña Carmelita Romero Rubio de Díaz with the hypnotist Onoffroff (who commands a member of the audience to have toothache).

This is a society that is both refined and religious, where parties – essentially the occasion for communication – are a matter of devotion. To Good Friday corresponds the celebration of Saint Anne; the burning of Judas is a cathartic act; while no one who is anyone will forget to pray to the Virgin of Guadalupe on 12 December. A decent society with noble sentiments loves the home as if it were the nation, and venerates the nation as if it were a mother: there is no such thing as virtue outside official engagements, no true love outside marriage, and no civic pride that is far removed from the respectful laying of bouquets and wreaths. Patriotism is commemorative and magisterial, as is clearly illustrated by the cultural fusion of both in the building of the Independence Angel, using white stone from Pachuca and white marble from Carrara. There is no television: Society comes together at oratories and at musical and literary evenings. There is no cinema: society fulfils itself in celebrations.

With the great exception of the nuclei of provincial Liberals (see Mariano Azuela's novel *Los fracasados* ['Failures']) and the forms of bourgeois and bohemian lifestyles in Mexico City, in 1910 a feudal morality still reigns in Mexico, according to a very simple equation: 'the defence of the natural right to possess women, land, workers and nation = spiritual fortitude = pillar of society

= sexual repression'. The Church verbalizes, amid homilies and absolutions, the landowners' dream: that history and society do not change, and that respect for owners will be eternal. It is a Mexico that is at once ideal and tragic, sombre and repressed, ferociously cruel and silenced, that acts itself out – with literary excellence – in the pages of Agustín Yáñez's *Al filo del agua* ['The Edge of the Storm'] and Juan Rulfo's *Pedro Páramo*.

What Yáñez registers almost exactly in his novel of 1947 is the *Via Dolorosa* (all metaphors must possess a hint of Christian expiation here) of feudal morality: the succession of strict norms, chastity as the glorification of a code of prohibitions, the masturbatory rhythm of a collectivity, the accumulated sweat of social and sexual containment. The dominant spirit of the landowners is that appearances be kept up at all costs. Dissimulation, not being an ethical defect, is a requirement of both public and private life, and their watchword, 'blow them away' ['*mátalos en caliente*'] is proof of their being in a hurry rather than of their cynicism.

A sense of balance. The Conservatives may have been defeated during the post-Independence Reform Wars, but in practice, Liberal secular legislation has no effect at all on religious belief or ecclesiastical tyranny in the country villages. A novel like Emilio Rabasa's *La guerra de tres años* ['The Three Years War'] is perfect in its caricature: the use of women by the Church to challenge the silence or abjection of the political apparatus in order to defend a perpetual past. Similarly, the novels of the second half of the nineteenth century cultivate homely virtues, glorify female dependence (virginity in, before and after marriage), distrust politics – the source of all evils – and fear the dissolving tendencies emanating from the capital city, the administrative centre.

What Yáñez contemplates is typical in its dense immobility. The correspondences between Clarín's novel *La Regenta* and *Al filo del agua* ['The Edge of the Storm'] are fundamentally thematic: the priest (the Church) watches everything from the bell-tower and takes advantage of everything from the confessional. The difference lies in Clarín's morbid observation and exploration of the Regent's wife's sexuality, compared to Yáñez's asexualized version of the perpetual frustration of a village in the state of Jalisco. Not even the coquettish Micaela has access to sensuality, since her flirtatiousness constitutes more a plan of escape than one of surrender. Luis Gonzaga's trip to the countryside in the novel is a fantasy that mixes mysticism with 'pre-Freudian' orgasm (which, of course, does not recognize itself as such). The political manipulation of religion is lavish in its creation – there are witnesses in abundance – of tortured consciousness (subdued souls). In these country villages sexual guilt contributes greatly to political stability. The Holy Sheet (cut in the middle so that the nakedness of the wife might not be revealed) is a sign of the fear – and the laziness – aroused by both Law and Church. If it is allowed, it is of no interest. Let not the Marriage Bed be stained: remember, the place for sex is an extension of the brothel! The ruling class could be described *politically* in a prayer to be whispered before the sexual act: 'What we are about to do, oh Lord!, is not out of vice, nor a desire for fornication, but to produce a son in your service.' Exclusion is the most intense nationalist sentiment, and a Duty Obeyed – either in bed or in the Chamber of Deputies – is the forced contribution to a strategy of domination invested in the public renunciation of pleasure. During the thirty years of the Porfirian period, private virtues were, notoriously, a political plan.

After years of foreign invasion and civil war, banditry, administrative anarchy and the absence of a sense of nationality, it was demanded that the dictatorship impose order and peace, and that Society should disseminate respectability. Now, the terms Decency and Good Manners come to us packed with the ridiculous pretensions of an elite elevated to their position by plunder and assassination. Then, however, being Decent and having Good Manners was something more than fabricated amnesia, more than the arrogance which improvises a past and invents traditions that credit and legitimize it. Porfirian Decency also constitutes a project for internal cohesion. There is no national conscience, no pride in a country so far from Europe; instead, the elite unites around a set of conventions, its first identity. . . . Decency thus becomes, in a very strict sense, a nationality more important than being 'Mexican'. Similarly, the Decency of the few intimidates the many who, not possessing it, feel themselves to be inferior or belittled. Anger and embarrassment felt by the Decent at the manners of others, their theatricalized horror and outrage at nudity or 'swear words', all spread and strengthen feelings of incomprehension and rejection among the people at their own behaviour.

Porfirismo: the elites and forced labour, literary and musical evenings and the Cananea and Río Blanco strikes (and subsequent massacres), Justo Sierra and Ricardo Flores Magón, respect for others and persecution. Splendour and misery, ritual and crime: the contrasts are obvious, but without the obviousness of the contrasts there would not have been a revolution.

II 'Porque no tiene, porque le falta . . .'

From among the mud and huts, and before the bewildered expression of the curious, a people and a Revolution emerge simultaneously. The people share their inheritance: the decision to die just as long as it guarantees a word shouted in their favour, fatalist resignation, damned resentment, the centuries-old perseverance it opposes to Porfirian stuccoed rigidity. Before and beyond the caudillos, the proclamations, and the patriotic calls to arms ('In the light of the above, I invite all citizens to rise up in arms'), the people rise up, grow and become. In an avalanche of sombreros and cloth trousers, the Zapatista masses spread another tone of the colour white across the nation. Let's head off for the hills, join in the fun; and take note, you fucking beggars: *The people exist only during Revolutions*, and between 1910 and 1917 the revolutions last all day, all year, and as long as they last the revo' is an organic mixture of historic events and everyday life.

THE 'SOLDADERA'

'And the young gal, she bravely followed them. . . .' When the battle ends, women remain. She, the fecund (the ideal slave), gets up and, suddenly, moves on. Not with much luck: after prodigiously long marches, Revolutionary women are mythified and the myth, stipulating the usual characteristics and conditions, confirms and guarantees slavery, bitterly transforming natural virtues into a dead weight for their descendants. Couldn't women of the Revolution have produced a lighter inheritance? In the event, they were forced to pass on to their descendants a fatal load of abnegation, silent suffering, stoicism and stubborn veneration for their men.

But let's not get ahead of ourselves, since in the end the process holds real interest. From being chattels and decorations, women become, in these years of violence, tireless and generous allies, the other army alongside the army, the fighters who brave long marches, and months of suffering behind horses and trains. Stubborn faithfulness: women become fighters, providers, cooks, gatherers of wood, lovers, nurses, and collective mothers. Women take on the fight and obstinately dissolve it: they take part in guerrilla action, map the country in reconnaissance activities, ride and bear arms. Today the *soldadera* is an oppressive myth: saintly sweetness. Then, in both a stoic and a brave way, she was the profanation of a destiny of invisibility.

The *soldadera*, a sum of commands: she gets the water, collects the wood, fornicates wherever and whenever, and gives birth amongst the scrub. While such servitude exemplifies masculine tyranny, the *soldadera* also represents the irruption of peasant women into history, the fertilization of the nation by legions whose disposability is synonymous with patriotic duty. A witness of the first order: the character of Pintada in Mariano Azuela's *Los de abajo* ['The

Underdogs']. She is disrespectful, mobile, and affirms her love for her man without circumlocutions; she is – in her own way, and during the battles – a woman fully in possession of herself. The rest of the time, she behaves without inhibition.

While resting, recounting adventures, preparing what passes for meals, sardonically attempting to transform – through laughter – a misfortune into a party, the people make a revolution with the same stubborn intensity as (moments before or moments after) they take to the battlefield, brandishing old rifles and ancestral curses:

> Hicimos de cuenta que fuimos basura
> vino el remolino y nos alevantó,
> y al poco tiempo de andar en la altura
> un nuevo viento nos desapartó . . .

[We thought that we were just rubbish/Then a wind came and blew us away,/And after being on high for a while/Along came another wind to blow us away. . . .]

The metaphor is hardly surprising: a man in the Revolution is like a leaf in a storm. But those wasted whining voices, which match exploits and romances to the impulse of a complaint without any hope of being answered, furnish (on intoning this war hymn) the missing unifying fact: the great *brawl* provides a great opportunity for self-criticism. The nation is broadened and recognizes its inhabitants, verifies and contradicts itself, invents and recovers itself, ceases being a sum to become a synthesis.

Metamorphosis: the military conflict becomes a (non-hierarchical) succession of horses, cannon, dust, a desire to escape the chaos which should not be confused with flight. *The gift of ubiquity:* the same people are firing the shots on both sides: the Federal troops are the people, the *villistas* too, and so are the *carrancistas*, and it is the people who are executed and the people who make up the firing squad; the people are both vague randomness and precise law. From a short distance two groups of combatants insult each other, challenge each other and expose themselves to danger. There are no tricks, nor can there be. Meanwhile, the photographer risks himself (and it is his duty to do so) while the combatants remain calm – they lack 'self-consciousness', are ignorant of their destiny (to decorate the official speeches of tomorrow) – and train and sharpen their aim.

THE EXECUTED

'And if I die in battle. . . .' The realities behind the 'if' of this song: a trail of
ephemeral cemeteries, the nationalization of old metaphors about Greek gods
and French tribunes. 'And they're going to bury my body.' This is all that was
needed! They're still harping on about the special relationship between Mexicans
and death. 'And if I die in battle . . .', and the theme has now been trivialized.
But that was what it was like then, how confidences were informally exchanged,
the daily exchanges with fucking eternity. The classic images belong in an epilogue: on firing his last bullet the soldier jumps out of his hiding place and
throws himself down the hill, crumbling amid the insults he hurls at the government forces; he jumps the trenches at a gallop, shouting 'Long live Madero,
sons of bitches!', and spurs on his horse, throwing himself at the walls of the city
of Torreón.

And a body is dragged and trampled on, and another one falls and is blown
apart and, among the cries of agony and the shots and the puff of dust caused by
the falling body, the country is made.

They are about to execute him, and the shots are about to ring out. But the
condemned man is boastful; he delivers a diatribe, smiles scornfully, and shuts
himself away in a mutism that denies the executioners their pleasure; and so that
no one can say that he cracked, he opens his shirt, and makes a farewell gesture
as if he were receiving the final applause he deserves.

It is as if everything were suspended: the command to fire; the oratorical gesture; the curse; the slow-wittedness of the firing squad; the objectivity of the
photograph.

The reiterative testimony of the corpses: there they remain, gathered in the
streets, dotting the roads, stacked up by the artillery. Mexico is a common grave.
Bodies dangle from branches, telegraph poles and lampposts: a strange fruit
which, with every swing, becomes natural, serene. And the Revolution unifies
lives and deaths. In the conflagration, hierarchies collapse and the will of the
people, however betrayed and victimized, returns again and again so as to remain
on stage long enough vehemently to change it. And the railway and the peasant
masses, and the rifles and the sandals, and the multi-galloned hats and the
ammunition, and the banners and the defiant expressions, and the signing of a
new plan that causes the region to rise up in arms – all have been incorporated
into the gaze of the hanged man, of the firing squad, of the *soldadera*. Before the
camera the Revolution is momentarily still. Like that, just like that. . . .

III   An intimate knife to the throat

The Revolution secretes a new class. And this new class opposes the aristocratic pretensions of the Porfirian oligarchy with its enthusiasm to rise and rule. Generals who become financiers, sergeants who double as landowners and bankers: this is the age of *Compadre Mendoza*, the character from Mauricio Magdaleno's story and Fernando de Fuentes's film. Social morality demands it: opportunism must be judged historically and on its own terms. The Revolution begins to create its own frames of reference, disseminating its own implicit and explicit legislation. Within this moral and social space, what appears today as opportunism (and as a function of the ideals of a minority, which in effect it was) can also be seen as the benefits of opportunity, or of a social mobility that makes it possible to age in comfort. Moreover, the reigning opportunism refused to be recognized as such, demanding instead to be considered a symptom of the uncertainties of Mexico at the time and, at most, a question of survival – where there are no real options, it is pointless to talk about concessions. What does it matter if literature vents its anger on all those slippery characters who repeatedly change their colours in order to survive: the toff Luis Cervantes, in Mariano Azuela's *Los de abajo* ['The Underdogs'], is this character's prototype.

'The Revolution is the Revolution.' While awaiting the invention of a new Constitution, Luis Cabrera's phrase becomes the law that replaces the over-thrown codes. It also reflects the shifts in social values that silence Fulfilled Destiny, Immutable Hierarchy, and Pulchritude, each blasted away by the Greed, Vulgarity and Bravery celebrated by the revolutionaries.

The witnesses of the time are almost infallible. In his memoirs *El río de mi sangre* ['The River of My Blood'], an intimidated Genaro Fernández MacGregor evokes the revolutionaries in Mexico City:

> Whoever owned a car hid it, so as not to attract the attention of the saviours of the nation, who had a particular weakness for such vehicles. . . . At that time we lived next to the hordes bivouacked in the Central Railway Station. The trains arrived with their carriages crammed with soldiers dressed in blankets and sandals; they travelled, elbow to elbow, standing in those stinking carriages like cigarettes in a packet.

This belief in the *immorality of the physical presence of the poor* attenuates the horror of possible violence. The *appearance of the hordes* complements the entelechy of the pure ideal. Although in practice it is happy with any and every alliance, in theory the bourgeoisie worships its moral absolute, the lack of all fissures, abominating the breakdown of order and anathematizing any attack on private property. The idealists in the novels of Mariano Azuela and Martín Luis Guzmán condemn the armed movement in name of an immanent structure (everlasting Justice) which consecrates Civilization before Barbarism, surrender before victory, harmonious calm before pillage. It is possible to derive an aesthetic from moral condemnation ('How beautiful is the Revolution, even in its very barbarism!', says the idealist in *Los de abajo*), without failing to stress that no visual enthusiasm can postpone the severity of judgement.

From within the remnants of Porfirian society, there emerges – sheltered in the untouchable and sacred – an absolute and theological morality that declares the revolutionary 'usurpation' an abominable crime. For one reason or another, many coincide – a tacit homage to the previous regime – in their repudiation of the newcomer. Essentially, a network of condemnations rooted in two certainties – the permanence and irreplaceability of the ruling class – remains intact.

The moralists tend to be those who have suffered defeat. Pitiless, the hasty condemnation of the great historical transformation intervenes to feed their bitterness – which will have repercussions in the long term. Right from its inception, the nation-state that emerges from the Revolution gives way to the opposition. Widely reviled by real or imagined exiles, the State, with formative modesty, reserves for itself the right to self-worship and the sowing and reaping of heroes. (Now one might say: self-critique as vainglory, and the discovery of elective affinities with those who might well have been our ancestors but chose to be our precursors instead.)

Mariano Azuela, Martín Luis Guzmán and José Vasconcelos (like the poets Jorge Cuesta and Salvador Novo later) all take the ethical foundations for their diatribes against the new morality from the cultural system in which they were formed, *porfirismo*: the mixture of positivism and Catholicism, nationalism as the hope for another nationality, and their Siamese love for dictatorship and progress. The moral judgement of the present entrusted to the past. This 'paradox', one of our historical constants, is also explained by the inconclusive character of the social and political transformations. Madero not only leaves the structure of the Porfirian armed forces intact, he also protects – and, fundamentally, worships – the tablets on which the laws that remorselessly judge him are written. The social Revolution triumphs, however ephemerally, but imposes its own rules only half-heartedly. Cabrera – who pointed out, with some lucidity, that Revolutionary morality was engendered and sustained only through armed force – would eventually complain about the success of his insightful phrase, which seemed to justify and authorize the excesses of the Revolutionary rabble.

Trotsky once suggested that moralists really want history to leave them to their books, magazines and common sense. Among the moralists who hounded the Revolution were some of the country's best writers and intellectuals, who, in successive stages, resisted – through internal and external exile – becoming its accomplices. And this happened because criticism was endowed only with the task of tracing the paths of hopelessness, anger and impotence.

Meanwhile, in the National Palace. . . . Another group begins to take control of this forced amalgamation of factions and tendencies which makes up the Mexican Revolution. They are 'the barbarians' from the Northern state of Sonora who, in turn, will invent 'the barbarians', now the forces led by Pancho Villa (the *villistas*), while bringing new attributes to the fore: particularly their ferocious pragmatism and laicism. They never belonged to the Porfirian Nation, and in widening and extending the parameters of the nation, they find in power – money, industry, business, estates, and the suppression of any opposition – the only patriotism they can understand. They have very few political debts to the past – and even fewer to the present. . . .

IV   How not to be overwhelmed by marble and glory

Abstractions have no meaning in periods of political volatility, and virtues or defects come alive only when they take control of people and lead them to mystification. The different kinds of social morality at the time are embodied in the figures of Plutarco Calles, Pancho Villa and Luis N. Morones. Villa's behaviour assimilates the landowner's grinding power over the lives and self-esteem of others, and translates it into peasant enthusiasm for justice and revenge. The stories of Villa's (historical and legendary) cruelty produce a diagnosis: he is the victim who inherits the brutality of the victimizer while also being determined or configured by the complex superstitions of his class; a condition which eventually leads – as the accusatory story continues – to that moment of fetishistic anxiety in the National Palace around the Presidential Chair. Calles, in turn, embodies efficiency. Defeated, the President's rival recognizes the reasons for his humiliation in one sentence: 'Mexican politics knows only one rule: be an early bird', thinks Aguirre, who represents Francisco Serrano in *La sombra del caudillo* ['The Shadow of the Caudillo', 1929] as he dies. Calles is a very early riser, and becomes the paradigm for the new morality of his age. He endows corruption not with the characteristics of plunder (consecrated in the verb 'to carrancear' from President Venustiano Carranza) but with those of necessary social equilibrium.

During the armed phase of the Revolution, the limits of behaviour were set by Pancho Villa: excess, vindicatory eagerness, and primitivism – attributes which authorize his folkloric metamorphosis by the bourgeoisie in both film and literature. Later, during the institutional stage of the Revolution, Luis Morones, leader of the Regional Confederation of Mexican Workers (CROM), defines a new limit (moral judgement as simultaneously a mark of admiration and reproach). His rapacity hones and accentuates the style (exhibitionist waste, enormous mansions, the cultivated atmosphere of the court and seraglio) of caciques and governors. Morones fine-tunes the gestures of the powerful and the tics of the influential. The traditional respect once held for those in power becomes the flattery of men surrounded by girlfriends and gunmen, posing as if they were in charge of the destiny of the nation.

The devastation associated with the period dominated by Plutarco Elías Calles finds in Abelardo Rodríguez (gambling joints, hippodromes, the Tijuana casinos, the appropriation of huge amounts of land) on the one hand, and Luis N. Morones on the other, its paradigmatic figures. Locations near the borders and in the interior are made free zones so as to attract tourists; casinos are built and the growth of prostitution is encouraged. The image of Mexico as a *hang-out*, a noisy and luxurious hideout from Prohibition, is disseminated throughout the USA. The Calles period pulls Luis Cabrera's statement in 1917 ('You must take money from wherever it is found') from its necessary context and transforms it into an invitation to plunder: it may be found in hippodromes, at roulette, poker and baccarat tables, in cockfights, in the *Agua Caliente Casino* in Tijuana, the *Casino de la Selva* in Cuernavaca and the Foreign Club on the outskirts of the city. It may be found in the budget and in government contracts. It is as simple as this: if you lend your services to the nation, it is only right that the nation reward you.

Not everyone accepts this self-compensatory nationalism. There is much protest, complaint, reproach, insult, and condemnation as the massive acceptance of the new meaning of the Revolution – sudden wealth – becomes routine. Public morality is secularized and freed from religious sanctions, and it is now time to create civil and social sanctions for it. What it receives, however, is ostracism, repudiation, and the grinding experience of lack. The twin supports of these punitive efforts are inevitably *machismo* and the idolization of private property. Trotsky also noted that moralism inevitably leads to the acceptance of a particular 'moral sense', an absolute, which is no more than a philosophical stand-in for God.

The 'absolute' admits of two possibilities here: nationalism and opportunism.

The State adheres to the former and indifferently abandons its memory to the latter. To give moral form to nationalist consciousness, the identification of the State with national history is sought in a synthesis of historic conquests and virtues. Class morality, wholly accepted and assumed by those who suffer it, works through a single idea: all education rests on the normalization of grandeur. For a time, this grandeur is concentrated in the teaching of History, in the heroics which articulate the moral rectitude and legitimacy of each and every one of the State's own fables. Muralism is the synthesis of such an irreproachable education. Blown up and inflated, Pancho Villa and Emiliano Zapata ride by on horseback while the Promethean man reaches out from among the vaults. The triumphant Revolution pedagogically administers its past. A *guerrillero*, a subversive, can always be the source for impulsive inspiration just as long as, on becoming a figure in the civic pantheon, he supports the System that honours him with statues with his own meaningful silence.

'Revolutionary morality' finds its models of behaviour and identification in nationalist sentiment. To be a nationalist is to do good for the fatherland, to become one in solidarity with your compatriots. On discovering – or rediscovering – the contents and forms of the nation, the primordial pacts of a collectivity are revealed and elucidated. Nationalism is the social morality which the State and progressive sectors accept and extol. Moreover, it is the impetus that runs alongside and accompanies the naked struggle for power. *Caciquismo* is overcome in order to strengthen the caudillo; the regional party bosses are unified and subjected to central powers in order to benefit all the more from their sectional autonomy. And another nationalism emerges. The National Revolutionary Party is the all-embracing solution created by Plutarco Elías Calles, which institutionalizes as it continues to pursue the conquest and maintenance of power, clarifying the panorama from within its own coalition: the Mexican Revolution has been the great Darwinian metaphor; political expertise is the sign of immortality, so to whoever survives the chain of coups and assassinations intact go the spoils. And nationalism as a moral impulse (in any radical sense) is attacked and finally destroyed by a corruption that will become the social basis *par excellence* of the regime's discriminatory and unequal distribution of wealth. In other words: let's sort out the bribes so that we don't have to share out the land.

V   At a banquet at which all the men hate one another

From Historical Grandeur to the Force of Sentiment. The familiar uses of grandeur gradually begin to wane as the nation's heroes ascend or descend in order to fit into primary-school mythology. Education now turns to the administration of feelings; to the tune – before the age of television – of a bolero trio made up of film, radio and popular song: have you heard the story of the mother who washes clothes all day so that her son can go to Harvard? The economy of this 'magnificent sentimentalism' moves between two poles which are, in reality, one: the family and *machismo*. The second protects and animates the first, projecting a historical reality structured by Judaeo-Christian morality and patriarchal ideology into the realms of myth and finance. A woman's fate is to be subjugated, anatomy marking her place on the social scale.

Before, *machismo* had been the first and last nationalist pride, the valour required to live like a Mexican and die at the first opportunity. During the high points of the Revolution the meaning of *machismo* was neither self-affirmation nor the ratification in public of private valour. It was, rather, an act of social obedience. 'If I'm to be shot tomorrow, let's just get it over with now' is not a cocky phrase but, rather, a realistic appreciation of the facts. In the Revolution, life and death are not heavily loaded with the clumsy significance endowed to them by a society of property-owners. The socialization of death changes death's significance.

Bravery, nobility and mettle are supreme commodities because in them are condensed concrete political commitments and historical judgement. An example: the episode called 'The Death of David Berlanga' in Guzmán's *El aguila y la serpiente* ['The Eagle and the Serpent'] when Rodolfo Fierro, charged with executing Berlanga, remembers him with admiration:

> 'Really,' he added slowly, 'I'm not as bad as they say. I've also got a heart, I've also got feelings. . . . What a brave man that Berlanga was, and strong! Look' – and he showed me his cigar – 'since this morning I've been trying to smoke a cigar without letting the ash drop; but I can't manage it. My fingers, I can't control them, so the ash falls. And that's even with a good cigar, I assure you. Whereas he, Berlanga, had a steady hand, and kept it steady for as long as he wanted, right up to the moment when we were going to kill him. . . .'

Machismo as a *commercial spectacle* emerges towards the end of the 1930s. In decorating established codes of behaviour, it folklorizes and depoliticizes. No one questions it, perhaps because no one took the massive reach of this industrial campaign seriously enough. The fact, for example, that the so-called 'love of death' is the product of the vulnerability of the popular classes is ignored. Those who have been educated under repressive regimes do not endow life with the same absolute value as dominant morality does. Consumer-*machismo* is, right from the start, the product of bourgeois ideology; and the starting point of their mass strategy is a class one: only the excess of physical bravery redeems the mortal sin of poverty. As a *cultural value, machismo* was, at first, presented as a definitive and defining characteristic of what it meant to be Mexican, the indispensable quality needed to appreciate and take pity on a nationality. As will be the case later, in the 1950s, when, protected by a critical and/or apologetic literature about Mexicanness, there emerge critiques of the ruthless conduct towards women and the barbarism of circus and vandal-like behaviour. However, the impulse at the heart of this 'show' hardly exhausts all its possibilities. For *machos* do not only want to crush women. They also need to locate the compensatory technique of their social, economic and cultural inferiority, and their victories over already defeated beings are not compensation enough. They also need to acquire a personality which will allow them to forget, one which attenuates or denies their everyday exploitation. From another point of view, *machismo* is also a complaining demand for recognition: 'Believe me, if I weren't just a nobody, I wouldn't exhibit my need to be with such anguish, I wouldn't negate the humanity of my partner, I wouldn't risk my life so stupidly.' Having been dispossessed, the never-quite-adult *macho* from the popular classes offers up the credulity of his puerile, deteriorated and sacrificial ego for commercialization. A section of the Left has also resorted to *machismo* in order to provide itself with quick 'heroic personalities' while still exploiting women, and offering indifference to all risk as its only political programme. Generally, the Left's sexual politics has duplicated Conservative orthodoxy: the family providing its central axis, defending strict monogamy for women, and rejecting all birth control as an anti-imperialist strategy.

In the dominant classes, *machismo* becomes a technique of concealment. The *macho* (he knows how to party and to seduce, and will take on all comers) tends to reveal the deep roots of its cause in his very actions: *machismo* comes from repression, is to be found in his drunken deterioration, and moves towards renewed subjugation. Those in control of society know that in the self-delusions of *machismo* (in the fascination of being defenceless before one's most deplorable fantasies) there lies an endless source of control.

VI   *Who will tell me who you are and who you were?*

Stop the clock! Oh, what a sublime moment! The country affirms its stability in 1929 with the creation of the *Partido Nacional Revolucionario* (National Revolutionary Party), which will become the *Partido Mexicano Revolucionario*

(Mexican Revolutionary Party), which will become the *Partido Institucional Revolucionario* (Institutional Revolutionary Party). The story of subjugation is told in the changes of acronym (PNR/PRM/PRI). Inside and out, the Party of the Revolution – a politico-bureaucratic totem – provides, rents, and proclaims myths: the only possible way of getting anywhere near the dispensers of goods, prestige and rewards has been massified. The PRI becomes a party (a whole way of life) which – especially in the provinces – also provides patterns of behaviour, gestures and sayings. Moral and visual lessons: you speak as if you belong to the PRI, you wave your arms about as if you belong to the PRI, you become instantly morally incensed as if you belong to the PRI, you obtain pride of place as if you belong to the PRI. The religious monopoly has come to an end: the PRI gathers disciples just as faithful, and much more ambitious.

Cardenismo does not constitute, despite the admirable efforts of Lázaro Cárdenas himself, an interruption in this process of consolidation. On the contrary, the attempt at a Revolutionary nationalism becomes instead a series of loud poses. What does change – and radically – is the realm of governmental public morality. A populist or revolutionary nationalist programme calls for moral credibility, and needs support and exemplary behaviour. In December 1934, President Cárdenas writes in his *Apuntes* ['Notes'] that, among other major difficulties: 'Centres of vice, operating with the backing of local and federal authorities, make me realize that my task is a difficult one, that I will find major obstacles to the clean-up campaign. . . . But I am confident that with the support of the people I will be able to resolve these problems.' Next, he closes down the casinos and prohibits gambling.

The most genuine moments of Cárdenas's government make for a mixture of loyalty, opportunism and demagoguery. In 1936 Vincente Lombardo Toledano said: 'He who makes a mistake backwards dies, and he who makes a mistake forwards guarantees his future.' In this case, nationalism finds a person who passionately wants to represent the nation, and the national becomes identified with such policies as Agrarian Reform and the nationalization of oil. Nearly everything is centred around the President, his moderation, and his popularity with the masses, especially the peasantry. And then: capitalist development requires a calm bourgeoisie and solid administration, and in 1940 this inflexible logic is provisionally embodied in the new President, Manuel Ávila Camacho. Again, more shifts and reaccommodation, involving the solidifying of institutions and techniques that 'Mexicanize' capitalist mentality. Despite the recovery of control over the land during the Cárdenas regime, and the moral commitments to Abyssinia, Finland and Spain, the popular meetings, artists' leagues and rural missions, the visits to the nation's co-operative farms and the fiery speeches in the Confederation of Mexican Labour (CTM), not one dent is made in a stubborn individualism, the adoration of bank accounts, or the celebration of those who impose themselves whatever their methods. Soon, it makes no sense whatsoever (and no one is going to propose it anyway) to advocate an ethics of solidarity.

The Second World War is being waged during the Ávila Camacho government. Translated into the terms of government propaganda, this provided the occasion for more nationalist campaigns: patriotic sentiment increasing the autonomy of the State. The project flounders amid speeches, while immigrants arrive in waves from the countryside to stir up High Society.

There is a great change in social morality. Between songs, dancers share Stock Exchange tips, and the sinful replaces – to great applause – the subversive: so let's just enjoy this delicious alternative to the parish meeting and political gathering. From the confessional to the conga, passing through the mythic number of one million dead, from excommunication to the boogie-woogie, from the Dutiful Daughters of Mary or the political cabals to the romantic bolero. *Ego te absolvo*, they tell the Lord. *Ego te absolvo* dances mambo and *danzón*. Thanks to the cinema, popular song and social fantasies associated with Night Life, Vaudeville's prediction that the plebs are also an integral part of the city is finally accepted – after only four-and-a-half centuries.

The first task is to foment and dissimulate the effects of what is quickly becoming the centre of all national life: the taste/distaste, hate/love of corruption. By the 1940s it is already one of the main topics of conversation, its aura being the inevitable result of a morality solely dedicated to appearances, which, once the rituals of austerity and democracy have been reverentially kept, believes only in personal aggrandizement and the maintenance of the status quo. In precarious opposition, the *idée fixe* of the conservatives: we are a people condemned by our intrinsic corruption. *Ars Combinatorium*: dominant morality obtains unlimited admiration from those who possess all the stocks and bonds; dominant morality obtains general adherence to corruption; the middle class remains forcefully critical of corruption while practising it.

During the government of Miguel Alemán, corruption has a technical name ('Developmentalism') and great public and national significance: from the accumulation of wealth will spring general prosperity. Let everything be subordinated to this general purpose. Alemán doesn't want to corrupt the whole country, only to make sure that the royal road to greatness is devoid of all revolutionary implications. Society as showcase and pedestal: there is a frenzied desire to exhibit one's possessions, and both the banks and the cabarets become the twin voices of this one chorus.

Here is the testimony of the film star María Félix, published in an interview with María Elena Rico in the magazine *Contenido* (October 1976):

> Jorge [Pasquel, a prominent member of President Miguel Alemán's clique] was the most splendid man I had ever met. When we were filming *Maclovia* in Pátzcuaro, he left his hydroplane at my disposal – for anything I might need. One day the hotel ran out of ice, and within hours the hydroplane was back from Mexico City with an enormous fridge. He accompanied me to Pátzcuaro, and we travelled with six Cadillacs following behind us carrying uniformed waiters, hairdressers, a cook, a valet, three maids, a masseur. . . . We ate at a pretty spot on the road: in a twinkling of an eye, the servants put up tents, a 'stand' so that Jorge could practise his shooting, and a table with a long tablecloth where the cook served up a fantastic banquet. . . .

VII *'And the present/is already the future, and forgotten'*

It is not enough, says Tocqueville, for a government to have the power and will to commit acts of violence and injustice; the habits, ideas and passions of an age must also lend themselves to them. During the government of Alemán, and the years that follow, habits, ideas and passions are driven by the ideal of self-fashioning, the dazzling story of the ego. Nationalism becomes a noble sentiment demanding occasional support while, economically, the country is gradually, but systematically, denationalized. The Land of Tomorrow receives foreign investment, and in exchange co-operative farmers are assassinated in order to generate divisions and conflict, while workers stubbornly remaining within free trade unions are locked out, beaten and imprisoned with the complicity and complacency of shared habits, ideas and passions. If, as Whitehead suggests, an idea that is generally held is always a danger for the existing order, the general idea to be destroyed is – surprise, surprise – the class struggle. The idea of National Unity is fabricated instead: 'I will govern for everyone', says Ávila Camacho, as the CTM crowns Miguel Alemán the 'Worker of the Nation'. Despotism is tempered by assassination, fraud and pillage, and given prestige by whatever charitable donations the booty allowed. From the point of view of power, everything must become a question of social and economic success. The fate of the working class and victimized peasantry is the concern only of political commentators (and the families of the deceased). Everything is absorbed by the spectacle of national growth, the show at which dams, motorways, stadiums and universities are unveiled. The monument to Miguel Alemán in the University campus is no mere anecdote: it is one more reiteration of the fact that symbols of greatness constitute manuals of good conduct. A Zapotec Indian may or may not want to be President of the Republic, but what surely matters to him – and by now has become a shared breviary – are the splendours of a well-situated residence, a pool and a cool whisky, served pronto.

The government protects economic denationalization by identifying itself more and more absolutely with the Nation. In this regard, paternalism and depoliti-cization are the best techniques. The paternalism of the Cárdenas government even becomes irrational ('You have to agree with the Indian even if he isn't right', says a compassionate high bureaucrat), pretending to give the masses a direction, to guide them in their political orphanhood. The paternalism that follows sees in philanthropy the medium, and in the demand for gratitude the message. Win the sympathy of the people through good works, building roads, dispensing favours and free hats, and offering the best student grants. If the government is every-thing – gifts and threats, force and benevolence – all individuals can do is either to please or to deceive it. Communal actions are not only useless now, they may also imply a disadvantageous and risky comparison with the government.

It is no longer freedom that is the ideal of citizenship, but gratitude. From Benito Juarez to Porfirio Díaz to Carranza to Calles to Miguel Alemán to Díaz Ordaz to Echeverría, this idea subsumes and clarifies not only a panorama of fic-tions but also a historical project: the country will grow, and its better classes will benefit if only they let us govern in peace. Depoliticization is a petition of prin-ciple: doesn't the government do it well?

VIII   No more tears or reproaches

The figure of President Ruiz Cortines is exactly right for a colourless period that was apparently benevolent. Everything about him is both in and out of tune: his appearance, age, and bureaucratic ancestry; his austerity and parsimony; his erotic inclination for grand slogans, bow ties and billiard-and-domino binges. Nothing about him echoes the brashness and waste of the previous years; and the modesty and sparseness of ceremony that surrounds Don Adolfo produces a rather grey figure, not at all suitable for any of the usual excess. Intense com-mitment has become a thing of the past. Eloquence is restricted to slogans ('The March to the Sea'), the grandiloquence of rhetoric seems out of place, and productivity falters very much like the failed poetic tones: 'Forward to creative and fecund work'!

Before its liquidation by 'the desire for universalization', cultural nationalism battles to retain some 'public credibility'. Emerging against it, an expanding field: described culturally as the middle class, it is averse to singularity, terrified of betraying itself as merely colourful, and hungry for glamour and 'international status'. Who cares now for the idiosyncrasies to be found in either the Mexican cowboy [*charro*] or the village Indian girl? This freeing of the middle classes has a number of different but complementary causes: the rampant North-Americanization of the country; the exhaustion of the cultural and political resources on offer which had emerged with the post-Revolutionary rediscovery of the national; the rapid diffusion of the most important international currents and artists (the 'global village'); the disdain for politics as a source of social prestige; the deterioration in the bureaucratic use of the myths of the Mexican Revolution.

The 1950s were the decade when a struggle was lost. The petty bourgeoisie is bored with muralism, fed up with national films; it glances at 'archetypical features' with a slight false condescension, and is now ashamed of its most intimate predilections. During the Ruiz Cortines period the concept of nationhood is irreversibly ruined, to be replaced by another kind of mentality – not devotedly colonial, still linked to very deep national ideas, but indifferent to tradition, unable to fabricate coherent versions of the national past and future. Only the most fatuous and local of customs are saved. What can take the place of the faith in the creative and regenerative features of the Mexican Revolution for art and culture, once it had been lost? An administrative communiqué: we must continue to believe until another institutional source of such a stimulus can be found. Such trusteeship obtains an identical response in the years that follow: if no one can establish what does and does not belong to tradition, and if nationalism has ended in a demagoguery whose logorrhoea has neutralized genuine findings and conquests, it is time – never mind the injustice – to put peculiarity, the essential, the national and the regional to one side.

In the midst of a tranquillity both real and apparent, the middle sectors begin to desert the practice of 'Mexicanness'. What was once acclaimed as *national essence* (the merry-go-round of fatalities and fatalisms) is now interpreted by those who benefit from capitalist development as *folklore* – that is, as commerce. Troubled by the spectres of an undefinable entity, 'Mexicanness', the dominant classes renounce what is *sui generis* to demand the colonial right to hybridity. In fewer than three periods of government a considerable proportion of the bourgeoisie and petty bourgeoisie morosely, but clearly and lavishly, modifies the ways in which it lives Mexico. This transformation takes place without disturbing the codes of verbal communication, the unalterable rhetoric, the same slogans as always which refuse, in their increasing deafness, to recognize the existence of a different audience.

Is the period of the Ruiz Cortines government a crossroads of subterranean tendencies that eventually emerge during the period of López Mateos and finally explode in 1968? From this point of view, the Ruiz Cortines period would be something like the (managed) calm before the storm that set out to destroy it, the transition towards the breakdown of much more than confidence and much less than institutions.

(In 1959 the mayor of Mexico City, Ernesto P. Uruchurtu, utters an impeccable thought: 'All establishments should be closed by one o'clock in the morning so as to guarantee that workers' families receive their wage, and that the family inheritance is not frittered away in centres of vice.')

Melodrama – a direct route for the expression and fixing of socially recognized sentiments – remains the classical form in which society registers its moral temperament and bears witness to its intimate convictions. Even literature confronts the theme of the institutional revolution (for many the revolution betrayed) through melodrama or mythification. Over here a Secretary of State comes to power; over there a businessman appears. Meanwhile, the working class extends like a folkloric shadow waiting to be defined. In melodrama dominant morality is extenuated and strengthened, governed by a convulsive, shuddering faith in the values of poetry.

The message is clear: melodrama is the midpoint between social success and absolute pessimism. Mexico cannot be understood if you do not know why the actress Sara García sheds a tear in silence, if you do not accept that social life is the martyrdom that each family passes through before its happy end. What the bourgeoisie and proletariat, middle class and lumpenproletariat look for throughout the length and breadth of the culture industry, and find without knowing it, is a systematic understanding of society unified and transfigured by melodrama.

IX Like me, many and nobody

The Loudest Disagreements usually hide or dispel the true ones. What are the programmes of the independent candidates to the Presidency over the years – of José Vasconcelos, Juan Andrew Almazán, Ezequiel Padilla, Miguel Henríquez Guzmán, or even Vicente Lombardo Toledano? None that differs *radically* from the doctrine of the Revolution, if by doctrine one means the short- and long-term offers made on behalf of the ruling classes. The outbursts are in the main sentimental, and the elemental democratic convictions of the *vasconcelistas* carry with them the grievances of the 'decent', passed over and shocked by the barbarism of the long line of post-Revolutionary rulers from the Northern state of Sonora. Similarly, the campaigns of Almazán and Henríquez are fed by the desperation of the middle classes, which is condensed into slogans about honesty and an easy and ephemeral manipulation of popular discontent. The exceptions: the messianic movements of the extreme Right – the *Cristeros* and *Sinarquistas* – who, in their condition of servants of the Kingdom of God, are (at their height) truly out of the ball park, refusing to indulge in the obedience and patience demanded by the representatives of atheism and apostasy.

Without ever theorizing nationalism, the Establishment always took it into account: while nationalism controls both public buildings and private feelings, there will be no major demand for ideological dissidence. The coercion and legitimacy provided by nationalism have emerged from structural conditions and a certainty in what is ours: cornucopia. To a great extent, nationalism was the historic result of the entrenchment in both existing values (and fears) and the array of anticipated pleasures at a very probable greatness to come. We have experienced what might be called a 'prospective nationalism', a vanity associated with the inevitable Mexico to come, mixed with a smiling forgiveness for the defects and customs of compatriots whose descendants will also inhabit a splendid future. This faith in things to come is, psychologically and culturally, the driving force of nationalism's demobilizing power.

Any discussion of political struggle in the 1930s inevitably comes to the moment when an old militant polemically isolates the reasons for his defeat: 'If we hadn't made that historic error in that meeting, the working class would now clearly be an independent force.' Resistance to the past: there has been a constant refusal to accept that the power of the hegemonic bloc relied in part on the confidence of the defeated in the foreseeable greatness of the nation; there has been insufficient appreciation of the contribution made by the nationalist candour and confidences of the marginalized; nor has the mythological power that produced the project for a new nation been sufficiently understood.

What social and cultural spaces have been made available for Mexican dissidents, fighting for democracy or socialism or for alternative lifestyles? Prisons, common graves, tolerance, silence, negation, clandestinity, ridicule by the mass media, complaints of conspiracies, scams, funereal elegies, posthumous defamation, the ghetto, the endless succession of ghettos, confinement, and the asphyxiating alleys in which the hopes and illusions of bohemians, feminists, radicals, anarchists, homosexuals, have been born, and – rebels or not – have found it possible to disaffiliate themselves from the State, Society, the System, Official Trade Unionism, Convention and Moral Prejudice, *Machismo*, the abstractions that name everyday oppression. Periodically they have been jailed, raided, murdered, their publications have been closed down and they have been the object of hate campaigns, moral lynching, insult, their careers destroyed and their work ignored amid the promotion and praise of the mediocre and the pros-titution of criticism. Periodically, too, the minority representatives of the minorities have been assimilated into the institutions, with jobs, deferential treatment, the recognition of the importance and bravery of their struggle, promises of immunity, prizes, the snapshot that seals the pacific coexistence of the powerful, their voluntary and involuntary politeness.

The strategy – and the situation has changed only slightly since 1968 – has been one of identifying this great marginal saga of the subaltern with the osten-tatious claims of its leaders' obvious failures (or what have been considered such). The other – not perceived or unwritten – history is that of a people whose anonymity included the refusal of all concessions, the unknown militants who chose prison or losing their jobs rather than giving up, the feminists who suffered decades of insults and ridicule, but just kept on fighting all the same, the railroad workers and electricians sacked just weeks before their retirement because they refused to sign up for the corrupt official union. What gets in the way of understanding this other admirable history is insisting on thinking about it in the redemptive terms (sacrifice, abnegation, martyrdom) of the liberal ideal of heroism by, for example, introducing the possibility of a kind of postmortem victory, of 'rewards-to-come' in a 'society-to-come'. All or nothing: sacralizing words tend to encourage forgetting the actual and implicit victories of merely not giving in or conforming to the norm. It has never really been admitted that the reservations into which the dissidents are crammed both make possible and extend that minimal democratic space the rest of us inhabit.

X *I believe I hear the busy murmur of the multitude at dawn*

Adolfo Ruiz Cortines, Adolfo López Mateos, Gustavo Díaz Ordaz. Presidents come and go as the old governmental style of understanding and living nation-hood reveals its cracks, its slogans so memorable because they are so open to satire: *The Abuse of Freedoms is Preferable to Any Hint of Dictatorship; I Do Not Harvest for Myself: I Harvest for Mexico.*

You can invent them, too: *All Freedoms Except One: The Freedom to Exercise*

Them. Even if President Ruiz Cortines never uttered this phrase, he should have. Because an X marks the place of your signature: *One-Way: Mexico. . . .* According to President López Mateos there is only one way, too, so the stubborn attempts at creating independent trade unions are met with the criminalization of strike action, murder, the imprisonment and harassment of workers. For more than eleven years Demetrio Vallejo, leader of the railroad workers, the Communist Valentín Campa and a group of revolutionary leaders are left in prison with hardly a protest. Because the silent majority is deaf too. Stability is frivolity. Already in the 1960s, amid the periodic crises of nationalist doubt, the middle classes who enjoy the commercial and spiritual delights of Modernity accept – when the goal is cosmopolitanism – that it is worth being apathetic when it comes to political rights. What is important, however, is the extension of that other dimension of individual rights, the making of egoism into an ideological adventure, vindicating psychoanalysis as the universal right of the bourgeoisie, rummaging about in one's infancy or poking about in one's loss of identity looking there for the prestigious or licentious roots of conventionality. Television begins to unify the reactions and speech of the whole country; even the luxurious up-market *Zona Rosa* ['Pink Zone'] becomes a moral proposition: understand it once and for all, you beggars – democracy will be possible only if you share in the admiration of cultural modernization. The rumba of False Consciousness visits art galleries and conference-shows, the Theatre of the Absurd, experimental films, the novels of Salinger and Robbe-Grillet, enthusing about the Civil Rights movement in the USA and the Cuban Revolution. Cultural modernization also involves some political struggle, and in their own meagre way the struggle against censorship and the mocking of chauvinism and prudishness are liberatory. This is the context in which the events of 1968 take place: one marked by parodies of the law, denationalization, demands for modernization, the desire for direct participation in the changes that are taking place. In the beginning the Student Movement (with the capital letters of historical singularity) offers unexpected parameters: faith in democracy and the immediate and emancipatory quality of their perspective. Everything, from the chants ('*Get down from the balcony, big-mouth*') to the pretensions of creating an independent State-within-the-State ('*University City. Free Territory of Mexico*') is a continuous act of faith in the liberatory potential of the country, a potential which the Constitution of the Republic recognizes, demands and defends.

The idea that the basis of political modernization can only be moral recovery is at the centre of the National Strike Council's petition that starts a dialogue in which the government never takes part. It demands the release of political prisoners (including Campa and Vallejo) because their continued imprisonment is unjust. It demands the resignation of the chiefs of police and the dissolution of the cavalry because of their involvement in violent acts of repression. The crime of 'social unrest' is a constant threat for the student militants, so they demand the repeal of Article 145 of the Federal Penal Code. At the same time – and this complements rather than contradicts the above – the vanguard of this middle class that has benefited so much economically demands the strict observance of the promises and decrees of Westernization: laws that really are respected, a functioning multiparty system, full participation in the nation's decision-making process. The Student Movement subsumes all these demands and desires, and articulates them in magnificent demonstrations, courageous gestures, irrefutable passions. From 26 July to 2 October 1968 – to give a chronological temporality to a phenomenon whose consequences are still present and determining us – the Movement is literally a massive displacement of energy that makes use of civil liberties in order to affirm its existence, recovering the street in the name of the people in order to proclaim its faith in the progressive contents of the juridical institutions of Mexico.

What, in the last analysis, does the Student Movement want? The official recognition of public injustice and demagoguery (in the style, for example, of the much-advertised 'Mexican Miracle'), the elimination of the most grotesque elements of the system, the renovation of the State Apparatus. When Javier Barros Sierra, rector of the UNAM (National Autonomous University of Mexico), fixes the national flag at half-mast because of the occupation of the San Idelfonso campus by the armed forces, a challenge is made: for the first time in many years the official version of a national event is not accepted as the only one. It's your turn now: in accordance with an old tradition, the State affirms its domination of the streets of Mexico (Public Space) with armed cavalry and police: in this country only those in power have a voice, a Movement and political ideas. Power is unidirectional: the affirmation of democracy can exist only in declarations to the press; revolutionary pronouncements can be made only by presidential decree; and if anyone protests, the source of the Plot will be identified in all of five minutes. The political apparatus, whose anachronistic flag is summed up in and held aloft by President Gustavo Díaz Ordaz, concedes nothing under pressure, and personalizes its answer: 'I do not hear the insults, I remain untouched by libel, the hate is not mine.' The State is not flexible, and a tragic solution soon becomes inevitable. The government refuses to accept its errors and arbitrariness, and demands clear submission to the power of the State. The students refuse to see things the same way, and so become its victims.

Such inflexibility is expressed in architecture. The buildings in Tlatelolco are an extension of the reason of state: gigantic proportions must exorcize its inferiority complex and prove us to be the equals of any nation. What is expressed in the constructions built for the 1968 Olympic Games, and in the buildings at Tlatelolco? Let me venture a hypothesis: the will of Mexican leaders to elevate themselves over and above the realities of their time, as well as pointing to a psychology and morality (ideology) that are to be translated into massacres and mass imprisonment. Those who have offered to host the Olympics must protect it (if threatened) at all costs. The limitations of a colonial or semi-colonial nation are obvious: on the one hand, the presence of the USA; on the other, a lack of recognition or admiration from the rest of the world. The USA cannot be eliminated, but the Olympic Games will bring international respect. The Olympics signify the coming of age: as the centre of the world's attention, Mexico becomes mature. Maturity, that is, understood in a very special way. From the government of Alvaro Obregón to Díaz Ordaz, Mexican public architecture symbolizes not only structural chaos and an almost pathological disdain for rational administration, but also a repugnance for technology and the technological age that is deeply imbued in the ideology of the Mexican Revolution. Nevertheless, one should not exaggerate the archaism of government policy, for it is perfectly possible to combine a romantic desire for the past with a disinhibited use of the means and materials of the present. And in Mexico, strong anti-modern sentiment goes hand in hand with the project of full industrialization.

The massacre of hundreds of demonstrators in Tlatelolco Square on 2 October 1968 is a historical break: it has been interpreted within a Christian schema (the offering of victims); it has imposed an extremely *macho* self-definition of Power that will not be taken advantage of by anyone; it has pretended to affirm the impossibility of democracy; it made for the reiteration of fatalist claims which – as of the 1950s – see in underdevelopment the form of oppression *par excellence*, the inescapable destiny, a hole. Already during the government of López Mateos, underdevelopment (the word and its devastating implications) excuses defeatism and upholds predestination. Even in attempting to think about it, recourse is made to its mere existence: there is underdevelopment because there has been underdevelopment. A grinding economic reality becomes a psychological fatality, a theory that legitimizes impotence. We are underdeveloped, and there is nothing we can do about it; we will never be whole.

The student movement of 1968 – despite its myriad mistakes and distortions, not to mention inexperience (exacerbated by defeat) – represents a splendid moment of moral, political and social consciousness, brilliant even in its most tragic moments. Nineteen sixty-eight: the tragic and the pathetic. The pathetic: the waning rabid nationalism, still desperate to identify national destiny with personal destiny. The tragic: the events of 2 October. The significance of the Tlatelolco massacre is not that 'to govern is to depopulate'.* Rather it established once more, as a limit case, that our system is paternalistic, and that it punishes; that it is boastful, and defiantly assumes the monopolization of the power to punish; that it is melodramatic, and displaces its guilt on to the punishment of others; that it is insecure and vacillating, publicly proclaiming the abolition of punishment; that it is didactic and has circular arguments, and punishes the victims of punishment. The process that ends in Tlatelolco Square is, despite its chronological brevity, vast. It contains heroic acts and great communitarian intuition, democratic feelings and practices, frustration, cowardice and false starts, professional moralists and provocateurs, total participation and the discovery of 'unforeseen' national leaders, radicalization and ideological conversion. In 1968, both the manufacture of a public history and the forging of a true history are known and recognized in synoptic and violent forms. In the first case, the official methods of constructing events are verified; in the second, the limits and weaknesses of manipulation and cover-up are observed.

XI Open chance or secret law

Between 1969 and 1970, after the defeat and dispersion of the movement, feelings of asphyxiation and self-mutilation take hold in centres of higher education, because students are marginalized by unhappy consciousness, myth and opportunism. It is now the State's turn to appropriate the demands for modernization, and during the government of Luis Echeverría a Third-Worldist discourse and a so-called policy of Democratic Opening emerges to incorporate the dissident sectors and take charge of the opposition from above, suppress the traditional isolationism of Mexico and provide it with a new rhetoric.

The guiding obsession of Echeverría's government is to eliminate the effects of '68 – in other words, the idea that the State has lost its most praised resource: the ability to negotiate and conciliate. Because Díaz Ordaz did not believe in

---

* According to the post-Independence Argentine critic Juan Bautista Alberdi, 'to govern is to populate'. As in the USA, the stimulation of immigration – preferably from Northern Europe – was a racist policy of nation-state formation among the new ruling classes of Latin America. [Translator's note.]

flexibility, the State cannot now count on its tacit allies, the intellectuals, and its most important supplier, the universities. Reinstating those lines of supply, privileging executive power once more (and to the maximum), re-energizing a political apparatus eternalized through the generation of need: these are the main themes of the Democratic Opening, Echeverría's proposal condensed in the opportune slogan '*Public Opinion, Return. The Government Forgives You!*'. Indeed, the Democratic Opening has a baptism of fire: a strike by civil servants resulting from the massacre of 10 June 1971, when the urban lumpen demand admission to our history in the form of the *Halcones* ['Falcons'] paramilitary group. The unforeseeable takes place: the union boss Fidel Velázquez states: 'The Falcons do not exist because I have never seen them', but the head of the Central Department is sacked and the Attorney General disappears (only to reappear again), while the intellectuals gloat over the union leader's incredible phrase. The Democratic Opening is, at first, an invitation for criticism, perceived with some suspicion – unsurprisingly – in a context where the invitation to criticize is taken as a demand for praise ('We thank the President for the clean, Mexican and brave opportunity he has offered us to thank him'). But the offer is also taken up from below, in journalism, in the development of certain academic trends and in the work of young people in popular neighbourhoods in the capital city or in the countryside, where they feel the need – not without some naivety, alarmism and sectarianism – to take part in the task of providing a voice, organization and critical leadership to the majorities, however weakly or rhetorically to begin with. In this sense – as in its exemplary support of 'Popular Unity' in Chile and of political refugees from all over Latin America – the Democratic Opening is part of a strategy, something a little more than the usual glory any regime desires for itself as the embodiment of virtue. It is a technique of internal persuasion: to postpone or suspend fascism in Mexico. The cost of this measure is the extension of corruption, attacks on the independent trade-union movement, economic and repressive desolation in the countryside, and the failure (political impossibility) of fiscal and administrative reform. For the minimal public opinion that exists, the 'Opening' finally means the failed attempt to modernize without conceding, or being able to concede.

From the point of view of publicity, the government presents itself as *energetic*: an insomniac President, 'working breakfasts' that last all day, endless openings of new institutions and trusteeships, an official architecture that extinguishes underdevelopment with its mere presence, endless speeches, spectacular tours, the dissemination of our Third-Worldism. Quick march! The 'Echeverrían style' is discursive, ubiquitous, and obsessed with the appearances and essences of nationality. And in order to reconstitute the prestige of nationalism, the integration of regional craftwork into everyday life is proclaimed – and on show in the Los Pinos Presidential residence: leather chairs from Jalisco, blown-glass china, paintings of volcanoes and naive impressions of village weddings, flowerpots, curtains, jugs, masks, carpets, statuettes, lamps. The ornamental parade is at one with the parties put on for illustrious visitors at the National Palace: stylized, the national costume puts on a nostalgic struggle before being recognized in public as fancy dress.

The conflict that most obviously characterizes Echeverría's government is statism versus 'the spirit of free enterprise'. It is not clearly visible at first, appearing only timidly, but with a verbal impetuosity that effects interests and sensibilities, and produces serious conflicts between the State and its long-time partner and beneficiary, Private Enterprise. (Meanwhile the government is still referred to as the Mexican Revolution, just so as to evoke the dust that precedes the signing of contracts to build dams and highways, while the Left proceeds to dissolve: sectarianism, spontaneism, Stalinist stigma, totemic inhibition before the State, technocratic jargon, hurried slogans, the confusion of the future of Humanity with the correlation of forces, superstitious invocations against capitalism.)

Among the middle classes, the 'Spirit of '68' dissolves and wanes. Democracy? A hopeless goal! People took to the streets motivated by a desire to participate, the anxiety to be citizens of a developing country which now demanded political participation and the equal distribution of wealth. All for nothing. Tanks and prisons were the only response. The desire for Democracy is refuted, or considered an impossible dream, and replaced by small groups made ever more desperate by ideological decline, a lack of any sense of reality, and the sordidness of impatient violent formulae. This all fails too, and terribly. The awareness of being the forced vassals of a corrupt autocracy is accepted reluctantly in the spaces of an enlightened middle class, amid the *unthinkability* of a rupture with the State or the idea of a State (dry land, mother protector, cruel father, close friend, secular provider of all reward on earth), protected by personal career 'success', the lack of will, or the absolution provided by protest songs or the oversimplifications of 'academic Marxism' (obsessed with verifying the notes at the foot of the page of the struggle for socialism), or tirelessly insisting on the new 'theory of the Trojan Horse': Revolution-from-within, the-transformation-of-structures-from-the-position-of-power.

From 1968 to 1976, what the mass media unify, politics separates. The complexity of the country is accentuated regionally, and the attempts at trade-union independence, or the organizational efforts of dissident groups, or the contradictory emergence of popular neighbourhoods (the demographic response to urban *latifundismo*) are all phenomena which, at the level of the national, are of only secondary importance. Way ahead is the Statist ambition to diversify, modernize and internationalize. And when an unspoken deal is believed to have been struck between complaint and the minimal spaces of freedom available, when the looming economic crises hit, and the devaluations follow, and what is left of the dream evaporates, collective misery is flaunted as the extension of progress: to whom do you direct your trust when everything is for sale?

2

Identity Hour or, What Photos Would You Take of the Endless City? (From a Guide to Mexico City)

Visually, Mexico City signifies above all else the superabundance of people. You could, of course, turn away from this most palpable of facts towards abstraction, and photograph desolate dawns, or foreground the aesthetic dimension of walls and squares, even rediscover the perfection of solitude. But in the capital, the multitude that accosts the multitude imposes itself like a permanent obsession. It is the unavoidable theme present in the tactics that everyone, whether they admit it or not, adopts to find and ensconce themselves in even the smallest places the city allows. Intimacy is by permission only, the 'poetic licence' that allows you momentarily to forget those around you – never more than an inch away – who make of urban vitality a relentless grind.

Turmoil is the repose of the city-dwellers, a whirlwind set in motion by secret harmonies and lack of public resources. How can one describe Mexico City today? Mass overcrowding and the shame at feeling no shame; the unmeasurable space, where almost everything is possible, because everything works thanks only to what we call a 'miracle' – which is no more than the meeting-place of work, technology and chance. These are the most frequent images of the capital city:

- multitudes on the Underground (where almost six million travellers a day are crammed, making space for the very idea of space);
- multitudes taking their entrance exam in the University Football Stadium;
- the 'Marías' (Mazahua peasant women) selling whatever they can in the streets, resisting police harassment while training their countless kids;
- the underground economy that overflows on to the pavements, making popular marketplaces of the streets. At traffic lights young men and women

overwhelm drivers attempting to sell Kleenex, kitchenware, toys, tricks. The vulnerability is so extreme that it becomes artistic, and a young boy makes fire – swallowing it and throwing it up – the axis of his gastronomy;

- mansions built like safes, with guard dogs and private police;
- masked wrestlers, the tutelary gods of the new Teotihuacan of the ring;
- the *Templo Mayor*: Indian grandeur;
- '*piñatas*' containing all the most important traditional figures: the Devil, the Nahual, Ninja Turtles, Batman, Penguin . . .;
- the Basilica of Guadalupe;
- the swarm of cars. Suddenly it feels as if all the cars on earth were held up right here, the traffic jam having now become second nature to the species hoping to arrive late at the Last Judgement. Between four and six o'clock in the morning there is some respite, the species seems drowsy . . . but suddenly everything moves on again, the advance cannot be stopped. And in the traffic jam, the automobile becomes a prison on wheels, the cubicle where you can study Radio in the University of Tranquillity;
- the flat rooftops, which are the continuation of agrarian life by other means, the natural extension of the farm, the redoubt of Agrarian Reform. Evocations and needs are concentrated on the rooftops. There are goats and hens, and people shout at the helicopters because they frighten the cows and the farmers milking them. Clothes hang there like harvested maize. There are rooms containing families who reproduce and never quite seem to fit. Sons and grandsons come and go, while godparents stay for months, and the room grows, so to speak, eventually to contain the whole village from which its first migrant came;
- the contrasts between rich and poor, the constant antagonism between the shadow of opulence and the formalities of misery;
- the street gangs, less violent than elsewhere, seduced by their own appearance, but somewhat uncomfortable because no one really notices them in the crowd. The street gangs use an international alphabet picked up in the streets of Los Angeles, fence off their territories with graffiti, and show off the aerial prowess of punk hairstyles secure in the knowledge that they are also ancestral, because they really copied them off Emperor Cuauhtemoc. They listen to heavy metal, use drugs, thinner and cement, destroy themselves, let themselves be photographed in poses they wish were menacing, accept parts as extras in apocalyptic films, feel regret for their street-gang life, and spend the rest of their lives evoking it with secret and public pleasure.

The images are few. One could add the Museum of Anthropology, the Zócalo at any time (day or night), the Cathedral and, perhaps (risking the photographer), a scene of violence in which police beat up street vendors, or arrest youngsters, pick them up by the hair, or swear that they have not beaten anyone. The typical repertoire is now complete, and if I do not include the *mariachis* of Plaza Garibaldi, it is because this text does not come with musical accompaniment. Mexico: another great Latin American city, with its seemingly uncontrollable growth, its irresponsible love of modernity made visible in skyscrapers, malls, fashion shows, spectacles, exclusive restaurants, motorways, cellular phones. Chaos displays its aesthetic offerings, and next to the pyramids of Teotihuacán, the baroque altars, and the more wealthy and elegant districts, the popular city offers its rituals.

On the causes for pride that (should) make one shiver

It was written I should be loyal to the nightmare of my choice.
(Joseph Conrad, *Heart of Darkness*)

Where has that chauvinism of old gone for which, as the saying goes, 'There is nowhere like Mexico'? Not far, of course: it has returned as a chauvinism expressed in the language of catastrophe and demography. I will now enumerate the points of pride (psychological compensation):

- Mexico City is the most populated city in the world (the Super-Calcutta!);
- Mexico City is the most polluted city on the planet, whose population, however, does not seem to want to move (the laboratory of the extinction of the species);
- Mexico City is the place where it would be impossible for anything to fail due to a lack of audience. There is public aplenty. In the capital, to counterbalance the lack of clear skies, there are more than enough inhabitants, spectators, car-owners, pedestrians;
- Mexico City is the place where the unlivable has its rewards, the first of which has been to endow survival with a new status.

What makes for an apocalyptic turn of mind? As far as I can see, the opposite of what may be found in Mexico City. Few people actually leave this place whose vital statistics (which tend, for the most part, to be short of the mark) everyone invents at their pleasure. This is because, since it is a secular city after all, very few take seriously the predicted end of the world – at least, of *this* world. So what are the retentive powers of a megalopolis which, without a doubt, has reached its historic limit? And how do we reconcile this sense of having reached a limit with the medium- and long-term plans of every city-dweller? Is it only centralist anxiety that determines the intensity of the city's hold? For many, Mexico City's major charm is precisely its (true and false) 'apocalyptic' condition. Here is the first megalopolis to fall victim to its own excess. And how fascinating are all the biblical prophecies, the dismal statistics and the personal experiences chosen for catastrophic effect! The main topic of conversation at gatherings is whether we are actually living the disaster to come or among its ruins; and when collective humour describes cityscapes, it does so with all the enthusiasm of a witness sitting in the front row at the Last Judgement: 'How awful, three hours in the car just to go two kilometres!' 'Did you hear about those people who collapsed in the street because of the pollution?' 'In some places there is no more water left.' 'Three million homes must be built, just for a start. . . .'

The same grandiose explanation is always offered: despite the disasters, twenty million people *cannot leave Mexico City or the Valley of Mexico, because there is nowhere else they want to go; there is nowhere else, really, that they can go.* Such resignation engenders the 'aesthetic of multitudes'. Centralism lies at the origins of this phenomenon, as does the supreme concentration of powers – which, nevertheless, has certain advantages, the first of which is the identification of liberty and tolerance: 'I don't feel like making moral judgements because then I'd have to deal with my neighbours.' Tradition is destroyed by the squeeze, the replacement of the extended family by the nuclear family, the wish for extreme individualization that accompanies anomie, the degree of cultural development, the lack of democratic values that would oblige people to – at least minimally – democratize their lives. 'What should be abolished' gradually becomes 'what I don't like'.

To stay in Mexico City is to confront the risks of pollution, ozone, thermic inversion, lead poisoning, violence, the rat race, and the lack of individual meaning. To leave it is to lose the formative and informative advantages of extreme concentration, the experiences of modernity (or postmodernity) that growth and the ungovernability of certain zones due to massification bring. The majority of people, although they may deny it with their complaints and promises to flee, are happy to stay, and stand by the only reasons offered them by hope: 'It will get better somehow.' 'The worst never comes.' 'We'll have time to leave before the disaster strikes.' Indeed, the excuses eventually become one: outside the city it's all the same, or worse. Can there now really be any escape from urban violence, overpopulation, industrial waste, the greenhouse effect?

Writers are among the most sceptical. There are no anti-utopias; the city does not represent a great oppressive weight (this is still located in the provinces) but, rather, possible liberty, and in practice, nothing could be further from the spirit of the capital city than the prophecies contained in Carlos Fuentes's novel *Christopher Unborn* and his short story 'Andrés Aparicio' in *Burnt Water*. According to Fuentes, the city has reached its limits. One of his characters reflects:

> He was ashamed that a nation of churches and pyramids built for all eternity ended up becoming one with the cardboard, shitty city. They boxed him in, suffocated him, took his sun and air away, his senses of vision and smell.

Even the world of *Christopher Unborn* (one of ecological, political, social and linguistic desolation) is invaded by fun ('relajo'). In the end, although the catastrophe may be very real, catastrophism is the celebration of the incredulous in which irresponsibility mixes with resignation and hope, and where – not such a secret doctrine in Mexico City – the sensations associated with the end of the world spread: the overcrowding is hell, and the apotheosis is crowds that consume all the air and water, and are so numerous that they seem to float on the earth. Confidence becomes one with resignation, cynicism and patience: the apocalyptic city is populated with radical optimists.

In practice, optimism wins out. In the last instance, the advantages seem greater than the horrors. And the result is: *Mexico, the post-apocalyptic city.* The worst has already happened (and the worst is the monstrous population whose growth nothing can stop); nevertheless, the city functions in a way the majority cannot explain, while everyone takes from the resulting chaos the visual and vital rewards they need and which, in a way, compensate for whatever makes life unlivable. Love and hate come together in the vitality of a city that produces spectacles as it goes along: the commerce that invades the pavements, the infinity of architectonic styles, the 'street theatre' of the ten million people a day who move about the city, through the Underground system, on buses, motorbikes, bicycles, in lorries and cars. However, the all-star performance is given by the loss of fear at being ridiculed in a society which, not too long ago, was so subjugated by what 'others might think'. Never-ending mixture also has its aesthetic dimension, and next to the pyramids of Teotihuacán, the baroque altars and the more wealthy and elegant districts, the popular city projects the most favoured – and the most brutally massified – version of the century that is to come.

3

Tradition Hour

Year after year, on the evening of 11 December, popular faith gathers in its thousands at the Basilica of Guadalupe. If devotion to the Virgin of Guadalupe ['Guadalupismo'] is not exactly the national essence (millions of people are not Catholics, which does not strip them of their citizenship), it is the most extravagant expression of our religious life, manifesting itself in the communal effort of many – trade unions, families and street gangs – and in the conviction that when the calendar – or, indeed, pain – demands it, faith returns as the need to dazzle God with an abundance of suffering.

Those who serenade the Virgin are, for the most part, adolescents or young men. For two whole days people of all ages file by, but the night of the eleventh belongs to the kids carrying blankets, guitars and huge pictures of Guadalupe on their backs. Their celebration is multiple: of surrender to a symbol that doubles as both doctrine and nation; of demographic relief at the realization that there are thousands just like themselves; of satisfaction at being born into the bosom of Guadalupan favour (as expressed in their unions, their neighbourhoods, towns, or countless relatives). The reasoning runs as follows: from our families we get our looks, our names, and even a couple of memories; from our compatriots and comrades we get aspects of our style; while from you, Virgins, Christs and saints, we get. . . .

Bicycles flood the atrium area, rivers of people merge into each other and dissolve. Walking is impossible – it is much easier just to go with the flow – but the weariness is the preamble to transfiguration. In the squeeze the people have become a mass of clearance-sale clothes, their bodies disappearing as they adapt themselves to the lack of space. And what remains hidden the rest of the year is now revealed in those with no access to the trickle-down effects of modernization.

An inventory and a litany

Lord help us. Look at these your people. If you do not intervene, who will? Lift us from this hole, Little Mistress. We offer you everything we have: our faces as inexpressive as they are revealing, the nopal cactus spines buried in our knees, our bleeding feet that betray kilometres of sorrowful jostling, our vision blurred from alcoholic sustenance, our willingness to dance endlessly until tomorrow noon. . . . You favoured no other nation like ours, Little Virgin; you accompanied the liberator Miguel Hidalgo and overthrew the foreign Virgin of Remedios; you never left Emiliano Zapata's side; you shine on bare walls and allow us to adore you in shops and garages, on the roads and on coaches, in the slum housing where we live. . . . Lend us a hand – the minimum wage is a mockery, and they've just put up the prices of petrol, tortillas and beans. . . .

Historically, *Guadalupismo* is the most embodied form of nationalism, signifying belonging and continuity. But what happens to all of this in a post-traditional world? What is the contemporary connection between *nationalism* and *Guadalupismo*? Today, rather than thinking of them as bellicose passions, I believe one needs to think about the ways in which they function to resolve questions of poverty, destitution, custom, an understanding of the world that works through ritual acts, the fearful love of symbols, syncretism as a means of adaptation (first to the Conquest, then to the nation that emerged amid battles, and later still to modernization), and a fanaticism that is simultaneously the bodily experience of incomprehension. Blind faith: the strength within the weakness of believers who are Mexican, of Mexicans who are also believers.

She's the Queen of Mexico. Here we don't have a monarchy, but in the heavens above she's the Queen of us all – that's because she's Indian.

So that they respect us cyclists, we have to come in our hundreds. If not, we'd never get here.

I promised the Virgin that if I make some money and marry next year, I'll name my firstborn Guadalupe, whether it's a girl or a boy.

Lucky you didn't make that promise to the Virgin of Fatima.

What more is there to be said about Guadalupe? She is, on the one hand, the pacific moment in the Christianization of the Indian peoples and, on the other, the Mexicanization of faith (1531 was the official date of the beginning of syncretism); she is the great reservoir of reverence for Mexicans abroad, and has pride of place in bedrooms, trade-union headquarters, bars, brothels, goods trucks. . . . But at the end of the twentieth century, one finds condensed in Guadalupe the experiences of marginality and suffering that are concealed by the pride in being Mexican. Present in the childhood of all Mexicans (be they Catholic or not), she constitutes the landscape of tutelary convictions and is the sign of normality in poverty, the formidable pretext for the exercise of intolerance.

11 December, 9 p.m.

The pilgrim advances falteringly on his knees, worry written into his face: wounded piety, trembling hope, the possibility of imminent alleviation, blurred and illustrious pain, faithful prayer, not to mention the noise from the traffic and the blare of transistor radios.

The next few feet open up like an abyss before the pilgrim. Then he will quench his thirst, be pardoned and blessed, expiate his need for atonement. He will be happy because his permanent unhappiness will have acquired, as if by miracle, a meaning. The family lay out blankets for the pilgrim as he passes by, deaf, oblivious, but silently grateful, knees bleeding, his prayers now low, now loud. And he will prevail (a religious vow is a sacred commitment), not because his life will change – his crop will not be lost (he doesn't have one), his daughter will not run away from home (she died young), nor will his father's health improve (he never knew him) – but, rather, because a promise made to the Virgin, whatever the state of health of the one who makes it, is the equivalent of a deathbed vow. And on the threshold of death you do not fail your most important creditor, the fount of all wealth, the greatest beauty you have ever known. This is why his chastised body will yield – not because his weakening crawl exorcizes the future, nor because the Virgin can be bribed by martyred flesh and prayers (she is not a low- or, indeed, a high-ranking bureaucrat) but, rather, because the pilgrim loves her to the point of weeping, to the point where unnecessary pain is transformed into justified suffering.

Who shares the faith of this supplicant nowadays? To what end such penitential zeal if nothing changes? Would it not be better just to direct any felt mortification into the short cut of indifferent prayer (because ultimately, nothing else is expected), and so neutralize the obvious character of exhibited sacrifice? The public stands back, absorbed in its own mortification.

The Basilica, 11 p.m. Live on TV

The young quartet – so reminiscent of the Cuban groups of the 1950s – sings, as harmonious as a jukebox from another world:

Brown-skinned Lady,
Beautiful good Lady.
Brown-skinned Lady,
You, you kissed me.

The unquenchable thirst produced by advertising is transformed here at the Basilica into such sweet melody. And now an abbot initiates yet another catechistic session. After four centuries of undivided Christianity, and one of popular faith, only now has the country finally opened itself up to evangelization. . . . The singer María de Lourdes and her group, redeemers of tradition all, ease the instruction of those who are on the point of suffocation, not forgetting the vendors, who still – at least for the moment – have customers. The typical regional costumes (a generous helping of forgetting how we once dressed) evoke 'a beautiful mosaic of what is Ours'. For in this Festival of Fervour, we all intone Juan Zaizar's song 'Guadalupe': 'Guadalupe, beautiful flower on the tunic of Juan Diego' . We have been singing just like this since 1531, and this is how we have dressed, too: in ponchos, embroidered dresses, palmleaf hats, the Mexican dawn glittering on our eyelashes and emerging from our Mexican throats.

Up to what point can a crowd whose exhilaration comes from its televisable potential remain reverential in the old-fashioned sense? Who knows? Traditional customs have been devastated over time, and it is not the same to pray alone as to pray before the camera, nor is brotherly love experienced as well in poorly illuminated parish churches as it is in a spectacle sponsored by the wine merchants Casa Domecq. As I ponder these difficult issues, a clergyman unleashes yet more allegorical manna: 'Mount Tepeyac reflected the divine glory of the Lord. . . . She revealed to them the God in which the Aztecs had always really believed.' And the master of ceremonies interrupts to remind us again of the unforeseen: Mexican singers are distinguished by their *Guadalupismo*.

The Festival of Fervour needs no jury. The television is here, and it tells us: within each Mexican, however dressed, there lies a peasant who sings or recites 'Guadalupan Compliment' by the bard López Méndez:

Virgencita linda, mi Guadalupana,
la mejor amiga de mi fe cristiana. . . .
Bendita tu eres entre todas ellas,
entre las mujeres y entre las estrellas.

[Pretty little Virgin, my Guadalupe,/Best companion of my Christian faith. . . ./Blessed are you among all,/All women and stars.]

The evangelizing impulse provokes an academic conceit: 'What can you tell us, Reverend Abbot, of the latest theories of the image? How many homes has Our Lady of Guadalupe?' I hear the next group of serenaders led by Lola Beltrán and, for lack of a better interlocutor, ask myself: what can these singers be thinking about? Not the publicity, nor being sanctified on national *and* international TV (as the commentator promised). If their faces are to be believed, they rather discern miracles in the surrounding hills, and rejoice in the memories of a historic visit made by an Indian to a bishop – without forgetting the cosmological shift from Thomism to our very own, national, religion that *Guadalupismo* entailed. Nor forgetting the practice of preaching first through interpreters, and then by way of mass conversion – which, for better or for worse, at least according to the priest, was no such thing anyway because, being monotheistic ever since their departure from Aztlán, the Aztecs were Christian in general long before being so in detail.

Dressed in unblemished white, as if attending his vocal cords' first communion, and the very embodiment of the stylized *charro* freed for ever from the countryside, Fernando Allende sings Gabriel Ruiz's '*Despierta*' ['Awaken'] to the little brown-skinned girl: 'Awaken, sweet love of my life,/Awaken, if you are still sleeping. . . .' The lyrics, written to celebrate earthly love, straighten as they make a beeline for the divine: 'Listen to my voice sound beneath your window-pane. . . .' Words that for the cinefile evoke *La Virgin del Tepeyac* ['The Virgin of Tepeyac'], an unforgettable film – mainly for extra-artistic reasons. I still remember Allende (as Juan Diego) walking along with those short choreographed skips, like a small woodland animal, inaugurating in New Spain what was to become the stereotypical hybrid speech of the Hispanicized Indian and/or urbanized peasant as seen on TV: 'Well, ya see, Papa Bishop, that while walkin' in them 'ills, myself, this stupid illiterate Indian, who knows nowt neither 'bout theology nor metaphysics, was bedazzled by the splendance of a beautiful lady. . . .' Or something like that. I turn back to listen to the murmurs which, along the way, have become the Virgin's 'birthday greetings' [las mañanitas], and towards the faces illuminated by duty, projecting their innocence at the new altar, the television camera – that Great Beyond – a new totem which demands neither adoration nor entranced contemplation, but gets it, in abundance.

'These are the birthday greetings [las mañanitas] that King David sang'

My unconditional support for tradition crumbles. *Is this possible?* Yes, yes, it is. The congregation is *reading* the lyrics to the greetings from bits of paper handed out at the door. If the people don't know that song off by heart, what destiny awaits the Constitution of the Republic? . . . And the band plays on: boleros and rancheras are deposited, as always, at the feet of the Virgin, but not quite in the same manner as always. With one of those extraordinary feats of memory, capable of inventing anything just as long as it prevents us from remaining at odds with ourselves, I remember the first television transmissions made from the Basilica of Guadalupe, with Pedro Infante intoning songs to Guadalupe with extreme unction, and other artists offering serenades to the Mother of God in solicitous faraway tones – not far away from her, of course, but from the camera. Back then, in primitive times gone by before the video age – what backwardness! – people seemed simply to feel alive.

The 'serenade' is an institution, and each year in the Basilica it forcefully revives and unfolds the costumes of Mexicanness thanks to which Mexicans continue to recognize themselves in the multicultural firmament: blankets, shawls, braids, colourful bows, futuristic *charro* suits, hats held respectfully in hand, embroidered blouses, quexquemetls, Tehuana costumes. All worn by our ancestors for the noble purpose of liberating us from the lack of tradition.

'On this clear night/of bright and restless stars/I have come to tell you/That it is you I love. . . .' María Victoria sings 'Randalla' by Alfonso Esparza Oteo – a song that will last as long as there is a need for midnight serenades. The singer, once upon a time distinguished by her sensuality, submits now to the discipline of mortification, adopting one of those glazed looks straight from a film specially made for Easter, and an appearance that seeks to make the worldly invisible, arms crossed patiently awaiting a deluge of absolution. And around María Victoria ecstatic faces abound – or are they, rather, the exhausted expression of recent assaults on Mount Carmel from which the assembled crowd has just returned with the puffed-out aura of celestial day-trippers? The *mariachi* bands continue where the Gregorian chants leave off: 'I knew a pretty brown girl/And I loved her a lot./Every afternoon I went enamoured to see her./And on looking into her eyes my ardour grew./Oh brown girl, my little brown girl I shall never forget you.' *Y quedéme no sabiendo, toda ciencia tracendiendo* ['And, there remaining, knew no more, Transcending far all human love.']. St John of the Cross should have written boleros. And as I reflect on this, the pictures of Bethlehem are interrupted to make way for a commercial break and more popular religion (it will never be the same again).

'The overabundance of technology signals the end of mysticism.' I don't know who said this, or if anyone did, or indeed if it is not just one of my own posthumous premonitions (the new species of this neo-liberal age). But what is certain is that, squeezed tightly into the new Basilica, without space enough to imagine the idea of space, I am witness to a sleight of hand: the replacement of the observation of piety with piety observed.

Reflections which, for lack of a sponsor, remain on the edge of heresy

An unworthy comment: how many of the assembled performers are exploiting the opportunity merely to promote themselves here and throughout Latin America? A thought that negates such unworthy comments: how many will affirm, with their example, the spiritual exercises of the viewers? If one falls into the temptation (to use a pompous phrase) of feeling that the electronic media have been overrun by faith, all one needs do to be brought right back up to date is to imagine the activities of the hundreds of thousands, or millions, of families actually watching the programme: they get up to go to the refrigerator, comment on each other's clothes, tell office stories, smile, hug each other, send the children to bed, ask what time Elenita and Roberto will get back in tonight, flick channels to 'keep an eye on all that devotion', talk about yesterday's programmes, and suchlike. . . . And if I lie, let me be excommunicated by Channel 2!

Television disseminates belief and, in transmission, transforms it into something slightly different – not irreverence, of course, but a consciousness split between intimate prayer and the mass disclosure of intimate prayer, between sacred representations and the screen. Does this actualize piety? Probably not, but it does not foreground disbelief either. Television, the focal point of all contemporary belief and unexplainable idolatry, is itself neither a believer nor an unbeliever, but a rush of images that become indistinct, a routine that instantly acquires the appearance of a burning bush.

One might ask: will audiences end up looking at the set as if they were at Mass? The sceptical reply: will audiences end up immersed in Mass as if they were watching TV? Two *fin-de-siècle* powers meet to become that moment previously known as – in the absence of abbreviations – eternity. With TV, the multitude belongs to spectacle in ways that can never be offered by the Church. The serenade concludes, the pontifical Mass comes to an end, and all are convinced that there is still yet more (to come).

The atrium of the Basilica: midnight

The singers off-camera are . . . how can I put it? . . . aggressive. They resent the silence, the weakness of spirit and, above all, the absence of gold, frankincense and myrrh to offer Her, the Mother of the One True God. Their monotonous, profound, piercing, beautiful song exterminates sin and indifference. . . . And suddenly, dreams and vigils are added to the noise – today's liturgical language – creating a great synthesis that overwhelms prayer, the songs dedicated to the Little Brown Girl of Tepeyac, the ranchera elegies of José Alfredo Jiménez and Tomás Méndez, the blessings (dispensed like curses), the exhortations, and the parents' warning not to get lost whatever you do. Not to mention the sounds of *mariachi* bands, the commercial announcements, and the complaints of TV technicians. . . .

Every 12 December the religious community gathers at the Basilica. Does what liberation theologists call *ecclesiogenesis*, the creation of the Church from below, from the people, occur here, and if so, how? The question is beyond me, but whether *ecclesiogenesis* occurs or not, I do hear the roaring, thunderous throng that equalizes and drowns out all differences, maddens the mountain and cures the mad, undoing all hierarchies; all this, moreover, while providing the noise I have attempted to describe with a quality that presages the empty and disordered earth before the Beginning or the Apocalypse, granting faith repose during the dance numbers – which still, of course, demand our undivided attention.

In the religious crush belief comes and goes, vents itself eurhythmically, retreats, shops, eats, fasts, is robbed blind, loses heart, recovers, certifies that there is no sensation more heretical than pure doctrine, joins a new queue every five minutes, emits phrases that impede conversation, entangles itself among the shawls, shakes the bells on its feet, speaks with teponaxtles and drums, becomes both pilgrim and tourist, moves equally to pre-Hispanic rhythms and to the marches of John Philip Sousa, heats tortillas, drinks itself sober, deposits flowers on the altar, crosses itself, becomes annoyed at not feeling struck by blessed mortification. . . . In the crowd, faith is democratized.

Necessary syncretism

The dancers exercise their monomania for hours on end in the atrium, placing repetition – the fire of patience – at the mercy of the Here and the Great Beyond, and the circular desire that She may recognize them in the lap of the nation, belief, race, the people, community and, of course, the resurrection. Each year the number of dancing tribes grows, probably the result of the return to religion (or the study of religion, which has become, mainly because of the academic industry, more of a theme than an experience) and a fascination with primeval rhythms. The dancers are conscientious, their dignity apparently unaffected by the traditionalists' attacks on their multicoloured plumes and their wholesale trousers. But the dancers' rigour sets fantasy aside and makes of ritual their greatest temple, their catharsis, their terrestrial and angelic biography. This must be the way religion was 'nationalized', through the endless adaptations that poverty imposed on adoration (as well as through the awe of the conquistadors).

Tradition also involves a certain availability of materials. For some time now the tribes of dancers have dressed themselves as best they could. But the clothing that had filled generations with pride was in tatters, or tourists had come in times of hardship and, for a few dollars, made off with the costumes and extraordinary masks. Whatever the cause – the dancers are not concerned with their heterodoxy, since God is offended only by wickedness of the heart – in practice, the typical costume has been supplemented by wrestlers' masks and outfits; the Caballero Aguila is now associated with Octagón, the Tlatoani with El Santo, and the Enmascarado de Plata and the flyer of Papantla alternate with Spider Man. If the intention is pious, their use of the contemporary bears its pardon with it.

The new syncretism is very simple; it admits hybrids because it considers them variations on a sixteenth-century theme. It refuses all feelings of guilt because they hinder the wedding of the culture industry to the cosmic legacy. Traditions are replaced by spectacle. In anticipation of spectacle, tradition. The visual explosions of yesteryear are replaced by the chromatic regularity of the Mexican curio, and to the Mexican curio is counterpoised the originality of attitude. The faithful use of original indigenous clothing is displaced by the wardrobe of the *Ballet Folclórico*, indebted in turn to 1950s Hollywood design – which invented gods for the sole purpose of paying them choreographic tribute, and dreamt of pre-Hispanics so bedazzled with catwalks and tropical scenery that they celebrated their idols merely for allowing them to play the tom-tom, wear loincloths and garlands of flowers, and dance lasciviously. That Dance: stunning colours, incandescent plastic, an ambitious style that dreams of the glamour (yes, that's what they called it!) of Tenochtitlan before the arrival of the Spaniards.

With all respect. This phrase is one of the most frequently heard in Mexico today and is, in fact, the great excuse for the ways in which traditions are being forced to change. *I know that you will eventually be lost, but we've given you a place. It grieves me to push you aside, but such is the nature of change.* With all respect, Mr Mayor. . . . With all respect, housewives. . . . And why not? With all respect, Little Mistress . . .? These were not your colours, nor were these the clothes of my ancestors. Nor do these carefully unpolished masks have anything in common with those carved with care and character in the villages. But look, Mistress, no one makes those clothes any more, those cloaks and masks. It's all so expensive and impossible to buy. That's why you must accept us now; we bring all we have – and there'll be no more. And don't be angry, either; you should be happy just to see us. Between us and fashion, rags.

In the atrium, dancers pull on their wrestlers' masks and make an offering of their collective face, that principled abolition of individual features, to Tonatzin-Guadalupe.

2 a.m.: the echoes of popular theology

Oh, he understood all too well that for the humble soul of the common Russian peasant – exhausted by toil and woe, and even more by perpetual injustice and perpetual sin, both its own and that of the world – there was no more powerful need or consolation than to find a holy object or person and to fall down before it and worship it. Even if among us there is sin, untruth, injustice and temptation, at least in certain places, somewhere on the earth, there are men who are holy and exalted; to make up for it, those men have truth and justice, to make up for it, those men know truth and justice, so it has not been lost to the world, and one day it will come to us, too, and will reign in all the world, as was promised. (Dostoevsky, *The Brothers Karamazov*)

I observe observers of popular religion. Until very recently, only the most paternalistic of statements were ever made about 12 December by institutional Catholicism: 'That's how the people are! Their education merely furthers their excess. They take only their frustrations to the Virgin, their rapture and their filth. Admittedly, yes, they do offer their incandescent faith, too, but the cult is fundamentally pagan.' This was before, when no one really paid attention to popular religion, or analysed the carnival from a Bakhtinian point of view, or talked of sacred spaces and times, or of Christianity's 'preferential option for the poor'.

She is the Mother of God, Jesus Christ's own little mum.

The Virgin was a humble woman, a peasant, specially chosen to start from below.

She's the same as us, just prettier.

As far as I'm concerned, Juan Diego was the first Mexican. Before Guadalupe there was no real nation, because the only ones around then to dispense favours were foreign saints.

I share God, but not my saints.

I pray when I'm ill, when one of my children is ill, when I don't have any money, when I've recovered, when I have money, and to show God that I am not just self-seeking. I pray in good times and in bad times.

The worst thing about the rich is that even though they already have everything, they use up all God's time asking for more.

If God wanted to, he'd put an end to poverty. But who'd pray to him then?

The saints are our advocates before God, but they're good ones: if God concedes the miracle, they don't take the best part.

The saints are saints because they're nearer to God. The greater the distance, the greater the sin.

As I understand it, those who haven't been baptized wander through life weighed down by original sin.

Me and my late husband are Catholics: me, as a precaution; and him, I'm sure, out of gratitude.

I got married after living for twelve years with my wife so that my children had nothing to reproach their mother with.

They put a cross in my uncle's mouth so that he didn't take his wicked tongue to heaven with him.

They put flowers out for one boy I know, so that the angels didn't mistake him for a dwarf.

And a group sings for the umpteenth time:

> The Virgin Mary is our protector,
> Our redeemer, there is nothing to fear.
> We are Christians and we are Mexicans.
> War, war against Lucifer.

In the small hours, a number of young lads are still awake: how wonderful it's been to stay awake all night just sharing our belief. And this central concern persists, even though the conversations are sidetracked along the paths of romance, past girlfriends, shows, work (real or imagined), illness and New Year parties. Nothing of what they say appears to be sacramental, although even if an outsider cannot perceive it, it must all be. Because the boys are exhibiting (and this is only an intuition, because I could obviously be mistaken – after all, who am I? – especially since I don't share their faith) their intimacy to the Virgin: *this is all I can offer you, what I feel and what I imagine,* given the state of the economy; and anyway, they are what they are, and theirs is a relationship with the Virgin, not Anthropology.

In the atrium, while waiting for the new dawn, fun ('relajo') and reverence are, by now, drowsy forms of transcendence.

4

Dancing: The Funky Dive

Genaro is not confused, nor has he heard of the sociology of youth movements. He couldn't give a shit about 'alternative lifestyles' either, or the System, Alienation or Manipulation. He lives in the Moctezuma neighbourhood and he needs a job; he is nineteen years old and his fancy T-shirt (which he wears everywhere) has *Let's Fuck* written all over it in capital letters. It's 6 p.m., and time to go dancing at *Nothing Changes*. Not that Genaro is bored. Why? Because boredom belongs to another world, with different notions of time and speed, and implies having Made It in Life. How can you be bored of nothing?

In 1968 and 1969, a number of young dynamic businessmen surveyed the scene and came to a unanimous conclusion: rock music is popular, but there's nowhere cheap to listen to it; so let's make money doing something for the poor – buy or rent halls, disused shops, old houses; we'll also get some paint and posters, hire groups that don't charge too much, prohibit alcoholic drinks, and provide these kids who are forced to stay in their neighbourhoods with discotheques. The places are known as *funky dives* (*funky*, according to the dictionary, means 'passionate', 'authentic', 'earthy', 'smelly', 'soulful'). And these places that appear and disappear, go bankrupt, only to reappear again unlicensed and, under the heavy burden of payoffs, disappear again, only to re-emerge . . . live up to their name. And they survive, to become, not long after the Avándaro pop festival, a social need. Every week, in oxygen-free environments, groups set up their acoustic nightmares so that national rock can pay its homage to international rock while the kids get *turned on*, as if they were listening to some other music, in some other place.

'Sure,' says an old rock-and-roller, nostalgic for the good old days when groups called themselves Rhythm Mad, Rock Rebels and Teen Tops, 'everything's different now. Look, before, even when things were bad, we played garden parties next to pools in fancy districts like Narvarte, Las Lomas, El Pedregal; and when we played "Beach Baby", everyone danced, even the parents of the birthday girl, and nine times out of ten a member of the family would fall into the pool, suit and all. But then that lot from the Border came down, with their hair down to their shoulders, smelling as if they'd been on a second-class bus all day. That's when things went wrong, and now the *funky dives* are out there near places like Vallejo Industrial Park, or along Eighth Avenue or in Netzahualcóyotl.' The decline and fall of Rock and Roll!

Genaro has asked his old friend Armando to come along tonight. It's not such a laugh on your own. Picking girls up isn't such fun, and it's difficult to make the most of what's on offer at the dives: dancing with others to music so loud you can't hear it. Outside, youngsters unload amplifiers and guitars from the dark insides of vans, while at the door, standing still and lined up in the dark, the same kids as usual hand over the same money as usual to get in. 'Shine a light!'

On the steps outside, Armando recognizes an old 'raver', a girl who claims to have done everything, which includes stripping off at Avándaro, although it's clear she'd never been anywhere near the festival, and that if she had, the crowd would have put her clothes back on. Meanwhile, Genaro scrutinizes the poster. He knows all the bands playing in Mexico City – except the ones that broke up last week (instability is the norm) – even those playing in bourgeois discotheques. He also knows the bands that everyone else ignores, despite their names: The Constitution of 2017, Tragic Fortnight, Sleeping Shrimp. Inside, a notice reads: 'BROTHER, take your drapes or blankets to the cloakroom. You will DANCE better. (YOU KNOW!) Welcome to the cloakroom. One peso per coat or nappy.'

Improvised groups come together in corners. This must be how society (any society) is constituted: some people are already there, patiently waiting for others to disembark from ships or come down mountains. The first conversations are timid, charged with essential information: my name is such and such and I live over there. Then – neighbourly duties over – it is time to choose friends and interests, and wait for the big events, commenting on what had happened the day before. That's how Aztlan and New Spain came about. That's how it must have been, like in this dive. No shit.

What is the role of the *funky dives* in youth subculture? Who cares! I'd rather check out the redemptive function of sweat in this hell so at the margins of theology's concerns: its apocalyptic surge, artificial climate, ecological disturbance, the drop-by-drop resurrection of the body. It is through sweat that the identification of sex and rock and roll is produced, and it is in this sweat that the new morality of a generation becomes clear.

Every dance without rules is a celebration of the tribe; while all tribal activity imposes rules. The kids come together and separate aggressively; they jump, growl and invoke the gods of sport and orgasm. Dancing is a great adventure – with its own mountain passes, waterfalls and sea depths – the ever-changing story in which the body is both hero and villain, where – according to Theo Theological – crime and punishment fight it out in an intense choreography of guilt and expiation. Genaro dances, and his fevered condition calms him down – that's better, a pity it's been so long since he last had sex; first it was the wrong time of the month, then that argument over a film, and then all that stuff about the attacks on couples staying in the hotel they went to. But dancing restores and reinvigorates, and helps recover a sense of time.

Intimacy/proximity

The girl dances alone, and remains alone inside her twists and ballet steps. No one is disrespectful because, among other things, such an idea has no meaning here; people just come to listen to the band and dance, and if someone, in a song, in times too loud for innocence, asks the girl just to be nice, or asks a sweet baby for a kiss, it would take on another meaning, pornographic for sure: a kiss – where?

The point is to get as much as possible out of the music. Immersed and withdrawn, the girl dances *just fine*. Not a millimetre separates us, my vibrations and me. This is how you discover rock in your soul; don't break away, the girl is *just fine*, she moves her body without overdoing it on the rhythm (she does not want to break into a rumba); everything is *just fine*. Genaro and Armando dance alone, both of them, with the rest, alone and together. This Sunday, the *funky dive* is just fine.

The North

All popular innovation emerges in the North of the city first, in the labyrinth of snack bars, paint shops, garages, photo studios, steam baths, repair shops, bus stations, scrapyards, stray dogs. Deprived of green spaces and residential zones, the North is compact, tense, homogeneous in its diversity, and closed to any understanding of either traditional or avant-garde aesthetics. In this domain of visual oppression, where no one is depressed any longer by the dismal well-ruined façades, the buildings agonize from the very day of their inauguration. From the outside, from the point of view of social psychology, the North of the city wears noise like a shroud: strain, anger, defencelessness, hate, impotence. From the inside, it's all there is, and whoever doesn't like it can fuck off to Dallas.

Among all the other instant museums here, the oldest *funky dive* of them all still survives: the *Salón Chicago* (on Felipe Villanueva Street), which once upon a time most probably housed an exemplary provincial family, desperate to get out but frustrated for years trying to save enough to do so. Vaguely inspired by the guesthouses to be found in Mexican films, the *Chicago* has been the useless passion of its punters for two decades.

Week after week, between one thousand and one thousand five hundred kids come to the *Sálon Chicago* anxious for strong experiences and a place to let off steam. During the week they have been harassed by the traffic police, told off by their bosses in garages and shops, nagged at home because they can't find a job, and insulted by their girlfriends because they have nowhere to do it. It's Sunday, and all they want to do now is unwind.

The naco

Towards the end of the 1950s, the quintessential insult makes its appearance in Mexico City: *naco*. The word is the apheresis of *totonacos*, and refers to undisguisable Indian roots and blood. The term goes beyond socioeconomic identification (before it was said 'he may have a lot of money but he's still basically a peasant'; now it has become 'he may have millions but he'll always be a *naco*'), violently alluding to the most marginalized of the nation – distant, even, from the purview of the philanthropist. It eventually becomes one of the main vehicles through which the cultural contempt for the Indians is articulated. Who cares for the everyday life of the *naco*, for the links between their appearance and the possibilities of success? Whoever lacks power lacks well-defined features too, and even the best-intentioned end up finding in big lips and thin moustaches the key to the political understanding of the 'coppery hordes'. No story of origins here, no legendary profiles: the *naco* is not mythical but typical.

Like all their antecedents, *nacos* have their own history, their society and an aesthetic. *Their history:* hatred enthroned, disdain for the (non-verbal) brilliance of Vaseline, for the (non-traditional) splendour of the yellow army jacket, and for the education that at times concedes a certificate (uncopiable?) for the sixth grade of primary school – just enough to encourage and support the voracious reading of comics, photonovels and sports pages. *Their history*: oppression, distrust for all authority, endemic illness, slum homes with cement floors, a recent agrarian past and an apprenticeship in matters of corruption as a defence against real Corruption. *Their society*: chat (the only saving grace of having to carry so much water from the only local source for miles), beer and jeans (as cultural structures), the neighbourhood as the most basic form of communal identity (which spreads out into a series of baptisms, confirmations, first communions, weddings, deaths, graduations, godfather ceremonies of every kind, celebrations of the Virgin). *Their society*: a language taken from sports commentators, television comedians, films, radio plays, photonovels, soaps . . . and all this crowned with the ubiquitous 'swear word', the last recourse against an accumulated linguistic wealth that rejects and condemns, and an intellectual amusement that discovers in every use of the expletive *chingada* the gifts of both sex and death.

Their society, the vision of the vanquished: the *naco* wants to learn karate, and puts his very soul into understanding football; he optimistically takes English classes, although he will never even have the opportunity to engage in conversation. I'll synthesize: alienated, manipulated, economically devastated, *nacos* love what they don't understand and understand what they don't love. The unfortunate truth: they inherit what the middle class abandons.

The *naco*, like all generalizations about the economically marginalized, is a local instance of a fearful and triumphant 'Western *mentalité*' (by Western, here, I mean the institutional forging of myths). The refined gentleman of the nineteenth century invents the leper, and the cosmopolitan bourgeois of the twentieth, the *naco*. Without understanding or verbalizing it (what for?), the *naco* intuits it instead: those who want to define him consider him a projection of their own selves, and recognize him only in his resemblance to their projection.

The reaction of the pariah: for the *naco*, 'self-knowledge' comes from a resolved contemplation of the 'self' in the mirror of culture, and is founded in an absolute trust in what is contemplated there. The game is a double one: the mirror and its reflection are indissolubly linked. The *naco* spies on those who observe him: in their eyes, his mere presence alone negates and rejects what they hold most dear in themselves; he is, therefore, despised. And why not, if the interpellated himself – as *naco* – comes to consider what happens to him as just? Outside the culture industry, he is never the centre of any spectacle. He is definitively proscribed, especially in advertising, because he *contaminates*; and his physical, social or cultural presence causes (if it causes anything at all) either horror or pity – both feelings of moral superiority – among the ruling class. In the exchange between the economically marginalized and the elites, the emotional traffic is always one-way, going from the stupor of some (repudiation or philanthropic admiration) to the *ressentiment* of others.

On forming such an image of the *naco*, the elites then impose it while simultaneously obliging him to 'choose'. Provided with a script, the *naco* will act out his part. The elites, however, in their role as psychic managers, refuse to believe in his spontaneity, accusing him instead of showing 'authenticity' only when they themselves have programmed 'disinhibition'. An example of this 'spontaneity': drunkenness as the patriotic impulse of nationalist filiation. Fundamentally, as in sixteenth-century European illustrations of America, there is a terror of possible confrontation, of being ambushed, of what looks back at us from the dark, of what has never had a face, the visible multitudes composed of beings who have been made invisible. Let's give them names (lepers, *nacos*), and endow them with fixed characteristics, and oblige them to live according to our script. In the end, as the elites put it, this is a country 'with a buzzard's stomach'.

Meanwhile . . . back at the dive

The identity of the punters is constituted by cultural and racial signs. They set off along the difficult paths of 'modernity' glued to their transistor radios; noise is just another kind of music, a communal experience. The labyrinth of inequality: a tamed instinct when it comes to choosing shirts and jackets and cowboy hats and tailored or bell-bottomed trousers. In the beginning there was Babylonic advertising, and the Earth was empty, and advertising created taste.

How can one describe the punters? They are *nacos*, to use that fatal word once and for all, and you can tell – marginalized by a centre which hangs on to an exclusivity that only distances it from reality. *The naco in Mexico!* And his appearance confirms his belonging to the Bronze Race. The epithet isolates and degrades – *naco!* – which means: without education or manners, ugly and insolent, graceless and unattractive, irredeemable, complex-ridden, resentful, vulgar, moustachioed and shocking, fan of the wrestler *El Santo* – confirmation of the inferiority of a lesser country.

However much they try to shake off the name – and, given that the term is a racial one, who doesn't it apply to in a country of Indians and mestizos, no matter how people try and get round it? – whoever is a *naco* considers themselves the lowest of the low, without hope, or even access to a form of consciousness that might serve a process of revindication. The long arms of National Unity – away with class struggle! – have proscribed them, cast them aside – except, that is, when they have to be bused in to 'vote', or enlisted into expressing their contentment at 'civic' ceremonies. The *naco*, however, presses forward, numerous and overwhelming, from among the proletariat or lumpenproletariat, from among all those desperately in search of water, drainage and electricity in the new meeting of the tribes of Aztlán. This is the mass presence that now defines Mexico City.

Alarmed decency cries out and protests – here in the form of the architect Mauricio Gómez Mayorga, who, in a bellicose article, declares: 'They're transforming Mexico City into the Great Monkitlán!' The monkeys, the *nacos*! Their grim features so contradict the classical creole ideal. Great Monkitlán! Every three minutes the Underground station expels waves of *nacos* into the streets, their laughter and appearances indecipherable because they are so often deciphered. What a drag! How are we going to become a contemporary modern nation if this lot ruin, damage, and interfere with the view? Moreover, who will redeem Mexico from the lack of an aesthetic that could justify as well as celebrate the nation? Greece has the Parthenon and Rome the Sistine Chapel, and France has the whole of Paris, with museums testifying to the ideals of Western classical perfection. While all Mexico has are groups of ladies from wealthy districts like Las Lomas and Pedregal visiting ruins and chapels, lost amid the wordy explanations of colonial painting.

How respectable is Respectable?

'Letting off steam': functional relief, catharses (big and small), letting go, an identity structured by cries, backslapping and panting. In the *Chicago*, with its classic bandstand and catwalk, a not-very-well-known band introduces their singer, Nasty, a deliberately Felliniesque character who goads the crowd. He threatens to strip, takes off his shirt, and when his scarf is snatched away he fights to get it back, and people come to his assistance. Someone descends into the centre of the boiling mass to recover whatever is left. Nasty explains: it was a keepsake given him by an English musician in that band that started it all in Liverpool; but no matter, the pieces are in better hands now, those of the public who love and adore him!

Finally, Nasty loses his shirt, gets rid of his scarf, and threatens to throw himself into the human mass with the joke: 'The last time I did I fell on an eighteen-year-old guy, and they charged me for him, as if he were new.' Laughter greets the story, and Nasty disappears. The crowd becomes impatient, and whistles, because applause is no longer the lexicon of admiration and reclamation, and an ovation is less significant now than a shrill whistle or the solemn enunciation of 'swear words'.

Then the sound equipment breaks down, and the crowd goes mad. The pianist doubling as MC shouts 'Viva Mexico' as a peace offering, and 'the race' essentializes its response with a roar that approves of the idea, but disapproves of the demagoguery. The guy at the microphone repeats 'Viva Mexico', and the crowd lightens up, responding to the pantomime game of control – as when they all moved aside when Nasty threatened to jump, or when he threw them his last bit of scarf and the kids relived old birthday parties, throwing themselves after the treasures spilled by smashed *piñatas*, pushing each other and rolling around, having a great time trying to get their hands on anything (except the scarf).

Naco is beautiful

The new group from Guadalajara goes by the name of Toncho Pilatos. What makes them special is the band's leader and singer. He has strong cheekbones, copper skin, a prodigious head of hair that accentuates his Comanche or Sioux looks. By the second song, Toncho Pilatos has already defined its style and its purpose: to create a Huehuenche rock using Indian elements and fusing them with heavy metal. Indeed, in his figure, style and purpose condense and overflow: with his set of maracas he weds his desire to be Mick Jagger with being the patriarch of all the shell dancers in the Basilica of Guadalupe, so that the violence of rock is calmed by the monotony, the trembling repetition of the Indian dancer.

The message, which no one dictates and everyone elaborates, is transparent: '*Naco' is beautiful. Black has been beautiful,* and in certain sectors *brown has been beautiful* too. For now marginalized sectors endow themselves with qualities, undoing prejudices which, for example, accepted creole beauty only as a consolation for not possessing Nordic beauty. Mexican racism disdains the majority of the nation's population, literally throwing in their faces their lack of valued attributes, while praising the sublime physique of minorities, and brutally extirpating any dream *nacos* may have in front of the mirror. Who defends them, when even in the mass media platinum blondes are used to represent Indian servants or Lacandon Princesses?

Toncho, perhaps despite himself, is a revindication. *Naco is beautiful,* proclaims the arrogance and rhythm of those who offer their choreographed monomania to the Little Brown Virgin (of Guadalupe). The theatricalization of racial and cultural aspirations creates solemnity in the crowd, makes a concert out of dance, so that the *Chicago* now becomes the Palace of Fine Arts, and Huehuenche rock the classical music of this generation of *nacos* which contemplates and reflects itself in steps and cries and gestures of rejection and scorn. Toncho's presence vaguely, darkly and confusedly repeats the refrain that *Naco is beautiful*, and he is belligerently supported by a public alive to the aesthetic, psychological and social consequences of its affirmation.

5

Yes, Nor Do the Dead Speak, Unfortunately: Juan Rulfo

In 1953: *El llano en llamas* ['Burning Plain']. In 1955: *Pedro Páramo*.* Written in such a short period of time, Juan Rulfo's two books are nevertheless classics of a culture and a language. Classics, because they represent the splendour of a canon that is re-established by each generation of readers. Classics because, through the wide variety of reactions they elicit – wonder being the most common – they allow whoever opens their pages to feel themselves reflected and expressed there.

Classics are the objects of endless praise. They become secondary- and high-school textbooks, as well as the object of innumerable theses, essays and monographs, the subject of theatrical and film adaptations, and of national and international recognition. Rulfo's work, however, wonderfully resists such an apotheosis, keeping its revelations and stimuli intact. In refusing the Definitive Interpretation, his work demands the democratic renewal of rereading. This is one.

I

Juan Rulfo has been an absolutely trustworthy interpreter of our national culture (as long as he is not erected into a system): of the intimate logic, ways of being, and the secret and public poetry of peasant villages and communities,

---

* Rulfo's important novel has been recently published in a new English translation by Margaret Sayers Peden. See Juan Rulfo, *Pedro Páramo*, Serpent's Tail, London 1994. All quotations from this text are taken from Margaret Sayers Peden's translation. Other translations of Rulfo's work quoted here are my own. [Translator's note.]

marginalized by the forgetfulness that so defines power (an equilibrium of survival and exploitation) and nationhood (synonymous with the dominant classes). Indeed, marginalization and amnesia have been the indispensable twin tactics accompanying strategies of modernization and capitalist development that have only ever addressed this exploited community opportunistically – whenever it was necessary either to prevent social conflagration or to reaffirm the solid integration of the nation. In the light of the dense ideological mist that surrounds the rural world, interpretations from within – which permit us to glimpse and examine the real environments lived in by those sentenced by a barely concealed genocide – become increasingly urgent. Among other things, Rulfo's work furnishes a limited version of the wretched of the earth.

How do we read what is so strange to us? How do we approach without condescension this other half of the population which, while it is our own immediate past and tireless provider, is also so unknown to us? Enlightened ignorance immediately turns to mystification when we attempt to understand the rural, judging any literature concerned with it (and the reality evoked, described, transfigured and affirmed there) as being servile to 'exoticism' or 'atavistic primitivism'. The unknown becomes the stuff of legends or, preferentially, *myth*: the time-without-time of small hamlets, cultural isolation, and the stifling morality of the parish, the poverty and endless migration, the irredeemable extinction of a culture due to the development of the nation, the voracious wearing away of belief and custom, the changes in and persistence of popular language. Everything is mythical, everything is incomprehensible, far off, self-enclosed.

Incomprehension produces definitions that are ideologically coded. Critics all too quickly resort to clichés concerning 'the essence of a Mexico that was', the 'rural universe', 'fatalism', or the centuries-old 'isolation'. According to some, Rulfo's work consolidates such prejudices. I, on the other hand, think that he negates them, providing concrete causes and effects where others have offered only the prestigious terms of defencelessness. Without actually saying so, or even foregrounding it, Rulfo offers themes, environments and characters who not only possess their own specific literary lives, but also reveal the uselessness of the above condemnations. What is usually taken to be pessimism may merely be the ways in which constitutive events are related, while fatalism may really be interpreted as a form of historical memory; and where we see only the accumulation of symbols, what we in fact have are everyday occurrences. This is why it is important to eliminate culturalist mediations in favour of a reading whose point of departure is the questioning of the reader's assumptions. For example:

what do we know about the peasant mentality, its supposedly reiterative and slippery logic? Remember the passage from *Pedro Páramo* where Juan Preciado asks for directions to leave Comala:

'Don't worry on my account,' I told her. 'Don't worry about me. I'm used to it. How do I get out of here?'

'Where are you going?'

'Anywhere.'

'There's dozens of roads. One goes to Contla, and there's another one comes from there. One leads straight to the mountains. I don't know where the one goes you can see from here,' and she pointed past the hole in the roof, the place where the roof had fallen in. 'That one down there goes past the Media Luna. And there's still another that runs the length of the place; that's the longest.'

'Then that may be the way I came.'

'Where are you heading?'

'Toward Sayula.'

'Imagine. I thought Sayula was that way. I always wanted to go there. They say there's lots of people there.'

'About like other places.'

'Think of that. And us all alone here. Dying to know even a little of life.'
(49–50)

Apart from the many interpretations (many of them convincing) to which this passage has given rise, it can also be seen as a beautiful re-creation of a verbal dynamic which, traditionally, has made use of symbolic and metaphoric systems to give its message a strong impulse. Such an interpretation is as valid as the next. But like it or not, at first, confronted by Rulfo's works, the majority of readers and critics are armed only with their acquired linear or technical comprehension of literary facts. The other referents (social and economic conditions, ways of life, rural Mexican world-view) we know only through a glass, darkly.

II

At first literature offered only either bucolic or slightly critical testimonies and re-creations of rural Mexico, inventing a kind and gentle countryside with its corresponding parade of idyllic episodes. In the nineteenth century, *Astucia* ['Cunning'] by Luis G. Inclán, *La navidad en las montañas* ['Christmas in the Mountains'] by Ignacio Manuel Altamirano or *La parcela* ['The Lot'] by José López Portillo y Rojas, all describe a countryside in which innate goodness sustains abstract virtues in opposition to the city – itself portrayed as the devourer of all traditional values. In the first instance, this is because of Hispanic-American intellectuals' and writers' contempt for the vitality, inventiveness and powers of adaptation of oral culture at the time; a contempt – as Jean Franco has pointed out – rooted in their own perceived distance from metropolitan culture. At the same time, narrative is endowed with the social function of description rather than criticism. For example, there is little public interest in the corrosive intentions of Mariano Azuela's pre-1910 work – as was proved by the silence that greeted *Mala yerba* ['Bad Seed'] and *Los fracasados* ['Failures']. No one lets on that they are aware of these impious approximations to small-town hypocrisy and corruption. Rather, it is insisted, the role of the novel is to add its own entertaining testimony to those that already exist.

Those who want to make room for historical representations, and liberate narrative from its feudal chains, follow in the footsteps of the so-called 'novel of the Mexican Revolution', which colonizes literary space, so to speak, introducing into society many aspects of the rural world by exhibiting fate, desperation, terseness, and the mere symbolic value of life. However important an advance it may be compared to the previous literature, this new 'verisimilitude and reality' was still fundamentally allegorical. What was 'presentable' was chosen from a class perspective: the vignettes that idealized and slightly defamed those beings who, like shadows, personified the people and acceded to individuality only thanks to acts of cruelty or the very decision to exist (Margarito and La Pintada in *Los de abajo* ['The Underdogs']), or through simple persistence (Tiburcio Maya in *Vámonos con Pancho Villa* ['Let's Go with Pancho Villa']). The peasant armies, their specific forms of violence, have to be dealt with somehow: Mariano Azuela despises and revindicates them; Gregorio López y Fuentes endows them with a 'poetic tone'; Martín Luis Guzmán makes them slightly less barbarous; Rafael F. Muñoz exhibits them as impulses from a collective unconscious. Only exceptionally do narrators such as José Guadalupe de Anda (*Los cristeros; Los bragados; Juan de Riel*) attempt to grant them individual characteristics.

Although the country develops, the cultural and social understanding of peasant life is immobilized by such mythological representations as those of the muralist José Clemente Orozco or the novelist Agustín Yáñez. Without quite aestheticizing them, Orozco incorporates the peasantry into a tradition of painting that had represented them as Virgilian or ephebic. Aestheticizing them in his novel *Al filo del agua* ['The Edge of the Storm'], Yáñez presents the history of a village as a succession of both small and large acts of repression. Dominant culture is impervious to the differences of perspective and, indeed, insists on unifying and freezing them in its desire to expunge all movement from the rural scene.

On the other hand, these cultural presuppositions (which have made a clearer reading of Rulfo that much more difficult) provided the author with a certain epistemological security. As Rulfo once explained to the critic Joseph Sommers: 'In effect, the Novel of the Revolution more or less gave me an idea of what the Revolution was about. I learned history through narrative. That's how I understood the Revolution.'

This is true to some extent, since this series of novels rejects and looks upon the Revolution with much bitterness: the emancipatory ideal quickly faded, the best died, and the worst came out on top. Rulfo inherits this critical summary, but in his work armed violence does not have the same abstract meaning – 'the only language of primitive beings' – as it does in most of the other Novels of the Revolution. Violence in Rulfo does not just characterize the great moments of national history; rather, it precedes and follows them, it is the general atmosphere that explains the reasons for that apparently frozen time: the reason why, in Rulfo's world, the Revolution means so little and changes less (although we know that at the end of the narrative astonishment, the feudal society described there will fall). Such a view of violence, however, is only partial. The great distance between violence as a barbaric act (see 'La fiesta de las balas' ['A Feast of Bullets'] in *El águila y la serpiente* ['The Eagle and the Serpent'] by Guzmán) and violence as a natural act (the story 'El llano en llamas' ['Burning Plain'] by Rulfo) has already been pointed out. As Jean Franco has noted:

> In Rulfo you will never find a civilized narrator observing a barbarous people. On the contrary, as is clear in *Pedro Páramo*, priest and people, men and women, landowner and peasant are all in the same situation because the disjuncture between word and action is the result, not of a personal decision or an existential situation, but of the breakdown of an order.

In what ways are the different literary and historical traditions mixed and fused in this work? By what we might call today a will to demystify, to which both the sombre tone and the truth of the characters contribute. Hence the correspondences between Rulfo and the Scandinavian writers Knut Hamsun and Halldor Laxness, the Swiss Ramuz, the North American Faulkner, and even the Luis Buñuel of *Los olvidados*. Rulfo is not in the least interested in idealization but, rather, in showing the village man as a concrete being, in his terrible subjection, living under the terrible weight of the rules of a game imposed and sustained by others. The reader's task is to come to some kind of knowledge of social conditions, the persistence of

these oppressive systems that have fabricated and defended this subjection –
because Rulfo does not openly predicate, declaim or judge.

III

Rulfo's text for Rubén Gámez's film *La fórmula secreto* ['The Secret Formula'] is,
in many ways, exemplary:

> You might say that I'm stupid,
> that it's a mistake to complain about fate,
> especially in this stunted land
> where fortune has forgotten us.
> The truth is that it's difficult to get used to hunger.
> And even tho' you might say that a hunger
> shared among many
> affects few,
> the truth is that here
> we are all half dead,
> with no place
> even to die in.
> And it seems
> that things are going to get worse.
> Nothing about putting an end to all of this.
> None of that.
> Since the moment the world was world
> we've wandered its roads with our belly buttons
> glued to our spines,
> holding on to the wind by our fingernails.
> They even haggle over our shadows,
> but despite everything, we go on as we are:
> half dazed by the damned sun
> that breaks us up daily
> pestering day after day,
> as if wanting to revive the embers.
> Even though we know all too well
> that even burning
> our luck will not light up.

I have quoted extensively because the text summarizes magnificently the nature
of Rulfo's characters. Isn't this, rather than any merely simplistic idea of resignation, an enfolding of a vast historical experience, the way collective memory
illuminates narrative?

Similarly, the irrationality of Rulfo's work is not a matter of atavism but a question of culture. Comala and Luvina are communities ruled over by another conception of rationality in a historical space that stretches from the period of Porfirio Diaz to the Cristero War, in which history traverses the characters without defining them once and for all. There is no social development here, and agony, sadness and decadence reflect very real and overwhelming sadness and decadence. Comala transcends but also represents the common denominator of villages left to their fate, with priests whose weakness ends up dragging them off into reactionary guerrilla warfare; incestuous couples who defy disapproval in order to found a new species; madwomen singing lullabies to children who have not yet been born; sons of caciques educated in plunder and outrage. Behind the brilliance of *Pedro Páramo*, its sharp combination of poetry and realism, is the description of a community formed and deformed by a cacique, built in his image and likeness, which is best described as a chronicle of violent accumulation, of possession of lands and bodies, and of authority expressed through a series of rapes, murders and humiliations. The character of Pedro Páramo does not embody only the obsession for control, nor the disturbing love for an image from infancy transformed into unfulfillable fantasy. He is also the succession of women and young girls who surrender or are raped, enemies hanged or killed off with machete blows, the buying and selling of values and wills, the amassing of land and cunning. Without intending to denounce, *Pedro Páramo* reveals processes of injustice and dispossession, the ways in which the possession of wealth and money translates into sovereignty over lives and dignity.

IV

Religion is one of the main axes of Rulfo's world. The determining idea is not, however, the *beyond* but the *here and for always*. Secular experience reconfigures a community's conception of heaven and hell so that they are located within the confines of its daily life, rather than in traditional seraphic or satanic images. The theological words may be the same, but their meaning is different. Yes, sin is the unifying ground, but not any sin that the characters may have committed; rather, the sins of their fathers and grandfathers which have indebted them to eternity and which they will, deterministically, go on to commit so that they deserve the sad fate that causes so much anguish. A self-denigratory and unpardonable conception of the world has been absorbed from Catholic dogma and is lived from within the cracks and corners of language, from the carnal incorporation of omens and admonitions. In *Pedro Páramo*, Bartolomé San Juan says:

This world presses in on us from every side; it scatters fistfuls of our dust across the land and takes bits and pieces of us as if to water the earth with our blood. What do we do? Why have our souls rotted away? (83)

And Dorotea *La Cuarraca* confides in Juan Preciado:

Life is hard enough as it is. The only thing that keeps you going is the hope that when you die you'll be lifted off this mortal coil; but when they close one door to you and the only one left open is the door to Hell, you're better off not being born. . . . For me, Juan Preciado, heaven is right here. (64–5)

In Comala, heaven is a cemetery. Comala 'sits on the coals of the earth, at the very mouth of hell. They say that when people from here die and go to hell, they come back for a blanket' (6). If no one evokes paradise, it is because the pain of its loss is not felt. The choice of such terms, however, must be accompanied by the representation of their contexts. Here, for example, religion is no more than the fusion of illusion and conviction, of a faith that is the invocation of all memories and beliefs. It is the place of that popular theology that mixes heaven, hell, virgins, saints, grace, the fall and the impossibility of redemption, and adjusts it all to the profane order, to the dimension of personal will: 'The secret is to die, God willing, when you want to, and not when he proposes' (11). Such an intense and wounded faith could well be an incredulity that has not as yet found a new language.

Juan Rulfo tells Joseph Sommers:

I was born into an environment charged with faith, but I know that faith there has been transformed to such an extent that some question whether such men believe at all, have faith in anything, which is why they have reached such a state. I'm referring to a negative state. Their faith has been destroyed. They, the characters of *Pedro Páramo,* did believe once, and although they remain believers, their faith is in reality uninhabited. It has no support, nothing to hold on to. This may be why the novel is thought to be negative; which makes me think about those who think that the justice that is the most just is the best of all justices, when in fact it is the greatest of all injustices. So, in such cases, fanatical faith produces anti-faith, the negation of faith.

In such a religious culture, only anger and bitterness are encouraged. So, Juan Preciado asks Dorotea: "'And your soul? Where do you think it's gone?" "It's probably wandering like so many others, looking for living people to pray for it. Maybe it hates me for the way I treated it, but I don't worry about that anymore.

And now I don't have to listen to its whining about remorse'" (65).

Superstition is a dense, overwhelming cultural force that seeks either alleviation or the easing of social tensions. What is the 'grace of God'? What is it to 'die in sin' if not to die according to tradition, to respond literally to the belief that this life 'is hell' with extinction? What is 'sin' but obedience to the law that determines the impossibility of obedience? The incestuous sister says to Juan Preciado:

> 'Look at my face!'
> It was an ordinary face.
> 'What is it you want me to see?'
> 'Don't you see my sin? Don't you see those purplish spots? Like impetigo? I'm covered with them. And that's only on the outside; inside, I'm a sea of mud.' (50)

Sin has physical consequences, and the moral consequences are also physical (the 'sea of mud'). In the magnificent story 'Talpa', what stands out is not faith but illness, and the grotesque choreography of the dying man is a demand not for health but for actively bringing life to an end. Is it so strange, then, that the greatest sin is literally the absence of goods, and that the people, in their religious celebration, make 'a noise like a lot of bees frightened by smoke', or that they break out in 'a murmur that is transformed into a single moo'? The animalization of the devoted soul is the just retribution of a dogma which, at the limits of the earth, preserves of faith only the sanctions of guilt and the certainties of doubt: 'What did he know of heaven and hell?' Father Rentería asks himself: 'And yet even an old priest buried in a nameless town knew who had deserved heaven. He knew the roll. He began to run through the list of saints in the Catholic pantheon, beginning with the saints for each day of the calendar: "Saint Nunilona, virgin and martyr; Anercio, bishop . . ."' (31). Without such a fixed 'roll', there can be no certified heaven.

Rentería has accepted the destruction of his flock; he has submitted to Pedro Páramo's power, and officiated, despite his initial resistance, at the ceremony for the soul of Miguel Páramo, who murdered his brother and raped his niece. But if in his case religion is feverish hesitancy, in the rest it is eternal unfulfilment: 'What has their faith won them?' (29), asks Rentería. Such are the reasons for the weakness of those theories that imagine a Christian substrate in *Pedro Páramo*: similarities to *The Divine Comedy*, biblical allegories on every page. What is evident, rather, is the implacable originality of a use of religious symbols which never submits to them.

V

Does the work of Juan Rulfo represent that moment in a literature when it turns from naturalism to anguished subjectivism? If it is evident that developments in literary technique did make the structure of *Pedro Páramo* possible, it is also clear that the novel derives its complexity from its global vision: here are the reality and the beliefs that a community assumes as perfectly real. Rulfo unifies, joins and accumulates: ideology and legend, superstitious faith and reliable superstition, exploitation and innocence, solidarity destroyed by murder and brutality grounded in love of the family, life and death, blessed and tormented souls. *Pedro Páramo* would not exist without this totality. And for this totality to express itself, a cessation of movement in time and space is necessary. This is the only way in which a collectivity can exist, without fissures but always equal and faithful to itself. So that Comala might be a closed world and its story told in the present tense, it was necessary that the action had both taken place a long time ago and was still happening. That Comala be a dead village, in which the characters wander about as ghosts or make their confession from their graves, anchored in that one time which is eternity, was the perfect solution.

This is what makes literary labels so useless. How can 'magical realism' or 'fantastic realism' or 'the marvellous real' be applied to Rulfo's works? Nothing marvellous (always a laudatory term) can occur on calcinated plains, in villages become ghostly through poverty and emigration, in ruined souls. What can 'magic' – a term suggesting astonishment, mastery, surprise and entertainment – do here? What is 'fantastic'? Rulfo tells Fernando Benítez: 'I came across a reality that does not exist, an event that did not happen and people who have never existed.' But the removal of facts and people is not 'fantastic', because the devastating facts remain, burning and terrible.

Nor will the adjectival constructions which announce the intention to terrify be found in *Pedro Páramo*. Almost from the beginning, you sense that you are discerning (reconstructing) the life of a village of the dead, suspended in incredulity. But the purpose of the echoes and murmurs, the whispering of suffering souls, the weaving of voices which, from the grave or cracks in the land, begin to configure the character of Comala, is not to menace or destabilize the placid and sheltered reality of the reader. On the contrary, one only gradually – and even then, in fragmentary fashion – glimpses the endless reconstruction of the agony of a town and of a cacique, of postponed love and the accumulation of resentment. Each fragment responds to a totalizing intention of an almost muralist kind, without insignificant moments but also without grandiloquence or overblown reactions. An ascetic temperament directs this near-epic of disaster.

What is Pedro Páramo? The character whose strength feeds on the weakness of others? The two-faced symbol of power and submission? Both the simultaneity of levels and the interior monologue flow into an image that is never totally clear and always changing: a cacique who is as hard as granite and fragile, cruel and sentimental; a cacique who embodies ambition and indifference, accumulatory zeal and the abandonment of self, indiscriminate lechery and monogamous purity. His absorption of the town is accompanied, as in a circle, by the vigil of the unattainable, that flight which will never be an arrow, his absolutely abandoned and reverential demand – unto death – for Susana San Juan: 'Hiding in God's immensity, behind His Divine Providence' (13). The immeasurable eternal present tense of non-consummated love is added to the essence of *Pedro Páramo*, constituting its dazzling ambiguity. Everyone is dead, everyone has been destroyed. One only wants to bring to an end and contain the erotic madness of Susana.

In *Pedro Páramo*, love is the only conceivable gateway into spiritual wholeness (that which words cannot express; that which exists only on the basis of words). The rest – pleasureless sexual subjugation, rape, forced love, sexual duty, life that cages one with another – happens because that's how it should be. God's law is the sum total of required behaviour, and it seems that the people reproduce only so as to continue putting a curse on the species. Only the great figures of desire, Pedro Páramo and Susana San Juan, representatives of will and delirium, are endowed with the illusion of a spiritual life that lies outside the humiliations and hallucinations of a parish-controlled mystique.

VI

In his admirable creations, Rulfo truly endowed spoken Mexican Spanish with an intensity (an intimate exactness) equivalent to that accomplished by the poet Ramón López Velarde. His celebration of a community's linguistic know-how reveals authentic ways of naming, of approximating beings and objects, of realizing how words possess a social identity (a tradition) in both the hostile and cordial ways in which they are handled, of regarding them as sentimental supports or instruments of rejection and punishment. For Mexicans, Rulfo's language is immediately denotative: it registers tones and epochs, regions and cultural customs, comparative systems and the qualities for the creative use of words. Nothing is more deceptive, however, than to be trapped into believing in the ease with which this language may re-create and reveal peasant life; and to prove it, there is the pathetic destiny of Rulfo's imitators.

The comparison with López Velarde is necessary, since in his texts, as in

Rulfo's, the 'nationalization' of speech emerges from the intense knowledge with which expressions – which in themselves arouse the dual sensation of loss and gain, of that which has been lost and that which still has the power to make us – are evoked and developed. In both writers (and this is an aesthetic myth rather than a mythification) rural and provincial language is necessarily located in the past. Here are a few lines from López Velarde's *Suave Patria* ['Gentle Motherland']:

> Gentle Motherland . . .
> I want to kidnap you in dark Lent,
> on a stallion, in a rattletrap,
> among police gunshots . . .
> and our tearful youth hides
> inside you, the pummelled body
> of birds that speak our tongue.

To express a collectivity is, among other things, to endow it – perfectly – with irrecoverable voices and scenes, and whatever is permanent within the irrecoverable, in as up-to-date a fashion as possible. (Speech isolates, preserves and disfigures what disappears.) When López Velarde declares:

> My brothers from all times
> recognize in me the same pause,
> the same suffering and fury

he is also saying: recognize pauses, suffering and fury, because you still see yourselves in this language that is also spoken by the birds. In a similar fashion, *Pedro Páramo* describes a town and a people through the workings of a sharp and murky memory: the memory of a community that knows itself as such because it has only one language to unify experiences and feelings with. Tradition is not immobile respect here but, rather, a way of hanging on to the present, that infinite present that accumulates ancestors, inheritance, crimes, destroyed loves, murmurs, ennobled memories. Juan Preciado says: 'I was seeing things through her eyes . . .' (4). That is: I come with a perspective that will allow me to eliminate decades of difference and equalize a vision:

'It's a sorry-looking place, what happened to it?'
  'It's the times, señor.' (4)

It is the 'times' that no longer favour that unique infinite present shored up by backwardness and oppression. The perennial decadence of Luvina, or the metaphoric submission of Comala, or the dryness of the plain, all announce the Great Change, the advent of a regime with a past, present and future, where no one can bring you the eyes (the exact words) with which your ancestors looked at these things.

VII

What is *El llano en llamas* ['Burning Plain']? Thematically, a monstrous parade, always sad, always deadly: an idiot who kills frogs to eat them, a group to whom the government has given barren rather than arable land, the persecution and execution of the killer of a whole family, prostitution as the moral apprenticeship of poverty, the murder of a rancher by a farm worker, a pilgrimage to Talpa organized as the perfect murder by an adulterous couple, the Revolution seen as a series of criminal attacks, the execution of a man forty years after he committed a crime, a rural teacher who tells the story of the disintegration of a village, the escape of a *Cristero* soldier, the long march of a father carrying his agonizing criminal son on his shoulders, the killing of a faith healer who prospers economically and sexually from the innocence of his devout women followers, the banquet to celebrate the charitable visit of the governor which becomes a costly bacchanal for the town, the hatred between a father and son which is alleviated only in death. But the thematic list is insufficient and misleading, for it gives no impression of the diversity in narrative techniques, nor of the imagination involved. *Burning Plain* is an extraordinary landscape of the forms of life that the Revolution brought to the surface, only so as to leave them there dying, consuming themselves, damaged by its very own implacable rules. A point of fusion: in Rulfo desperation represents nearly everything. Deliberate irony has no place in an environment in which the climate does away even with the desire to talk, and supports psychic collapse with its heat, drought, humidity, dust: 'After so many hours of walking without finding even the shadow of a tree, nor the seed of a tree, not even a root, you can hear the dogs bark' ('They've Given Us the Land').

On the plain, human life is dispensable, and all that remains is the most ferocious adaptability – of arranging every day as if it were your last, and savouring 'the smell of people as if it were a hope'. This is why, in these stories, what we, from urban culture, call 'desperation' is the measure of all things. This is not for metaphysical reasons but because of the rough proof of the surrounding environment. Only in two stories – 'Anacleto Morones' and 'The Day of the Fall' – can verbal irony be found at work, as opposed to just the irony of the situations.

'Anacleto Morones', especially, masterfully captures the ambiguous zone of superstition and sex, religious fanaticism and sexual man. If its ironic end is out of tune with the rest of the book (which is unified by tragedy), its atmosphere, that desolation without visual respite from misery of all kinds, responds to the general tone, alien to any attempt at making the reality involved any kinder through aestheticization.

The rural world is existentially diversified. Rulfo begins from an essential knowledge of a region, its legends, mental habits, customs, ideas of honour and loyalty; he begins from a ferocious lack of distinction between subjectivity and objectivity. In his literature, men from the provinces and countryside are protagonists of the morality of the vanquished, where the norm is not the fulfilment of an abstract duty but, rather, the avoidance of a very concrete normality which, in a very evident way, predetermines them. They are sacrificed and postponed by a destiny anterior to any 'free choice', but not prior to weariness, drought, sexual humiliation, crime and escape (as a form of surrender-on-the-move). The Mexican Revolution is dissolved under a relentless climate, obscene in a way that words or acts – in isolation – will never be. There are no gratuities or gratitude: all violence extends and details the procedures of nature; all action synthesizes history, society and the landscape: 'It is difficult to grow up knowing that the very thing which we can grab hold of to take root is dead. That is what happened to us' ('Tell Them Not To Kill Me'). Like Pasolini, Rulfo looks at those who are predisposed to lynching with an eye for an image.

6

Dolores del Río:
The Face as Institution

A dazzling face. Timeless – not because it is immune to the devastation of age but, rather, for the radiant effect it still has on those who contemplate it. A figure boldly kept, accomplished in the slow sinuosity of its movements, in the care of its magnificent skin, in the way it incorporates elegance into facial movement, a stillness that denies languor, and in the Indian cheekbones that maintain both tension and imperial repose. The gift – we call it being *photogenic* – of knowingly administering one's looks for the camera, and keeping a wardrobe in which fashion pays homage to perfect features. A woman, the possessor of a face, who in the preservation of her beauty finds the meaning of her artistic life.

'No one ever leaves a star'

It is not only those who are given over to nostalgia who yield to the Screen Goddesses – beings defined for ever in only a few films and a number of images. In the renewed pleasure of spectators, in the impossibility of completely capturing their object of veneration ('Oh! You escape in the very instant/In which your best definition was achieved'), lies the persuasiveness of the *star system* – a cult of those who have resisted time and criticism, changes in taste, their condition as industrial products, even the pitiful vehicles in which they took part. The aesthetics may vary, plots may be pulverized by the aging of the morals that once made them believable, the memory may be kind or cruel . . . but, in a truly protean fashion, at every showing they are born again from the celluloid: Greta Garbo, Marlene Dietrich, Jean Harlow, Bette Davis, Katharine Hepburn, Vivien Leigh, Ginger Rogers, Joan Crawford, Mae West, Marilyn Monroe, Audrey Hepburn, María Félix, Lupe Vélez, Dolores del Río. . . . In *Sunset Boulevard*

(1950), a bitter reflection that is also the culmination of a myth, Gloria Swanson simultaneously embodies and negates herself as Norma Desmond, the silent film star confronted by death: the forgetting of a former glory that – now aged in the industry's eyes – still evokes gestures and provokes Pharaonic entrances.

'No one ever leaves a star. That's what makes one a star.' Norma Desmond's phrase contains in condensed form the power of the great feminine myths: the abundance of tactics with which to incite and submit, looks that are like mystical offerings, modulations of the Eternal Eve, representations of sensuality as *high life*, poses of abandon for a camera that continues (by other means) the work of the Renaissance painters of Madonnas, ways of walking and talking that describe an epoch, a new view of women, a catalogue of desired goods. 'No one ever leaves a star.'

Sunset Boulevard is a multiple commentary on cinema: the solitude of one who Once Was, stardom, awe adopted in order either to arrest time or to blur a sense of failure. 'I'm big,' says Desmond, 'it's the pictures that have become small.' With the waning of the experience of reverence, and the 'secularization' or 'democratization' of cinema, Stars are left to the mercy of memory and cultural judgement. Only a few (Greta Garbo, Bette Davis, Katharine Hepburn, Marlene Dietrich, Dolores del Río, María Félix) are never abandoned. *Sunset Boulevard* is the most cruel and most praised of Hollywood's apotheoses. George Cukor's *A Star is Born* (1954) is its elegiac retelling. In her demand for unconditional surrender, Gloria Swanson embodies the female star's wild abandon; and in her fragile eloquence, Judy Garland synthesizes the leap involved from being 'perishable' to becoming deified. Kenneth Tynan's phrase 'What others see in women when drunk, I see in Greta Garbo when sober' traces the boundaries of such a terrain's believability: the Goddess and the votary, the screen as temple. For decades the true sociological location of these women is ignored, attention being paid only to the series of changes undergone by shopgirls, starlets, well-to-do society girls, chorus girls. . . . Suddenly, the chosen ones abandon their original personalities, renounce the looks that once represented their innocence and, in the time it takes for the national or international success of their films, reappear, representing what is most desirable and unattainable, framed by the most brilliant of adjectives, their photographs reproduced millions of times on posters, giving invented interviews, in scandals suppressed (or strategically fanned), buying mansions in Bel Air or Beverly Hills, endlessly travelling and universally worshipped.

According to the director Joseph von Sternberg, glamour is produced by *chiaroscuro*, the play of light on the contours of a face, the aura of a star's hair, the creation of mysterious shadows around the eyes, and the compositional use of the surroundings. In Hollywood, stars as different from each other as Marlene Dietrich, Rita Hayworth and Dolores del Río acquire and possess glamour, the technique and will to refine their own beauty. They are – in films like *Shanghai Express, Gilda* or *Bird of Paradise* – the indecipherable magic of cinema, the dream material of one generation and the admiring rendezvous of the next. They underline the fact that – at least in one sense – *myth* is that which resists the familiarity that erodes. The effect of films by Griffith, John Ford, Lang or Eisenstein will never weaken for us; we will never exhaust a joke by Chaplin, Laurel and Hardy or Buster Keaton, or a close-up of Greta, Marlene or Dolores. Exalted (a legitimate recourse where film is concerned), it is understood that art sustains the glamour of such stars and renders it transcendent. The cinema of an epoch, however ragged, resists conventional histories, reactionary ideology, ludicrous ends, incongruences and arbitrariness. It cannot, however, survive the absence of ecstatic presences, faces with auras, imperious orders that the actor who receives them transfers to the spectator who reveres them.

On the inconvenience of Good Society

The official biography of Dolores del Río is scant in detail. She was born in Durango on 3 August 1905 (according to other versions, 1901), the only daughter of Jesús Leonardo Asúnsulo and Antonia López Negrete. The actress holds an idyllic view of her childhood:

> The house in which I was born – I remember it now as if I were there this very moment – was very small, with simple columns and rooms around a patio. It also had a garden in which I learned to walk holding on to the flowerpots. Inside, in the living and dining rooms, there were two windows through which I saw people pass by sitting in my wet-nurse's lap. I liked to walk in the countryside and watch the cows graze, the smell of the flowers, to wander along the furrows and sow cauliflowers. As a small girl I learned to love the land, and I still do now. I was very young when my mother brought me to Mexico City to meet her cousin Don Panchito – which is what she used to call him – Madero, then the President of the Republic, who sat me on his knee and gave me an enormous red balloon. (Jorge Guerrero Suárez, *Dolores del Río. La vocación de la belleza,* 1979)

The Revolution does not affect the fortunes of the family irreversibly (although an Uncle Asúnsulo is murdered during a military campaign). Dolores's father is

Director of the Bank of Durango, and in 1910 he flees to the capital with his family to escape Pancho Villa, who had taken possession of the bank and the family home. Dolores has the conventional education of the privileged: French nuns in the San José Convent, dance classes with the celebrated teacher Felipa López, gatherings hosted by the Best Families. A portrait of the adolescent Dolores painted by the then successful Alfredo Ramos Martínez shows her to be beautiful, distant, fashionable, an adolescent by John Singer Sargent in a *foreign country.*

In 1921 she marries the lawyer Jaime Martínez del Río, educated in England and France, and from a family considered 'aristocratic'. The portrait of her in her wedding dress (designed by the painter Roberto Montenegro) is misleading. It portrays a young woman subject to social conventions, prepared to follow the luxurious and impersonal course laid out for her by her class. They spend their honeymoon in Europe, naturally, and Dolores is presented to the Spanish Royal Family.

On returning to Mexico, Dolores exorcizes her boredom by studying dance and preparing 'intimate ballets. . . . It was my only emotional escape. And when I danced, I realized that I also wanted to act.' Not, however, without first paying her respects to Society. A photo, representing 'conjugal bliss', reveals not the life of a couple, but their idea of social respect: Martínez de Río concentrates on his reading in front of a chimney; Dolores contemplates him with the required attention. A homage to stability is fixed in poses.

A friend of the family, the painter Adolfo Best Maugard, takes the director Edwin Carewe to the Martínez del Río residence. A scene straight from a film of the time: Dolores dances a tango, Carewe is enthusiastic; Dolores dances some more, Carewe convinces Don Jaime to let her accompany him to Hollywood. Then conflict, complaints from the husband's family, intense doubts about the social inconvenience of being an actress. Dolores challenges these prejudices and goes, accompanied by her husband: 'Jaime wanted to escape an environment that did not satisfy him, hoping to develop his literary inclinations writing scripts for Hollywood.' In August 1925, the couple arrive in Los Angeles.

The primitive remains and endures

Hollywood in the 1920s, and the commonplaces that have not as yet become common: the jazz age, the zenith of silent cinema, the orgies that disclose the pastime of Kings, the flappers pursued by the longing gaze of philosophers. Carewe, the discoverer, directs Dolores's first three features: *Joanna* (1925), *High*

Steppers (1926) and *Pals First* (1926). Her first important film, *What Price Glory?*, is directed by Raoul Walsh in 1926. Dolores plays a character who, like Lupe Vélez and Raquel Torres before her, Hollywood will make her own: the 'exotic beauty' whose immaculate features in movement disclose primitivism, the impulse never to be conditioned by civilization. In *What Price Glory?* and *Bird of Paradise*, in *The Red Dance* and *Girl of the Río*, she plays the wild beast that can be tamed, the savage redeemed by love . . . and Western civilization.

Hollywood 'exoticism' is as understandable (once its grotesque impact has been assimilated) as the tales of Marco Polo or geographical maps of the Middle Ages. The 'induced fluster' is founded on a desire to weave, yard by yard, a geography of the imagination with its own scenery, language, orography, hydrography, music, urban rules, eroticism, wardrobe, cabbalistic signs, adventures, public morality, gods and cruel rulers. *Tlön, Uqbar, Orbis Tertius.* With a persuasiveness that is recognized only after the event, US cinema stages continents, countries and customs that are not to be found in enyclopaedias. Slanderous but stylish inventions – Baghdad, Casablanca, Istanbul, Shanghai, Canton, Zanzibar, Morocco, the Pacific Islands, Ancient Rome or nineteenth-century Seville – all possess, in Hollywood's reconstructions, the authenticity of childhood fantasy, the concreteness of dreams redeemed by the obsession to travel.

Dolores is asked to animate this sensual, racist, puerile (and not necessarily tropical) geography, which could just as well be a cardboard-cut-out Mexico as a vague 'South America', the court of Louis XIV, the Pacific Islands, the virgin forests of the Amazon, or the countryside in Tsarist Russia. Depending on the particular task at hand, she would be Carmen de Mérimée, the unfortunate Ramona, the Red ballerina from Moscow, the savage Luana, the whimsical Madame Dubarry or the Españolita. Such characters are moved either by praise or by sensuality: the unusual (read 'foreign') beauty is possessed by an uncontrollable psyche, the emotions of a native frightened by the gods of the volcano, or a Hispanic whose sophistication stops at her clothes. For Hollywood, the sensuality of the 'native' is inseparable from their religion.

Queen for a century

For decades, the film industry benefited from a mystical status. The big studios – Paramount, Metro-Goldwyn-Mayer, RKO, United Artists, Warner Brothers, Twentieth Century Fox and Universal – prove that when it comes to Sacred Monsters, spectators suspend all secular reason (of the religions of the twentieth century, cinema is the one that best exploits the cult of the Vestal Virgins). In an art that contains its fair share of science, awe is managed and processed in order to produce a Star who may become profitable as well as a sacred object of fascination. Hollywood publicists will dedicate their lives to such celluloid theology between the 1920s and 1950s, as do great directors like Cukor, Von Sternberg or Minnelli, make-up artists, dressmakers, costumiers – all those charged with producing glamour with light and shade, set designers who idealize the opulence that becomes, on screen (or in cinematographic myth), the consolation of the masses (Dolores, while specializing in peasant roles, embodies luxury and the gifts of fortune in her publicity pictures). Each star has a team specialized in the surgical creation of the Radiant Personality: secretaries, hairdressers, seamstresses who eliminate the traces of the everyday from their Object from Paradise in order to prolong the filmic fantasies.

'We had faces then!', screams Gloria Swanson in *Sunset Boulevard*. And Dolores's face is so remarkable that it simultaneously determines the apotheosis and impossibility of her artistic development. Nobody seriously demands acting abilities from the Star, and from the very beginning, in The Wampas Baby Stars of 1926 promotion (which unites her with Mary Astor, Fay Wray, Janet Gaynor and Joan Crawford), all that is demanded of Dolores is decorative acting, the endorsement her beauty brings, and the adaptation of her body and face to the needs of melodrama. Dolores is sensual and moving; she sings gracefully in *Ramona* and *Evangelina*, accepts and redirects the demands of photographers, wears Oriental hairdos aplenty, and hats whose colours match the swimming pool, and adopts poses desexualized by beauty. She is the Latino face of Hollywood, and this implies both devotion and sacrifice, the never-ending self-consciousness of a face forever under surveillance. In Cecil Beaton's portrait (1931) Dolores is the forbidden fruit, the spell before which the arms of civilization yield. In a hastily cobbled together 'tropical' scene, she is the delirium of the senses, the consecration of a Nature that technology will inevitably destroy.

Between 1925 and 1942, Dolores del Río takes part in twenty-eight North American films. Her presence is magnificent, but not enough to redeem inept plots, carelessness, mistakes. From the contemporary point of view the following sustain some interest (for a variety of reasons): *What Price Glory?*, *Resurrección* and *Ramona* (the latter two directed by Carewe), *Bird of Paradise* (directed by King Vidor, 1932), *Flying Down to Río* (directed by Thornton Freeland, 1933), *Wonder Bar* (1934), *In Caliente* (directed by Lloyd Bacon, with choreography by Busby Berkeley, 1935) and *Journey into Fear* (begun by Orson Welles and finished by Norman Foster, 1942). *What Price Glory?*, an excellent melodrama about the First World War, reveals her merciless vitality; the subsequent films attenuate her energy or direct it along the most puerile of channels.

Within the restricted economy of Hollywood roles, Dolores stands for the irruption of instinct or the serenity of beauty. Nothing more. In *Flying Down to Río*, she dances with Fred Astaire and exhales romantically . . . a mere stepping stone on the way to the Astaire–Rogers partnership. In *Wonder Bar* and *In Caliente* she participates in Busby Berkeley's prodigious 'optical choreographies', and submits to the idiocies of the scripts and the racist distribution of instincts and abilities. *Bird of Paradise* is the ideal showcase for 'exotic beauties'; *In Caliente* is an oblique denunciation of the rapacity and shamelessness of Mexicans, eternal strummers of guitars; and *Flying Down to Río* is merely the pretext for a series of great musical numbers. Racism brooks no exception, so that whatever is considered 'tropical' is the object of continuous derision. In Mexico, a film that starred Dolores, *Girl of the Río* (Herbert Brenon, 1932) was considered offensive and is exhibited only in a censored version. Dolores apologizes: she had insisted that the action take place somewhere in the Mediterranean, and behold, it turned out to be Mexico! Now wary, she turns down a part in Jack Conway's *Viva Villa!* for 'Mexican reasons'.

On live works of art

Dolores's triumph in Hollywood is undeniable. *Ramona* and *Resurección* confirm her status as a great star – so much so that the Pullman company baptizes three of its sleeper carriages in her honour: 'Del Río', 'Dolores' and 'Ramona'. In mid 1928 she signs an exceptional contract with United Artists to make seven films at a hundred thousand dollars each (the first being *Ramona*), her fee including six months' paid holiday a year (see Gabriel Ramírez's excellent *Lupe Vélez. La mexicana que escupió fuego*, Monografías de la Cineteca Nacional, Mexico 1986). Dolores belongs to that select group of stars who escape the monopolizing grasp of the studios, filming with whomsoever she pleases without suffering reprisals.

Dolores's crowning year is 1928. She participates in the great radio transmission organized by United Artists to demonstrate to the public that the voices of its great stars more than meet the demands of the talkies. Douglas Fairbanks is the master of ceremonies, John Barrymore recites a soliloquy from *Hamlet*, Gloria Swanson gives advice to the young on how to make it in Hollywood, D.W. Griffith discusses 'love in all its aspects, except the sexual', Charles Chaplin is inhibited, Mary Pickford talks to women 'intimately', and Dolores sings 'Ramona'.

Her image is to be seen everywhere; the great photographers lay siege to her *native beauty.* Soon, she is no longer the tamed little wild animal of *What Price Glory?*, and acquires the reputation of being distant and 'inaccessible' (very different from the lively and untamable Lupe Vélez). And she changes her appearance. 'I believe', says Larry Carr, 'that Joan Crawford's looks influenced Dolores's at the beginning of the Thirties.' In 1930 and 1931, when Crawford emerged as a striking beauty, women all over the world – but especially in Hollywood – imitated her way of dressing and her make-up. The pastel look, with heart-like lips, disappeared, to be replaced by sculptured features with an angular face. The camera, with the assistance of new ways of applying make-up and a different lighting style, produced a new kind of beauty, of which Dolores del Río is the precursor. . . . She discards her style of the 1920s, lets down her hair, enlarges the appearance of her lips, changes the style of her eyebrows and underlines her exquisite bone structure. Her face becomes one of the original Great Faces.

In 1928 Dolores is divorced from Jaime Martínez del Río (who, it seems, committed suicide some years later), and in 1930 she marries Cedric Gibbons, the prominent artistic director of MGM. From this very privileged position, she experiences 'Hollywood Babylon': fancy-dress parties in William Randolph Hearst's *Xanadu*, tennis tournaments, high frivolity – where no one took any notice of her protests against the succession of her decorative parts, of plots centred on her physique. *Resurrección*, she insists, approximates her artistic ideal, and *Resurrección* is a run-of-the-mill melodrama. 'My Hollywood pictures almost ruined me,' she declares, 'I was forced to play glamorous characters, which I hated.' But glamour endows Dolores with the aura of being a woman of her time – modern, blamelessly happy, and without prejudice – who embodied and offered the public the chic atmosphere and up-to-date taste which were lacking in Mexico.

In Mexico, Dolores del Río's career in the United States is the (inevitable) cause of peripheral pride: she is the compatriot-who-has-made-it-in-Hollywood, the local girl who is a delight on the universal screen. While her films are the object of intense scrutiny (and High Society Ladies imitate her, not without some disapproval), she is declared an honorary member of that select club of Universal Mexicans; and as such she is invited to the inauguration of the Palacio de Bellas Artes (Palace of Fine Arts). In their box, Dolores and Ramón Novarro *(Ben-Hur)* are proof that national art has crossed an important frontier.

Reality is a little different. *Hispanic film* in Hollywood loses its popularity, 'exoticism' is no longer of interest, and from 1932 onwards, Dolores – albeit a figure with great status – is of no consequence at the box office. Nevertheless, when she is offered the leading part in the film *Santa*, she declares (in other words) that not even in her wildest dreams would she become part of a film industry that was not up to her high standards – as was the case in Mexico.

In 1940, the relationship between Dolores and Orson Welles causes a great scandal. Welles, the Hollywood *boy wonder* and theatre director, whose radio version of H.G. Wells's *War of the Worlds* created such a commotion, who had directed *Citizen Kane* in such great secrecy, and planned to revolutionize the cinema. The success of *Citizen Kane* is followed by an angry persecution campaign mounted by the Hearst network against the film and its director, and it partially affects Dolores, whom Welles was thinking of directing in *Cortés and Malinche* and *Journey into Fear*, a thriller based on the novel by Eric Ambler. Midway through the filming, Welles resigned and was replaced by the very conventional Norman Foster. The result: an interesting but flawed film.

Opportunities in Hollywood exhausted, Dolores decides to return to Mexico. She declares: 'I want to choose my own stories, my own director and cameraman. I think I can get all this in Mexico.' In 1940, just before her departure, the writer Salvador Novo describes her in Hollywood:

> If, at times, there surfaces a consolatory belief that talent is a form of beauty, with Dolores del Río we are in the presence of a case in which extraordinary beauty is only the material form of talent. She has been gifted with grace, elegance, a fresh and vibrant nimbleness that, being natural, seems exotic. The most important fashion magazines fight over her latest photograph in which she wears a simple hairdo that she has just made up and which, soon, families will begin to impose as the norm; a thick amethyst bracelet, the only adornment to quietly set off her tiara against her black hair; or the sandals in which she goes out to the garden to look at the frogs and ducks with which she has populated it; or the place in which she has placed the orchids in her suit. She creates herself . . . just like any artist creates their best work.

Whatever you say

What could be better for the national film industry than the return of Dolores in 1943? Del Río: the artistic guarantee of excellence, the centre of all social life, the *de luxe* hostess. In her transplanted California-style residence in Coyoacán, anyone who is anyone comes to pay homage to her perfect taste in manners and wardrobe, or to plead for her presence at banquets in honour of the President of the Republic, the Minister of Education, the Director of the Institute of Fine Arts. If Cecil Beaton or Weissberger portrayed her in the solitary splendour of the Beautiful Savage or the Woman at Home in the World, Fito Best Maugard, José Clemente Orozco and Diego Rivera will paint her moving innocence, her candour and timeless majesty, the dual – pre-Hispanic and 'mestiza' – representation of warranted haughtiness.

Once in Mexico, Dolores is convinced of the need to change her image, and thus accepts supreme conventionality: to be the meek and ignorant barefoot Indian girl. To convince her to take the leading part in *Flor Silvestre* ['Wild Flower'], Emilio Fernández – recalls his daughter in her convincing biography *El Indio Fernández: Vida y mito* (Editorial Panorama, Mexico City 1986) – assures her: 'If to your beauty and fame we add the tragic spirit of the Mexican people, you can be sure, Lolita, that you will conquer Europe.' And he further impresses on her:

> You must win the love of the Mexican people who resent your disdainful attitude, and it won't be easy. You must show that you are Mexican, and proud of it; and what is more, that you feel sympathy for the oppressed and downtrodden. You cannot, and should not, distance yourself from the drama of the Revolution and its ideals. And if, in contrast, you participate in a film that praises and sympathizes with them, well, Mexico will not only love you again, it may even idolize you.

Whether these are actually the right words or not, the context makes them believable. According to Adela Fernández, Diego Rivera convinces Dolores: 'What is on offer is the opportunity to take part in a very Mexican-looking film at a moment when the Europeans are rediscovering Mexico, attracted by the mysteries they find here. Mexico is considered fascinating.' Dolores accepts and, without wanting to or really knowing it, becomes involved with the nationalist Left that sees in *Flor Silvestre* an act of vindication. Next – and despite Dolores's resistance to themes about the Revolution – 'el Indio' Fernández offers her 'a story of love and pain, Indians, flowers and death: *María Candelaria*'.

Dolores is surprised by the part, but 'el Indio' Fernández is quick to reassure her: 'With this film, Lolita, you will attain more glory than you have ever wished.' Dolores replies: 'I said that the story was interesting, not that I was interested in it. First a farm girl and now . . . now you want me to play a little Indian girl? Me . . . barefoot?' 'El Indio' Fernández's answer immediately brings to mind the expiatory journey of Ana de Ozores in *Regenta*: 'Of course, your feet will be the greatest nude ever; your feet are enough!' And *María Candelaria* is a triumph in Cannes and Locarno, and assures Dolores's second film career.

Suffering justifies the close-up

What function could Dolores del Río serve in Mexican cinema? In Hollywood she was asked to be *deeply spontaneous* (that is, 'primitive') in melodramas or comedies, and the camera registered her sudden excitability, the stirring of ancestral pain, her infantile happiness and whims expressed in dance or in *Madame Dubarry*'s demand that Paris be bereft of salt just so as to create the effect of snow in Versailles. But in Mexico, this 'exotic flower' will be allowed no such spontaneity. What follows seems, from a distance, like an operation of 'facial ideology'. In order to excuse the unrepeatable beauty of a native, local racism makes her hieratic – the negation of happiness, a reservoir of suffering and dignity. The sexist idea of mature femininity cancels out all naturalness.

Dolores is confined to melodramas, the theatricalization of family torment as joy through tragedy, and the inevitable pact between the film industry and a public who, from such modest catharses, extract didactic conclusions. Almost without transition – and setting in motion a set of expressive gestures which in *La malquerida* ['The Despised Woman'], become self-parody – Dolores passes from the forced gesticulation of silent cinema to passive gesticulation. The difference is considerable. She had been Ramona, lovesick for Alejandro, the Indian; Luana, snatched from the arms of her beloved and delivered to the appetites of the gods of fire; Katusha Maslova, the Tolstoyan heroine. Now, only exceptionally will she be given solid parts – *La otra* ['The Other Woman']; *Doña Perfecta*. Most often, Dolores will be the incomparable creature of melodrama, a genre that makes no concessions to real beings or situations, sweetened by the eternal Victims of Fate or, in the case of 'el Indio' Fernández's films, by the emblems of Nationhood.

If Dolores is experienced by the audience as both admirable and distant, this is first, because she is the perfect embodiment of a Society Lady, and second, because of her delirious succession of roles as the devastated and oppressed Long-Suffering Woman. . . . It is not easy to accept Dolores del Río, the great Mexican Beauty, as the grieving young woman of *Flor Silvestre*, cuddling her child on the ground; or, in *Bugambilia*, confessing to her nanny: 'Do you know who I'd like to dance the first waltz with? With a man who could dominate me with one look, one of those men who never ask because everything already belongs to them, a man as strong as a river, a man by whose side I would feel ever so small.'

The suspension of disbelief: the unconditional surrender of Screen Goddesses is never, in the last instance, convincing. How can we believe Dolores when she says in *Las abandonadas* ['Abandoned']: 'Juan, let me be your shadow in love!', if right there, as she appears shining at the top of the stairs, Pedro Armendáriz declares: 'Come down . . . please come down, and convince me this is not a dream!'? How can we accept her endless obedience if, in *Bugambilia*, her beloved endows her with the appearance and miraculous character of the Virgin of Guadalupe: 'Pretty? What we are accustomed to call pretty, no. She is . . . like an apparition'?

In her best moments (*La otra, Doña Perfecta*) Dolores is commanding, cruel, not the humiliated but the humiliator, the inverted apology of *machismo*, the woman whose fancy takes her in the opposite direction to traditional femininity. Nature – implies the logic of the melodrama – made her the gift of beauty so that she could accomplish her desire to control.

Dolores del Río will work with three important directors in Mexican cinema – Emilio 'el Indio' Fernández, Roberto Gavaldón and Alejandro Galindo – and with two extraordinary cameramen, Gabriel Figueroa and Alex Phillips. Gavaldón will make her the Virgin of Melodrama; Galindo will use her in his unusual anticlerical enterprise, and 'el Indio' Fernández will see in her the undefilable object of his nationalism – whose sources include Eisenstein and his cameraman Tissé, the muralists (especially Orozco), regional custom, popular song and the rediscovery of landscapes and customs that had not, as yet, been constituted as a tourist point of view. Emilio 'el Indio' Fernández believes that he has literally discovered – or rediscovered – Mexico, whose essence is to be found in the combination of unsuspected grandeur (a face, a twilight) and the *macho* attitude, the synthesis of Tradition and the Revolution.

Dolores del Río and Pedro Armendáriz, the dazzling origins of a 'Mexican Aesthetic', the Adam and Eve of a paradise of fire and fury where – in 'el Indio' Fernández's eyes – a nationality has set itself free from slavery. A couple who are both typical and classical, whose duty it is to embody the limits of masculinity and femininity in symbols, archetypes and myths, to live in a mythical time (corresponding to somewhere between 1850 and 1914).

The five films made with the Primordial Couple by the team of Fernández, Figueroa and the scriptwriter Mauricio Magdalena are important and, at times, even extraordinary: *Flor Silvestre* (1943), *María Candelaria* (1944), *Las abandonadas* ['Abandoned', 1944], *Bugambilia* (1944), and *La malquerida* [The Unloved', 1949]. *Flor Silvestre*, especially, which, despite its faults, is a classic that sets the tone for films about the Revolution, and makes of melodramatic delirium the 'potential neo-realism' of Mexico. Esperanza (Dolores), granddaughter of the farmhand Melchor (Eduardo Arozamena), falls in love with José Luis

Castro (Armendáriz), son of Doña Clara (Mimí Derba) and Don Francisco (Miguel Angel Ferriz) – despotic landowners who worship their own family background and refuse to let a peasant girl become part of it. Esperanza and José Luis marry in secret. His parents oppose the match, and insult Esperanza at a village fiesta. She gives birth to a boy. The Revolution breaks out, and José Luis takes an active part, but the followers of the treacherous generals Ursulo and Rogelio Torres (Manuel Dondé and Emilio Fernández) overrun Don Francisco's hacienda. José hears about what has happened, but reaches the hacienda too late: the place is in ruins and his father has been murdered. To take his revenge, he hangs the body of Ursulo, who has died of typhus. Torres captures Esperanza and their son, and threatens to kill them if José Luis doesn't give himself up. He does, and is shot. Esperanza screams and faints, and years later she tells her son of the tragedies that have made this modern progressive nation possible.

The synopsis sketches a somewhat demagogic work of 'operatic' taste, set amid a series of commonplaces. But it says nothing of the verve of the direction, Figueroa's marvellous images, and the visual eloquence that culminates in the faces of Dolores and Pedro – more like Events than Ideas, Founding Institutions than Events. Nor does it evoke Dolores's statuesque qualities: her slight smile, the movement of her face, and her predisposition to be shattered, all completely at the service of tragedy.

The 'ideological' hypothesis of these films – that the moral and physical perfection of 'the Couple' is the major obstacle to their happiness – persists in *María Candelaria*, a drama whose lyricism just saves it from the defects in its plot and the regrettable 'Indian' way of speaking forced on its characters. The plot is a classic of its type. In 1909, in the not-so-idyllic Náhuatl community of Xochimilco, Lorenzo Rafael (Armendáriz) wants to marry María Candelaria (Dolores), whom the village rejects because she is the daughter of a prostitute. Don Damián, a contemptible and exploitative shopkeeper (Miguel Inclán), desires María Candelaria, and pursues Lorenzo for the payment of his debts. All the couple possess is a little pig, which the resentful Damián shoots dead. There is a malaria epidemic, and the government sends Damián quinine to distribute free. María Candelaria becomes ill, but is refused medicine. Desperate, Lorenzo takes some quinine and a wedding dress for his beloved from the shop. She recovers, and just as they are getting married, Damián and two policemen burst in and arrest Lorenzo for stealing the dress and some money (which he did not take). He is condemned to one year in jail. A painter (Alberto Galán) is attracted by María Candelaria's beauty and invites her to pose for him, offering to pay Lorenzo's bail, but the judge is no longer there. María Candelaria refuses to pose naked, so the painter uses another model for the body. A neighbour gets a glimpse of the painting, and the gossip starts: María Candelaria in the nude! The villagers, their Catholic pride wounded, burn down the wretched Indian girl's hut, pursue her and stone her to death outside the prison. Lorenzo escapes and runs to María Candelaria, who dies in his arms. He leads her down the Canal of Death in a bed of flowers.

These days contemporary reactions to the film seem laughable, like those of the Stalinist critic Georges Sadoul, who said the the film was 'worthy for the authenticity with which it painted the rural life of Mexico', or those nationalists who praised its 'discovery of a poetic Mexico' (which Salvador Novo caricatured by rebaptizing it *María Calendaria* [María the Calendar Girl] on the day of its première). But many of the film's images retain their initial splendour, especially the pastoral scenes and the 'Indigenist' representation of Dolores, dressed in a shawl and a percale dress. These are the definitive illustrations of a mythological undertaking then in fashion: reverence before a pure and abstract Mexicanness which gradually spreads from people to objects.

From the point of view of plot, *Las abandonadas* mixes aspects of the political crime story – taken from the Grey Automobile Mob case (the underworld in the capital city protected by generals) – and *La mujer X* ['Woman X'] by Fanny Hurst, about a woman's decline produced by her desire to educate her son, who, now a brilliant lawyer, defends her without realizing that she is his mother. In *Las abandonadas*, Dolores looks magnificent as both the high-class prostitute and the cheap whore. Whatever the story may say, she is the inaccessible beauty; she is, again, the bird of paradise.

Dolores breaks with 'el Indio' Fernández during the filming of *Bugambilia*, 'the most lavish film ever to be made in Mexico', a melodrama set in the nineteenth century, the weakest of the five films made by the team. Already dominated and devoured by his own semi-apocalyptic character, Fernández insults everyone around him, gets drunk, and gets angry just because he feels like it. The injured party gives her version to Salvador Novo:

> He went on being arrogant with the whole cast, says Dolores, he even made Alberto Galán cry, and kicked the extras about. Then it was Dolores's turn, in the last scene shot in Guanajuato. He humiliated her in front of the extras, actors, and onlookers. From that day on, she refused to speak to him, except when it was professionally necessary on the set. Her next film will be directed by Julio Bracho – who, if less brilliant, will be more proper.
> 'So,' I asked, 'you've had enough of "el Indio" Fernández?'
> 'Yes,' answered Dolores, 'that's enough.'

(Salvador Novo, *La vida en México en el período presidencial de Manuel Ávila Camacho*, Empresa Editoriales, Mexico City 1965)

The basic defects of the nationalist cinema of 'el Indio' Fernández – its sexist content, the inconsistency of its allegories – are soon apparent. But in ridiculing and scorning his work, critics have made the same mistake of excess. Today, when there is no need to sacralize or desacralize, it is important to recognize the contribution made by this group, their promotion of the aesthetic transformation of what had always been there, but made invisible and ignored, and especially the way in which the films privileged faces and temperaments to infuse the delirious plots with a logic.

Dreams, the author of representations

Over a ten-year period, in addition to her collaboration with Fernández and Figueroa, Dolores makes three films of great interest: *La otra* ['The Other Woman', 1946], *Doña Perfecta* (1950) and *The Fugitive* (1947, directed by John Ford). In *La otra*, Gavaldón, still in search of 'quality cinema', resorts to lessons learnt from Orson Welles and Robert Siodmak, taking maximum advantage of the complexity of a screenplay written by José Revueltas, and the potential of a Dolores del Río unencumbered by familiar civic statuary. The story of twin sisters, one of whom murders the other out of frustration and anger, is a labyrinth of sensations, metamorphoses and false starts. The manicurist María kills the millionairess Magdalena and, possessed by the personality of her victim, falls into an alternating rhythm of modesty and arrogance, defencelessness and aggression. In her own eyes she will always be *the other*, and will be healed psychologically only when she is accused of a crime she did not commit. Without having to represent any National Essence, without the authoritarian *macho* to corner her, Dolores reaches her melodramatic height in *La otra*.

In an overwhelmingly reactionary context, *Doña Perfecta*, a transposition to the nineteenth-century Mexican milieu of Benito Pérez Galdós's novel, was a singular event in Mexican cinema. The young engineer Pepe Rey (Carlos Navarro), an open-minded Liberal Darwinist and reader of Spinoza, arrives in the town of Santa Fe. Initial distrust becomes hate when he refuses to kneel as a religious procession passes by. The first to attack him is his father's sister, Perfecta (Dolores), president of the Perpetual Vigil, the vigilant conscience of community morality. Rosario (Esther Fernández), Perfecta's daughter, falls in love with her cousin, but is coldly reprimanded. In the end, the unstoppable devout woman, ready to remove the sinner, stirs up the jealousy of Cristóbal Ramos (José Elías Moreno), a villager, who murders Pepe Rey. Rosario flees from her mother, who is left alone in control only of her exterminating faith.

A plea for tolerance, *Doña Perfecta* is perhaps Dolores's best acting opportunity. Lacking the brilliance of *Flor Silvestre* or *The Fugitive*, without the reverential scenes of *Las abandonadas* or *La otra*, Gavaldón's film allows her to be an actress without the constant support of close-ups and the constant hints to the audience that they are in the presence of a myth. Severe, transfigured by fanaticism, Dolores's Doña Perfecta is the nearest she comes to working with a total lack of conventional constraints.

In contrast, not even the abilities of John Ford and Figueroa, nor the presence of Henry Fonda, Armendáriz and Dolores, save *The Fugitive*, a hypocritical adaptation of Graham Greene's novel *The Power and the Glory*. It is a clerical writ that invents a Mexico of 'bloodied altars' and existential desolation. But in *The Fugitive* Dolores, the peasant who dances to protect a priest persecuted by government forces, is almost a devotional image. Photographed in shadows, captured in a sanctifying light, Dolores bears witness to the years in which the Star was a prolongation of the Madonna.

Need and conscious desire

Other films: *La selva de fuego* ['Jungle of Fire', 1945], *Historia de una mala mujer* ['The Story of an Evil Woman', 1948 – filmed in Argentina], *La casa chica* ['Love Nest', 1949], *Deseada* ['The Desired One', 1950], *El ninó y la niebla* ['The Boy and the Mist', 1953], *Señora ama* ['Mistress', 1954], *A dónde van nuestros hijos?* ['Where Are Our Children Going?', 1956], *La Cucaracha* (1958), *El pecado de una madre* ['A Mother's Sin', 1960], *Casa de mujeres* ['House of Women', 1966]. With the exception of *La Cucaracha*, they are all very badly made melodramas, orgies of gestures and crude scenes, in which Dolores takes on the responsibility of being the only possible moment of dignity amid the catastrophic acting and script. *La Cucaracha*, on the other hand, constitutes a case of legendary struggle against all odds. The director, Ismael Rodríguez, gathers together the stars that have survived the Golden Age – Dolores, María Félix, Gabriel Figueroa, Pedro Armendáriz and 'el Indio' Fernández – and sets them to work in his portrayal of the Revolution as *Grand Guignol*. For the one and only time, the two great myths of Mexican cinema, opposites and complementary, are united: María Félix is Cucaracha, the tough revolutionary; Dolores is Madame Isabel, whose way of life is destroyed in a matter of seconds, forcing her from being the decent Society Lady to becoming a 'soldadera'.

In the United States, Dolores makes *Flaming Star* (1960), in which she is the Indian mother of Elvis Presley, and the excellent *Cheyenne Autumn* (1964), directed by John Ford. In Spain she films *La dama del alba* ['Lady of the Dawn', 1965], and in Italy *C'era una volta* ['Cinderella Italian Style', 1970], directed by Francesco Rosi. Her last film is the Mexican–US co-production *Los hijos de Sánchez* ['The Children of Sánchez', 1977], directed by Hal Bartlett. Dolores remains a star in this period, no longer synonymous with eternal youth but with beauty that lasts, the highlight of a scene, the inevitable point of reference: winner of four Arieles for best actress, president of the Cervantine Festival, director of the nursery of the National Actors' Association. She takes part in US television programmes, marries for the third time, and acts in the theatre (*Lady Windermere's Fan*, *The Lady of the Camellias*).

With the exception of *Cheyenne Autumn*, the only recuperable aspects of this stage of her film career are her elegance and attractiveness to the camera. As far as Mexican cinema is concerned, it is not only a question of the deterioration of an industry but also of intimidation by the legend, now completely given over to consecrated formulae, to the detriment of her acting resources. From *Doña Perfecta* on, she only plays Dolores del Río, the filmic and social institution. She is exceptional in every respect: she survives her epoch, her contemporaries, the temptation to stop – just for one moment – that work of art renovated daily: the face, figure and behaviour of Dolores del Río.

For Dolores del Río, the need for beauty was a conscious desire and an endless victory.

7

Cantinflas: That's the Point!

Tents were everywhere to be seen in Mexico City during the 1930s, erected in abandoned lots, one in almost every neighbourhood: La Merced, Santa Julia, Tepito, Balbuena, Doctores. The *carpa* (tent) was the place where the circus met and mixed with vaudeville. Mario Moreno, a young member of the neighbourhood gang, decided to try his luck in *La Valentina* tent, put up in Tacuba. He wanted to make his friends laugh, and make something of a sense of humour already celebrated in the streets and pool halls. It was not a bad place to start: your pals got in for free, and you earned a few pesos for a day's work. The *carpa* would take an audience of three to four hundred people – whose appearance represented the price of the tickets quite faithfully – squeezed into collapsable chairs. It was just like home: garishly made-up neighbours sitting on peeling wooden benches, tattered curtains, the usual family get-together: singers, magicians, dancers, and clowns who couldn't decide if they were comics, and comics who couldn't stop being clowns.

Through real talent or, if all else failed, the goodwill of the spectators, the *carpa* inherits and betrays the circus tradition. The comfort of the audience is initially established with the march of the 'misfits'! If it is carefully announced, what passes by unnoticed in the streets can here alarm the audience. Then the novelties-that-never-were-novelties are brought on, and imposed: the soprano dressed in a ragged Indian dress replacing the trapeze artists, the tap dancers who are tap dancers only because of the tin toecaps nailed to their soles – animals are not included in the show, unless they can play the guitar – and on come Rabanito and Alfalfa, powdered up and happy because the lack of children in the audience means that they will not have to stick to 'children's humour' tonight. There are no dwarfs. The last ones left because they were treated so badly, while the Bearded Lady has become just another member of the chorus of old dears who rub their private parts, drink *pulque*, and generate with their happy grotesqueness that most superior of senses which, until now, the audience had not realized it possessed. There is drama, comedy, *zarzuela*; and the only real sign of originality is founded in the forgetfulness of jokes you have been listening to all your life. Sentimentalism, here, is the name of a singer who is unable to remember the words of her songs (which, in their turn, will never make her famous).

Late prologue: the glories of the city margins [arrabal]

During the 1920s in Mexico City, terror at the Revolutionary hordes wanes, and a *consolatory myth* is born instead. It is associated with the poor spaces located at the city's margins (the *arrabal*), naturally distanced from respectable Society, where tragedy is more real than real, and the poor experience the happiness of a suffering that has been denied the rich. The word *arrabal* – with its suggestion of pool halls, dens, taco stands, neighbourhoods, dust, hungry dogs, children with a supplicatory look – describes and invents what it names, an instant catalogue of realities and illusions: the Way of the Cross (poverty), shared purgatory (the neighbourhood), tradition (religious imagery decorating the rundown), irresistible sordidness (the Cabaret), redemption (family love and neighbourly solidarity), fallen angels (prostitutes), real men and real women, the born-to-lose and innocence-in-the-mud. It connotes, however, one benefit, rootedness – which, paradoxically, accompanies a forgetting of one's origins. Heaven and Hell, a reality that is equally distant from reality and conventional 'illusion', bars, tents, dance halls, cornerstalls, improvised football pitches and wrestling and boxing rings all fall within the circumference of the *arrabal*. To the *arrabal* belongs the wordplay associated with nicknames (which become written into their owners' faces) and the *macho* comments which redeem sexual failure.

This available and well-disposed multitude grows and is reinforced daily by peasants who arrive carrying with them their customs and feelings from the countryside, so that the *peladito** of the capital, and the farmer who only a week ago still lived in the sticks, are varieties of the same species. One example

---

* This word literally means 'little baldy' and denotes the process of having on the one hand, been shaved, and on the other, stripped. But for the author's discussion of the social and cultural significance of the *pelado* and its diminutive form *peladito* (as represented by Cantinflas himself), see pp. 98–9 below. [Translator's note.]

of such an identity is contained in a book by the poet Carlos Rivas Larrauri, *Del Arrabal* ['On the City Margins', 1930], which was read very widely for decades. The book's starting point is a sacred idea: that poverty is victorious ingenuity, the summit of its sincerity being the speech of an Indian just initiated into Spanish. Listen, everyone, to their garbled authenticity! But at the same time, however, you can already hear the voices of a new urban language in Rivas Larrauri's poems, which does not just come from the countryside, nor from a simple desire to corrupt the language of the conquistadors by adapting it:

> Mis güenos siñores:
> ¡ai les voy con mi hacha!
> ¡Pónganse muy changos!
> ¡Pónganse muy águilas!

['Hon'rable sirs/Here I come with my axe!/Be monkeys!/Be eagles!']

The phrase 'Hon'rable sirs' evokes eyes turned downwards, fixed on the floor, hats pressed on in nervous submission, the loudness with which the poncho stands out in a space made for the mackintosh. But 'Be monkeys' or 'eagles' is something else, and has to do with the experience of a big city, with the formative process of those who cross the street (watch it!) as if navigating a reef, with dodging the police and taking advantage of others so as to teach them a lesson in humility. Nevertheless, the prevailing tone when one refers to the poor is one of compassionate resignation. The most common response to social injustice is still a sea of pain, which Rivas Larrauri offers aplenty:

> porque en este mundo ni después de muertos
> los probes y ricos son la mesma cosa

['Because even dead the rich and poor/Aren't the same thing in dis ole world.']

Faithful reproduction becomes parody, almost immediately. This is especially clear in film: a linguistic model used without modification becomes a way of mocking the subjects so described, turning their 'sympathetic' qualities into submissive stupidity. Repeated *ad nauseam*, the speech of the hardly Hispanicized becomes a joke. Rivas Larrauri thus attains the reverse of what is intended, as if the marginalized were born just to get a laugh from their equals, and a gentle smile from the civilized:

'What's that you said about . . . Theo? Theo . . . what? What did you say?'

'Theories.'
'And who's that?'
'Well, who knows.'
But such are those tings
that're preached
and not done.

Rivas Larrauri recognizes a proscribed voice, and denounces its exclusion, but in the hands of populists and declaimers his verses become a confession of the verbal impotence (the derision) of the marginalized.

The *arrabal* has one genre: melodrama; a sense of humour: which can be found in the *carpa*; and one system of compensation: the penniless get drunk, the youngster hangs out with his Gang, while the sentimentalists adore the Little Mistress, kneeling before her for two whole days a year in the Basilica of Guadalupe. What cinema industrializes is a genuine way of being that becomes theatrical on seeing itself represented on screen, where the autobiographical is always communal, and experiences are meaningful only if they are told in detail.

Mario Moreno's self-description

According to Mario Moreno himself, he was born on 12 August 1917 in Mexico City – one of six children born to post office worker José Pedro Moreno and Soledad Reyes. He becomes a brilliant student and a good amateur boxer, the leader of a street gang, a tireless dancer, obviously popular, a great billiards player, and an apprentice bullfighter. In his own words:

> It's difficult to say exactly when Cantinflas was 'born'. In reality he never was. He took form gradually, over time. I should make it clear that my parents, with enormous sacrifice, were paying my way through the School of Medicine. But I abandoned it and began to work in the Tents as a singer and dancer in variety shows. My first contact with the public was very difficult. If you weren't liked they would let you know immediately by banging the wooden benches or clapping. And if they weren't with you they'd whistle or become violent, throwing – with great accuracy – empty beer bottles at your head. This is how Cantinflas learnt to dance. Once I suddenly got stage fright. For a moment Mario Moreno froze. . . . And, suddenly, Cantinflas took charge of the situation. And he began to talk, desperately muttering words and more words. Meaningless words and sentences. Stupidities. . . . Anything to defend himself from attack and get out of that rowdy situation! The spectators went quiet, bewildered, not understanding a word. . . . Then they started

laughing. . . . At first softly, then really loud. That's how I knew I had triumphed, and that's when Cantinflas was born! It is ironic that it was the desperate recovery from fear on stage that produced a word which is now officially incorporated into our popular language: the verb 'to cantinflate' means to talk a lot without saying anything.

Another version of events is given by Estanislao Shilinsky, a Russian immigrant who adapted perfectly to the world of the tent, where he got to know Cantinflas (they marry two sisters, also immigrants: Olga and Valentina Zubareff). In the *Pequeño Salón Rojo* in Santa María la Redonda, Shilinsky (the creator of the routine) begins a dialogue, and watches with some concern as Cantinflas fails to respond. He remembers:

> They were bitter seconds. I tried to get him to react and all of a sudden Mario began to speak and say things, mostly without beginning or end, as if his thoughts had sped past his words. I tried to get him out of the mess. Because of his nerves, he didn't know what he was saying. Then the audience began to laugh, and the laughs became louder and louder; then they applauded very warmly. We looked at each other, astonished. Mario came over to me slowly and came straight out and asked: 'What's happening?' I told him: 'They're laughing at you saying so much and so little at the same time. Carry on!'

Success brings its rewards: they are paid fifteen pesos a day for three shows.

Get off and milk it!

The 1930s. On Saturday or Sunday evenings in the neighbourhoods of Guerrero, Peralvillo, Tepito or Santa Julia, ordinary families wonder how to spend their free time. There are Mexican films showing in the Rialto, Goya, Colonial, Coloso, Cairo, and Bretaña cinemas; or, if you're scared of the dark, there's a *carpa* just round the corner. Fantastic! If the only consideration is having a whale of a time, the shows are neither *good* nor *bad*, but art-made-to-the-measure-of-your-pocket. There are tents all over the city (so many that a Variety Union is formed), and what is on offer is always the same. For ten cents, a four-act show, consisting of song-and-dance routines, puppets, ventriloquists and comedians. For ten cents, you can get your money's worth of fun. The musicians try their best, and smile as they painfully hang on to the piano, violin, drum, trombone or trumpet (they are unrecognized virtuosos, angels without wings: 'the simile may not be exact, but it gives you an idea'). The songs insist on telling their stories of oh-so-recent exile!, the desire to return to the abandoned ranch, the unharvested crop; past seductions and loyalties. The sketches repeatedly focus on one theme: the rascal who exploits the well-meaning innocence of those who have just arrived. An example: the city-dweller describes the advantages of a motorbike to the Indian. The overjoyed peasant offers him a cow for his bike. The worker responds:

'I'd look just great going down Madero Avenue on the back of a cow. I'd never get where I'm going. Everyone would laugh at me. I'd never get anywhere.'
'Yes, that's right,' answers the Indian, 'I'd never thought of it. But I'd look even worse.'
'What do you mean?'
'Of course: what would people say when they saw me milking the motorbike!'

In the *carpa*, there is no such thing as 'bad taste'. What may be found are the intimate details of intimacy, and security in the fact that any form of failure is funny: physical defects, the blunderings of physiological functions, unfulfilled desires. Coarse activities reign supreme here (unthinkable in the traditional middle classes, either inhibited by decorum or curbed by nationalist good conduct: 'the decent Mexican does not snore, nor get into undesirable positions when sleeping') – as does the double entendre which, in a not-so-virtuous circle, extracts innocence from lewdness and lewdness from innocence. For the People, the crux of the meaningless sentences is ecstasy before the prospect of sex, while funny walks and waves are paraded as confessions, complaints and petitions ('I move a lot or wiggle a little, depending on my place on the social scale').

The double entendre is much preferred to the political joke. This may be because, in the *carpa*, people feel themselves to be even further removed from their rights. Those who witnessed or took part in the Revo' love puns – they are more daring, more like life, which is a bitch and never leaves you alone. My next witness is one of the great figures to come from the *carpa* in the 1930s, Adalberto Martínez Resortes (interviewed by Abel Ramos):

'And what did they shout at you?'
'Not at me, but at those they didn't like. When an old dear came on they'd often shout: that old dear's got a dick! Giv'us a look! And the woman wouldn't answer, so they'd shout: Off, off! And off with your petticoats.'
'And if they'd have shouted "Off!" at you?'

'They never did.'
'And if I'd gone along to shout it?'
'Uuuuuuuhhh! This one's living dangerously!'

Because everything was implied, there were a lot of words. Back then, if the public was spoiled, the comics, in contrast, were not given much room at all – unlike today, when they can even insult the audience and get a laugh. Not then! There was the authority of the inspectors to contend with. Resortes continues:

> Once one of my sidekicks said to me: 'Your schoolgirl's mouth, drawn just for me', and I answered: 'Look what you've done to my willy.' Uhhh! They reported me to the manager. That's how things were, you couldn't let loose. But even we'd look down on it. Even if you came out with a 'Goddamn!', my God, you'd go all red. Those were other times. Other places.

What cannot be said is insinuated, and expressed in images made by the body. Among the people, eschatology (the 'obscene') is not a secret pleasure but a basic means of expression. Anger, parody and desire *need* 'swearing' (a bad word *here* is an unsubstitutable term *there*), and it is their absence in the *carpa* that produces the floods of laughter and the whistling which accompany the euphemism.

What did you say? No! You don't say! Really?

The 1940s, from Mario Moreno's fragmentary autobiographical notes:

> I took the stage name of Cantinflas so as not to shame my family, which was poor but proud. Mine was a third-class act, and I worked in the Tent where people with no money came instead of the theatre. Cantinflas was born and began to grow. Little by little he took on the physical appearance of Cantinflas and, mainly from necessity, adopted poor people's clothes: a long-sleeved cotton shirt that had once been white, crumpled-up small trousers held up at the hips rather than at the waist. And shoes that would look better on an hippopotamus. Overall this was a bit of cloth better known as a 'mackintosh'. Cantinflas's face is always the same, because Cantinflas has no age. He has a round face with a nose that is too small for the mouth – which is too big! Over the upper lip, two strands of moustache fall like a pair of out-of-place eyebrows. I tried to let a strand of hair fall over his forehead. But it wasn't worth it. And he needed a shave!

Mario Moreno becomes Cantinflas, and pleases a public whose future is as uncertain as the origins of his name: on the Night of the Metamorphosis, frightened or entertained, Mario Moreno speaks without saying anything. The audience celebrates, the news spreads, and soon the whole of Mexico celebrates his falling into the abyss of meaninglessness, his climbing the hills of no purpose. A not-yet-gigantic city enthrones a comic: look at the clothes of that guy whose disguise is his second skin, look at his shabby mac, his badly drawn moustache and his desperation to hold on to a language! *Stiffen 'im up there.* 'Everyone for himself/You see/Well, we'll see/That's enough . . .'

Have you seen Cantinflas yet? Don't miss him. Crowd scenes and ticket touts follow this new urban passion for 'baroque' gaits and postures. Cantinflas invents nothing and invents everything, improvises and synthesizes, and provides politicians with the opportunity to attack their enemies. For example, in summer 1937 Vincente Lombardo Toledano, leader of the CTM (Confederation of Mexican Labour), responded to attacks from the leader of the CROM (Regional Confederation of Mexican Workers), Luis N. Morones (who called him a 'traitorous, cowardly, trembling and wimpish Boy Fidencio'): 'If Morones wants to show off his dialectics, he should go and argue with Cantinflas', who was performing every night in the Folies Bergères. As was to be expected, Cantinflas intervened in the polemic and let loose a volley (partially transcribed in Alfonso Taracena's *La verdadera revolución mexicana* ['The Real Mexican Revolution']:

The first thing I did was think about going to see Lombardo to ask him what was the point. . . . But then I thought: Well, no! Because thinking about it, the truth is, he couldn't have picked a better person than me to solve the solution to the problem. [...] Because, like I said, naturally, since he can't solve anything while saying a lot, the same happens to me and we'd never come to an agreement. [...] Ah! But I'll let you know that I do have moments of lucidity and speak very clearly. And now I'm going to be clear! Comrades! There are moments in life that are truly momentary. [...] And it's not a matter of saying, but of seeing! What do we see? That's what we'll have to see. [...] Because, what a coincidence, comrades, that supposing that in the case – let's not say which one; but we do have to reflect and understand the psychology of life to analyse the synthesis of humanity. [...] Right? That's the very point! That's why I think, comrades, that that in which you are in agreement, when you are [...] because it might and it's rude just to return it [...] you have to be like the saying says! (I wish I could remember what the saying says.) So, just like I am in agreement with something I haven't agreed, we should all be unified for the unification of the emancipated ideology that struggles. [...] Why does it struggle, comrades? Well, you just have to look! You remember 15 September [...] which really hasn't anything to do with it [...] but we have to be prepared because life is like that and so am I. And how am I, comrades? [...] I'm a worker! A proletarian in the cause of the work involved in getting this cause off the ground. [...] And now, we have to look at the cause for us being like that. [...] Why has the cost of living gone up? Why does every living being have to live, in other words the gravitational point is the gravest thing. [...] And I don't want anything to do with that because I already am [...] and that's that, right? [...] And now comrades, I pray that you explain to me what I've just said.

This association with politics (with demagoguery) is an important aspect of Cantinflas's success. Salvador Novo has written about this process in *Nueva grandeza mexicana* ['The New Mexican Greatness', 1948], a celebration of the mestizo Mexico City during the government of Miguel Alemán:

> This was the dawn of a wordy age that made promises with no commitments, which was confused and oratorical. The cleverest newspapers called it *demagogic*. One sensitive antenna picked up these new vibrations, and hit the nail on the humorous head of the epoch's repression; it was called *Cantinflas*, a mature product of the city. If, thanks to cinema, the dyslalia which through Cantinflas attacks our times has become so successful and legitimized, it is because it is a reflection of reality. It so happens that for some years now, outside Mexico City, men have also been breathing the asphyxiating air of verborrhoea, confusion, promises that cannot be kept, oratory, unintelligible and vain wordplay. [...] In summing up such leaders, and in handing over the demagogic essence of their vacuous confusion to the healthy laughter of the people, lies the merit that assures the glory of Cantinflas, this stubborn son of the mixed and mocking capital city.

Cantinflas's technique

What is Cantinflas's humorous linguistic innovation that creates the strictly verbal ideology called *cantinflismo*? I venture the following hypothesis: he makes visible the outcast's vocation for the absurd – in part disdain and annoyance for a logic that condemns and rejects him – which finds its raw material in the rapid fire of words, where the objects are lost long before getting to the verb. Each night, in ferocious competition with *charro* singers, puppets and tenors who refuse to come on stage because they are still drunk, his body gestures organize the chaos of his words. *Cantinflismo* is the double language of that which seeks to be expressed and that which does not feel like being thought. (Which is why, when Cantinflas renounces mime, he rids himself of the essence of his comedy.)

A speeded-up body is translating urgent themes: how expensive everything is down at the market, the petty crime of the police, the incomprehension of the accused before the judge, the swindle that threatens in every dialogue between strangers. With choreographic flourish, Cantinflas's body rescues nouns and adjectives in mid-shipwreck, and on respecting his teaching, recently arrived peasants, workers and outcasts learn the new rules of urban living and distance themselves as well as they can from the fundamental fact of survival. Subject to censorship, the *carpa* is the most important school of *double meaning* in matters sexual on the one hand, and in learning how not to be taken advantage of on the other. The interrelation of artist and audience is the dialectic of poverty beginning an unintelligible conversation with strangers. Don't take any notice of what I'm saying, but of what I want to tell you; if you take no notice of my next sentence you're a cuckold or a queer; your best friend is going to betray you, your enemy is your brother, any conversation is a trap, the greatest good is free sex, and the worst thing is: your wife isn't cheating on you because you're still faithful. In this eulogy to confusion, there is little merit to be found in the memorable joke (the best joke is not knowing a joke).

But what could Cantinflas actually memorize? Sketch writers are few and in great demand, and it's impossible to renew one's repertoire of amusement daily. In fact, Cantinflas is supported not by his scriptwriters, but by his gift to improvise the things that *do not* happen to him. To a lack of resources, Cantinflas opposes a happy combination of verbal incoherence and bodily coherence. He frees the word from its logical bonds, and exemplifies the precise alliance of phrases which signify nothing (nor can they) with muscular movements that correct what has been said by no one. Logic knocks out the syllogism; the accumulation of words is what negotiates the relation (the symbiosis) between a body as tense as a boxer's and speech in search of the tension that clarifies meaning.

Examine the technique: his head begins a pendular movement and dodges the invisible enemy, his arms stretch out ready to meet the air, a sardonic expression laughs at the world, his eyebrows rise like guillotines, the tease is the same but different, *you don't say, why not, eh what did you say, you've made it, you don't say.* . . . The sounds slip from onomatopoeia to onomatopoeia, the phrases holding together the internal cohesion of the *nonsense.* In the verbal rough-and-tumble of the neighbourhood, *nonsense* carries a forceful meaning: you *say nothing* so as to communicate *something,* you confuse words so as to untangle movements, confound gestures with the intention of expressing virtues. So, then, start with 'From the moment I wasn't/Who I was/Just/The interpreter of my silence'. Become inebriated with words in the labyrinth where 'each one on their onesome/you see/let's see/that's it'.

An interval in which a species is described, and the
transformation of the pelado *into the* peladito *is remembered*

Who is the *pelado*? A person totally dispossessed – the inheritor and companion of the *leper* – who has endured the leprosy of poverty and a complete lack of social attention. (The nineteenth-century *costumbrista* novel and poetry inform only in contradictory and schematic ways about the *leper*, who merely inhabits the background.) Plays, comics, films and, at times, the parodies or compassionate sermons of novelists who noticed the masses, dealt with the *pelado*. Marginalized from the social distribution of income, he receives a generic name subtracting him from reality and burying him in abstraction. The *pelado* is the dangerous shadow of poverty in the expanding city, the nameless and almost naked threat, the figure of riot, robbery, assault; he is the inert shape on the pavements. . . . And all this is momentarily brought to a halt when the culture industry discovers the profitability of the *pelado* begun in the comic strip *The Adventures of Chupamirto* by Jesús Acosta, and in the cinematic grace – in their own disconcerting and imploring way – of Cantinflas, Resortes and Fernando Soto Mantequilla.

In 1936, the year Cantinflas goes into film, Samuel Ramos publishes his extremely important book *El perfil del hombre y la cultura en México* ['A Profile of Man and Culture in Mexico'], which includes the soon-to-be-famous hypothesis: an inferiority complex has broken our 'psychic balance'; so let's proceed to the psychoanalysis of the Mexican, choosing a social type in which all aspects of the process are present in exaggerated form, so that we can then clearly trace its history. The *pelado* is the perfect experimental rabbit, 'since he constitutes the most elemental and well-drawn expression of the national character'. Ramos goes on:

> We shall ignore his colourful appearance here. . . . We are only interested in describing him on the inside so as to determine the elemental forces that mould his character. His name defines him well enough. He is a person whose soul is completely out in the open, with nothing covering his most intimate urges. He cynically holds on to elemental impulses that others attempt to dissimulate. The *pelado* belongs to the lowest of social categories, and represents the human detritus of the big city. Economically he is less than the proletarian, intellectually he is a primitive. Life has been wholly hostile to him, and in

return he harbours dark resentment. He is of an angry disposition, and dangerous to deal with, exploding at the slightest opportunity. His anger is mainly verbal and is usually aimed at self-affirmation through crude and aggressive language. His anger is an animal performance aimed at frightening others and making-believe that he is the strongest and most resolute. Such behaviour constitutes an illusory compensation for his real life, which is the lowest of the low.

Before Cantinflas inverts the social significance of the stereotype by taming it, the figure of the *pelado* is still viewed as a dangerous anomaly who embodies an anger glimpsed in the shadows that are synonymous with poverty. Ramos discovers there what had already been associated with the figure of the leper: he is our untamed natural self, the urban primitive whose existence confirms us in our enjoyment of the benefits of civilization – without ever having the prestige of a Caliban. The *pelado* has never been chosen as a symbol; he did not learn how to swear by himself, either. He is the inevitable product of an environment marked by uncontrolled sexuality, representing a *negative machismo*. ('The *pelado* looks on fighting as excitement to heighten his depressed ego.') It is no wonder, says Ramos, that he should seek salvation in virility.

Without more ado, Ramos identifies the civilized with the desexualized and prudish, whilst simultaneously blaming the lower classes (symbolically represented by the *pelado*) for psychic repression. Now, with the help of Freud, this class chauvinism scores yet another victory. Ramos outlines the programme of the 'enlightened' fed up with a barbarism which, in their view, prolongs the violence of the Revolution into the everyday. By ignoring and casting aside the values of humanism, and identifying nationality with bravery, the *pelado* – the primitive – defames the Nation with his irrationality. In Ramos's view, which was to be extraordinarily influential in years to come, the *pelado*'s actions and (non-verbalized) reflections contain all the defects of 'angry Mexico', of the backward zones that prevent our immediate arrival at civilization's banquet. The *pelado* is this shameful hindrance, the being whose two personalities (one real, one fictitious) do not add up to enough to exchange for another that may minimally be worth it.

And this is where the *pelado* remained, subject to a mythical gaze, awaiting the mass treatment of film and theatre. Then, thanks to a comedian, he is rebaptized with the diminutive, the *peladito*, the smiling suburban [*arrabal*] rogue. It is not often that such a drastic transformation takes place in so short a time: the ferocious *pelado* awakens to find himself an inoffensive *peladito*.

The synthesis of resigned poverty

Cantinflas is a recapitulation and a point of departure. The trousers held up beneath the waist were already a commonplace of the comic strip (*Chupamirto*) and in popular neighbourhoods, speech encoded into the absurd (piss-take as a vocation and the confession of ignorance) abounded. But Cantinflas's style perfects and endows nonsense (the failure of eloquence) with humour and, in the entanglement of endless broken sentences, provides a glimpse of a frankly urban mentality, without rural comparison or allegory. His repertoire is wonderful: the mocking fear of the police, the ability of the rogue and the credulity of the tricked, the game with homosexuality that is both proof of malice and 'breadth of criteria', seduction as commercial rip-off.

The poor applaud in him what is close and familiar to them and, whether they realize it or not, become enthusiastic about a not-so-very-strange fact: the festive and vindictive representation of poverty. The rich are grateful for the opportunity to laugh at demagogues and the poor, and at the last gasp of small-town rural comedy. In the mid 1930s, the elites celebrate Cantinflas: he represents the perfect 'childishness' of the Underdog. And he reciprocates. The great cartoonist Miguel Covarrubias tells of a typical sketch: Cantinflas, a union leader, at the head of a group of workers, negotiates with the owner of a soap factory (played by Manuel Medel), and addresses the demands of the workers to him in a flowery proletarian language immediately approved by the boss, who is happy to find an opportunity to put up the price of soap. At the end of the speech, the owner calculates how many hours a year his employees do *not* work, if you take away Sundays, holidays, Labour Day, lunch times, birthdays, saints' days, union meetings, etc.; he adds up, manipulating the maths, and comes up with a total of four days a year of actual work. Cantinflas, visibly depressed, asks the owner of the factory how much they owe him for the privilege of working for his company.

This is my land: it has love in its heart

In 1936, Cantinflas alternates with Agustín Lara in the Folies Bergères, and his success announces his immediate move into film. But no comedian can become a leading man just like that. So, at twenty-three, Cantinflas makes his début in a secondary role in Miguel Contreras Torres's *No te engañes corazón* ['Don't Fool Yourself, Dear Heart'], making up a duo with the comedian Don Catarino. In 1937 he has a part in Arcady Boytler's *Así es mi tierra* ['This Is My Land'], with music by Tata Nacho, a typical rural comedy consisting of an endless very Mexican and Popular ranchera fiesta in which Cantinflas – albeit not very convincing in a rural environment – is both the Mexican and the Popular, abstract categories that precede, follow and blur him.

The story (if there is one) of *Así es mi tierra* reflects the desire for post-Revolutionary normalization at the time. In 1916, the General (Antonio R. Fraustro) returns to the village of his birth, accompanied by a sweaty politician (Luis G. Barreiro) and a group of loyal followers. There, he is immediately joined by the rogue Tejón (Cantinflas), who serenades the General with the *Calaveras Trio*, tells jokes, flatters, and personifies supreme innocence. In this film, Cantinflas's incompatibility with the rural milieu is clear. But with the character's move to urban environments in film, the bitter sharpness of the *carpa* is left behind, and the character is let loose in his most innocuous of forms.

In 1937 he makes a second film with Boytler, *Aguila o sol* ['Heads or Tails'], which also stars Manuel Medel (a traditional comedian capable of the most wonderfully detailed characterizations of popular physiognomies and languages). Underestimated on its release, the film still conserves its humour and imagination. It tells the story of three orphans who grow up in the world of the *carpa*, and is just right for Cantinflas and the re-creation of a 'neighbourhood culture' on the point of extinction. The scene between Cantinflas and Medel is especially good, transcending the very basic character of the script and reconstructing the forms and gestures of *carpa* comedians, their intimate relationship with the audience and the homely complicity of their laughter.

El signo de la muerte ['The Sign of Death'], made with very prestigious collaborators, was released in 1939. It was directed by Chano Urueta, with music by Silvestre Revueltas and a script by Salvador Novo. Almost a half century after its release, *El signo de la muerte* is a curious film, in which the most naive sections have aged the least. The plot promises much more than it delivers: Cantinflas is a *peladito* employed in a museum who, quite by accident, discovers the clue to a series of crimes caused by the madness of an Aztec grand priest (Carlos Orellana), attempting to restore human sacrifice and Moctezuma's empire. Like *Aguila o sol, El signo de la muerte* contains a dream sequence that includes transvestism, in which Cantinflas can show off his mimetic gifts.

In 1939, Cantinflas's own production company, Posa Films, is founded. It first makes a series of very professional short films, directed by Fernando A. Rivero and with scripts by Estanislao Shilinsky: *Cantinflas as de la torería* ['Cantinflas the Bullfighter'], *Cantinflas boxeador* ['Cantinflas the Boxer'],

Cantinflas en tinieblas ['Cantinflas in the Dark'], ¡*Olé mi gabardina!* ['Ole! There goes my Raincoat!'], *Siempre listo en las tinieblas* ['Ready in the Dark'], *Jengibre con dinamita* ['Ginger and Dynamite'], *Cantinflas gendarme y torero* ['Cantinflas the Policeman and Bullfighter'], *Cantinflas ruletero* ['Cantinflas the Cabbie'], *Cantinflas y su prima* ['Cantinflas and his Cousin'], *Cantinflas en los censos* ['Cantinflas and the Census']. Cantinflas owes his extraordinary diffusion to Posa Films and, among others, the expertise of his agents Santiago Reachi and Jacques Gelman.

In 1940, *Ahí está el detalle* ['That's the Point!'] by Juan Bustillo Oro, establishes Cantinflas in Mexico and – not so curiously – in the entire Spanish-speaking world. In *Ahí está el detalle* the aggression associated with the *carpa* becomes living-room fun, and the character of Cantinflas is defined: a runaway from the *arrabal* whose defects are the trademarks of his class: petty crime, stupidity, cowardice and being kept. This *peladito* does not reject society but looks at it from a distance, choosing the kitchen with the maids as his natural habitat. He hangs on to his clothes so that he does not lose touch with his origins. Nevertheless, *Ahí está el detalle* has many a recuperable moment, thanks to the popular force of Cantinflas and the mastery of the writer Joaquín Pardavé.

In 1941, Cantinflas makes two interesting films *Ni sangre ni arena* ['Neither Blood nor Sand'] and *El gendarme desconocido* ['The Unknown Policeman']. The first was directed by Alejandro Galindo, and includes a classic scene, a bullfight of shadows between Cantinflas and Fernando Soto Mantequilla in which Cantinflas justifies his fame as a 'brilliant mime'. In *El gendarme desconocido*, a 'grotesque farce', Cantinflas is an inefficient, clumsy policeman lacking any elegance or ability (hence the warning at the beginning of the film which insists on 'the valuable and respectable function of the police . . . of which Mexico is so proud . . . Cantinflas plays a part within a totally imaginary police force'). Cantinflas's policeman is a farce, a mocking of any possible fear of the police, the *peladito* who will remain one no matter what: 'At ya service, chief'. In representing the weakest, most ridiculous and incomprehensible aspects of authority, *El gendarme desconocido* becomes a classic of Mexican film comedy – not because it is very funny, but because it exemplifies the heights reached by comedy at a very particular time: the mass discovery of humour in cinemas (or sheds passing as cinemas). Cantinflian speech is aided and abetted by the simple quality of the jokes ('But doctor, my heart is on the other side.'/'Yes, but I'm listening to its echo.'), the minimal crime plot, and Cantinflas's well-oiled technique of, for example, taking insults literally so as to undermine their intention: 'Couldn't you sew my buttons on?' 'Why don't you ask your granny?' 'But she can't see.'

Posa Films becomes an associate of Columbia Pictures, which guarantees Cantinflas's success throughout the Spanish-speaking world. A number of journalists and – privately – producers see in Cantinflas a stepping stone for attracting US capital into the Mexican film industry. But Cantinflas remains unaffected by these implied accusations, nor do they concern nationalist viewers.

The laughter and smiles that any appearance of the old Cantinflas brings to many millions of Mexican or Latin American spectators are not incidental. In the first place, many collectivities have lived out and practised their sense of humour (laugh or get lost) thanks to him. What is it about him that is so celebrated? His incoherence, which is the coherence of multitudes; his aggression, which ignores hierarchies; the memorable joke, which can be repeated successfully.

Cantinflas: programmed murmur and conditioned reflex. He appears, moves, begins a verbal mix-up, confounds his interlocutor, and makes fun of the knowledge that can never catch up with the linguistic drift . . . and the audience is satisfied, enjoying the happiness and other people having fun. At first Cantinflas triumphs because his humour is new; then he becomes a tradition: this is what is really funny.

The myth of Cantinflas is founded on his origins, in the act of memory that exalts the times of the *carpa* in Santa María la Redonda. The minority who knew him there (there are not many left) and the majority who imagine it (there are more and more) agree: Cantinflas is a genuine Son of the People, the idiosyncratic and essential expression of what will be the new tradition. This powerful initial capital outlay will allow the comedian-businessman to absorb his numerous failures and generate permanent admiration for his one gag of talking a lot without saying anything.

The humorous in Cantinflas: his image and voice; Cantinflas's amusing message: his body. The myth: a function of memory. In a country without a comic tradition (comedy was a response to urbanization), whoever first represents Humour on a national scale becomes hilarious for ever. The middle classes gradually abandon Cantinflas, but his debt with the masses is long-term. He made them laugh and, therefore, undertook to continue to do so.

Mexican being

In the 1940s, Cantinflas becomes synonymous with the poor Mexican, representative and defender of the meek. At the same time, he is a one-man film industry and also a branch of popular craftsmanship: there are Cantinflases of every size and material in market stalls and shops. A legend (Cantinflas helps the needy) produces long queues at his front door. He is extolled to the point of acquiring a political dimension, and in elections to the Senate, and for the Presidency, his name appears on thousands of ballots. He is a celebrity on the point of becoming a myth, and politicians fall over themselves to evoke his name and authority. In his memoirs, the political boss of San Luis Potosí, Gonzalo N. Santos, tells of a dinner put on in 1945 by the Secretary of Communications, Maximino Ávila Camacho, for a group of politicians. Maximino rants about his brother Manuel (the President), swears 'on his Mother's milk' that Miguel Alemán will not become President because he will kill him, and declares Rojo Gómez (head of the Central Department) and Santos himself candidates. Then the declarations of support start. . . .

> Then Cantinflas began to speak and, because he wanted to be serious, his intervention was a disaster. He went on and on about the people, and ended up saying: 'here everyone is a politician except Mr Rojo Gómez and myself.' Everyone giggled and I said to Cantinflas: 'You've got no idea of these things, Mr Rojo Gómez is a born politician; as much a politician as me or any of the others here.' Cantinflas turned to Rojo Gómez and asked him: 'Is that true?' 'Not as good as General Santos,' he replied, 'but I'm a politician and nothing else.' Because Cantinflas was drunk and wanted to go on talking about the people, I said: 'Why don't you just shut up, you don't know a thing about the people, only the audience; so speak to us in your own language.'

In 1948 a philosopher, Ismael Diego Pérez, writes a book about the 'philosophy' of Cantinflas, declaring him to be a monument to 'Mexican being': his speaking a lot without saying a thing is the subtle and magnificent form of his disdain for demagogues, those who pervert the value of words. At the same time, the 'specialized' press constructs an identity: Cantinflas is the same as Chaplin – not because of his histrionics but, rather, because of the shared roots of both characters: the social defiance, the poetry, the wild romantic passion of the dispossessed. The Tramp and the *peladito*.

To service the myth of Cantinflas, Posa Films provides him with a fixed format: a more-than-routine director, Miguel M. Delgado, and a number of comic writers unified by their love for the petrified joke. The mechanism will be unalterable: Cantinflas will make one film a year, and will choose a 'humble' profession by antonomasia: fireman, shoeshine, film extra, bellhop, postman, and around him the most simple of plots will be constructed in which, at the end of 300 identical jokes, the (gorgeous) heroine, entranced by all that innocence, will end up marrying him. In addition, a pinch of transvestism in the style of *Charley's Aunt* is almost always guaranteed, as well as the double-entendre jokes, the poor who become millionaires in a day, the individual pursued by bad luck who comes across a gang of thieves and has them all imprisoned, the unjust accusation against the innocent protagonist, the couple helped out by an animal with brains, the loser who becomes a boxer (and world champion) by accident – all topped with a brilliant, sentimental last-minute speech by the comic hero. And the films roll on: *El circo* ['The circus'], *Gran Hotel* ['Grand Hotel'], *Un día con el diablo* ['A Day with the Devil'], *Soy un prófugo* ['The Runaway'], *A volar joven* ['Away with you, Young Man'], *El mago* ['The Magician'], *El supersabio* ['Brains'], *Puerta joven* ['Off with you, Young Man'], *El siete machos* ['Seven Machos'], *El bombero atómico* ['Atomic Fireman'], *Si yo fuera diputado* ['If I Were Senator'], *El señor fotógrafo* ['Mr Photographer'], *Caballero a la medida* ['A Gentleman Made to Measure'], *Abajo el telón* ['Down Curtains'], *El Bolero de Raquel* ['Rachel's Bolero'], *Sube y baja* ['Seesaw'], *Ama tu prójimo* ['Love thy Neighbour'] and *El analfabeto* ['The Illiterate'].

In 1953, Diego Rivera paints a huge mural at the *Teatro de los Insurgentes*. Cantinflas appears as the defender of the poor, the generous and just provider of redress. Once more scandal accompanies Rivera: on Cantinflas's raincoat he has painted the Virgin of Guadalupe, and the press and Catholic organizations accuse him of blasphemy. Cantinflas declares his innocence, and swears his respect for the Virgin. Rivera rubs the Mistress of the Mexicans from Cantinflas's clothes. This was his highest point. What follows is well known to all you fans of cartoons and adverts.

8

Tin Tan: The Pachuco

In my view, the secret of Tin Tan's continued appeal lies in an extremely effective combination of language and attitude. More specifically, in the way he condenses an attitude into language. With Tin Tan, anarchism and disorder do give way to solemnity, but only so as immediately to make way for more chaos. Dressed to the nines when his first films came out, he represented, then, a faint transcultural glimmer of modernity. Today, to those for whom Tin Tan is mainly a television experience, he represents the uncontrollable laughter of an otherwise grey epoch, when jokes circulated like memorial plaques, and respect had become society's death mask.

Tin Tan: the great comic actor whom a tamed film industry was loath to accept; hardly understood, and ruthlessly exploited. Nothing foreshadowed his explosive appearance in 1943, the year of his début. While Cantinflas, dominating a film comedy that was more verbal than visual, remained trapped in the prison of his one great discovery ('talking a lot without saying anything'), and the rest were mere variations on themes adapted from the Frivolous Theatre (vaudeville), Tin Tan was a leap in the dark. He had not escaped from the circus, nor was he the standard crook softened by the insignificance of his crimes; he was simply a young man who walked, talked and loved as if he carried a sinfonola brimming over with boogie-woogies and boleros in his head.

The comedians

In Mexican cinema, established comedians stick to a few variants on a few themes. Here is a list of their main duties:

- they must belong to the popular classes, expressing them in word and movement (not to speak of appearance). The comic must be both sympathetic and obedient, lascivious and controllable, a scoundrel but honest (an upperclass comic or a ladies' man is inconceivable);

- they must shy away from any idea of class conflict so as, rather, to represent the limitations of the dispossessed: their timidity, their false arrogance and mythomania. The function of such comedy is to make of social resentment a folklore of gratitude, and of humour a means of stifling all signs of rebellion;

- they must foreground the 'essence of comedy' (especially in love stories) purely in the industry's terms – as the prolongation of sentimentalism: when it comes down to it, laughter and tears are the same thing. Jokes, meanwhile, mould and temper the emotions. You laugh so as not to cry, and you cry because it hasn't occurred yet to anyone at this funeral to put an end to the wailing with a few good jokes;

- comic actors must maintain their original cultural capital – that is, the personality that took them on to the screen in the first place. If, for whatever reason, they change and lose their well-worn tics and techniques, spectators cry foul. In a medium in which what counts is tame verbal jokiness and an appreciation of the most simple of gags (the visual joke), the comics' initial resources (expressions, voice, gestures) tend to be their final ones;

- they must remain located, no matter what, within the popular domain: the comic character may experience unexpected success, wander through bourgeois mansions, travel, and even become famous, but in the last roll he will return, vanquished but victorious, to the wealth of poverty;

- comedians must put up with the most abject use of their talents. The function of even the most famous and gifted comic is to provide humorous relief in melodrama, to be the foils of successive Perfect Couples. Even if it had wanted to, the Mexican film industry could never have produced a Groucho Marx, or even a Bob Hope. This is because humour was a degraded form in the 1940s, and film (an instrument that can actualize and change its spectators) was a magic with eyes for melodrama alone – and considered significant at the time because it was the place where the resources of the industry and the public coincided;

- they must accept becoming the vehicle of puerile, mainly idiomatic, gags that legitimize a culture of submission through inversion (the reproduction of Indian, peasant and, most often, urban popular speech as the expression of a child-adult);

- they must respect the dogma that the joke – memorized and finely tuned – is the only redoubt of prestige in popular entertainment. Verbal wit, on the other hand, the spontaneous spark of light that opens out on to entirely new situations, is considered non-transcendent, just fun ('relajo'). Such a devaluation of inventiveness actually enthrones the joke: laughter at something which declares itself to be funny in itself, because it has always been there – the same words, occupying the same time;

- they must resign themselves to the stasis in comic roles imposed by the beliefs of the trade: throughout his career a comic develops one character, and one character alone;

- they have to accept 'natural' limits: Hollywood levels of production and the myth of Cantinflas. A successful comedian may become an idol, but he will rise no further in the identification stakes. It is not for him to represent the People – with a capital p – only examples of the 'popular'. This is because Cantinflas has monopolized the emblematization of the People to such an extent that audiences now amuse themselves in recognizing what they see and what they already know of the idol's 'proverbial ingenuity', laughing at the jokes they hear or, alternatively, at those they just imagine – all of which they will then ecstatically repeat for their friends the following day. The weight of the legend is such that, in the memory of the spectator, even the most pitiful of films become enshrined as yet another example of the 'national sense of humour'.

What sumara?

> Es el pachuco un sujeto singular
> pero que nunca debiera camellar
> y que a las jainas las debe dominar
> para que se sientan veri fain para bailar.
>
> Toda carnala que quiere ser feliz
> con un padrino que tenga su desliz
> vaya a su chante y agarre su veliz
> y luego a camellar pa'mantener al infeliz.

[There is nothing like a Pachuco/Who should never work/And dominate the 'honeys'/So that they feel 'very fine' and want to dance./Every sister who wants to be happy/Find a pimp full of tricks/Grab yer bag and off you go,/Off to work so as to keep the crook.]

(*Tin Tan's Song*, by Marcelo Chávez)

Tin Tan (Germán Genaro Cipriano Gómez Valdés Castillo) was born on 15 September 1915 in Mexico City. In 1927 the family moved to Cuidad Juarez, where his father was a Customs officer and his mother a housewife. He was brought up in a neighbourhood that was later to become a Pachuco bastion, did odd jobs and – something he often forgot – became a tourist guide. According to his brother Manuel, Germán's biggest influence was the city of Los Angeles, but the neighbourhoods of Cuidad Juarez and El Paso (full of with-it 'cool cats' with quiffs, their hands buried in deep pockets and shoulders slouched as they rhythmically strolled the streets) were also important.

'My first job', says Tin Tan in an interview,

> was to stick labels on the entire record collection of a radio station. To save spit, I found a street dog and taught it to stick its tongue out so I could wet the labels manually. Then I was an errand boy and later a sweep. But I owe my first real opportunity to a broken microphone. This is how it happened: I always liked playing jokes, and at the radio station I enjoyed imitating my friends and the bosses. Agustín Lara was fashionable at the time – I'm talking about the end of the 1930s – and I also imitated him. One day the microphone broke. When it was mended, Mr Meneses asked for someone to test it. They asked me. So I started imitating Lara. Mr Meneses thought someone had put one of Lara's records on, but it was me, fooling around! One week later I was starring in a show called Tin Tan Larara, scripted by Mr Meneses . . . I wanted to be a singer, but ended up becoming an announcer and impersonator. I impersonated everyone, and did it quite well. Then I was given my first stage name – Topillo Tapas – and I toured with it.

Not long afterwards Germán Valdés is a comedian (and singer) in Paco Miller's company – which tours Mexico and the Southern USA. The comic Donato also worked with Paco Miller. His sidekick – the 'other' comic, who represents high seriousness amid the custard pies – at the time was Marcelo Chávez, who became Tin Tan's 'buddy' ('carnal') for more than twenty years. 'One day we just started rehearsing, out of the blue. We went on stage that night, and it went down very well. We decided to stay together, write songs, and rehearse.'

The stories about Tin Tan usually leave out one important detail: his bewilderment at events in Los Angeles. Between approximately 1938 and 1942, in the Mexican-American neighbourhoods of Texas and, especially, California, the Pachuco emerges as the first important aesthetic product of migration, the bearer of a new and extremist concept of elegance – he is a dandy living on the outskirts of fashion – who, in the eyes of the Anglos (and the fathers of the Pachucos), is an outright provocation. The Pachucos' audacity in clothing and in gesture permits them to mark out their new territory with mobile signs, and – like their model, the Harlem dude – challenge discrimination too. The Pachuco is thus affiliated to the American Way of Life only eccentrically, and becomes a part of Mexican culture by confronting racism. Pachucos eventually become (not very voluntary) symbols of cultural resistance, and end up cornered and persecuted in the segregation campaigns that culminate in the Los Angeles Zoot Suit Riots.

By the time Tin Tan acquires his name, Pachucos had disappeared from the scene in the USA, while in Mexico they had become synonymous with the idea of a vagabond with radical taste and, furthermore, associated with the suburban pimp, or the embodiment of a new neighbourhood masculinity – as played, for example, by Victor Parra in *El Suavecito* ['Little Dude'] (Fernando Méndez, 1950) and Rodolfo Acosta in Emilio 'el Indio' Fernández's films *Salón México* (1945) and *Victimas del pecado* ['Victims of Sin', 1950]. In *El Suavecito*, the father scorns his son, the Pachuco, and eventually expels him from the family and society with the words: 'That's not a man but a hairdresser's dummy'. A traditional society – the only kind that existed in Mexico at the time – can see such an unrestrained wardrobe – jacket down to the knees, tails, incredibly wide lapels, a watch chain that hangs dangerously close to the ground, fantasy braces, a feathered hat, flowery shirts whose sleeves are long enough to cover the hands, and a sense of combination that sets the memory of decent clothes ablaze – only as an inflammatory provocation.

Ever since the Porfiriato, those Mexicans who became 'gringified' have been the object of disdain and fun. From the point of view of this dimension of popular culture, whoever so renounces the 'national condition' (dressing and behaving like grandads) becomes amusingly insubstantial. In his well-known novel *Al filo del agua* ['The Edge of the Storm'], set in 1909, just before the outbreak of the Revolution, Agustín Yáñez lists villager reactions to such 'Northerners' – those who had gone to North America, and returned:

'Poor people, poor country.' 'They're the cleverest, the bravest; just because of a handful of words they can mouth in a Christian tongue – even tho' they don't know how to read, like when they left.' 'And just because they've got those gold teeth they pick all the time.' 'Because they wear those big, thick boots, felt hats, wide trousers and cuffed shirts and shiny cufflinks.' '. . . And what about the way you talk? You've even forgotten the language your fathers taught you.'

With marvellous impudence Tin Tan undoes, without appearing to be aware of it, such a lack of understanding and rejection. His dress and style announce, for the first time, a popular modernity.

Guilty conscience

In Mexico City during the 1940s, Tin Tan triumphantly became the archetypical 'pocho', a category that was demonized both linguistically and socially. 'Pocho': a person who has lost caste [*descastado*], who has forgotten his Roots, and exchanged the vigour of idiosyncrasy for the plate of beans of superficial Americanization. In his column of 20 June 1944, Salvador Novo remembers an article of his on 'The Purity of Language':

> It is a good article, really. I was inspired by all that talk about Tin Tan, who stands accused of corrupting the language with 'pochismos' which the young repeat. Of course, I did not have the space to develop the whole theory as I should have, but essentially, and the intelligent reader would have understood, it rests on making of Cantinflas the representative of the Mexican unconscious, whilst recognizing that Tin Tan, when he bothers us, does so because he embodies the guilty conscience of our own voluntary or passive loss of caste [*descastamiento*].

Tin Tan elaborates to perfection the linguistic collage in which participate all those Anglo-Saxon words imposed by the necessity to name the new, and a rural Spanish full to the brim with archaisms, and sayings and expressions from the whole country. Tin Tan asks Marcelo, for example, about 'the "jale" that you got as "guachador"', and 'do your "relativos" still "forgetean" you?' One immediately has to translate: 'jale' is job and 'guachador' is 'velador' (watchman), and the 'relativos' who 'forgetean' are parents who forget. Nevertheless, Tin Tan does not emblematize loss of caste [*descastamiento*], as will become obvious in the years that follow; he only interprets the syncretism that marks the second half of the century. Many a reprimand still awaits the 'pocho', and will appear later in films, plays, radio programmes, sermons and editorials. The steady increase in migration, however, will eventually 'normalize' them: there are so many 'pochos' that the use of the pejorative collapses.

Tin Tan articulates a script opposed to known convention. He is the Pachuco: a word that in Mexico City oscillates between friendly irony and insult. There is a considerable leap from the riots in Los Angeles to the dance halls of Mexico City, and the Pachucos of the capital – who do not offend the 'other', the North

American, but, rather, the 'other', the man of respect – bet everything they have on this character who makes an adventure of dressing and an urban fantasy of the migrant's challenge.

'Turírurá tundá tundá tundá.' A classicism that feigns concern for correct syntax rejects innovations in the name of linguistic purity. And if Cantinflas is accepted in the name of an incoherence proper to the crowd, Tin Tan is rejected for his offence against immutable speech, the ideal property of the elites. Tin Tan is denounced by journalists and academicians of the Language who lay siege to his prefigurative attitude. More or less by force, however, producers and scriptwriters begin to incorporate the comic, the Pachuco, into their big-city neighbourhood scenes; and although they do not suppress the 'Americanisms' in his style entirely, they do lighten his linguistic experimentation.

Tin Tan's career was not as linear as it is usually presented. In fact, just as he was inspired by the Los Angeles Pachucos, his most recognizable influence was Cab Calloway, singer and director of the Harlem Orchestra and a huge star in the 1930s. Tin Tan takes his gestures of optimistic ecstasy from Calloway, his dress, a sense of movement on stage, and a syncopated malice that distorts, elevates and magnifies his songs. 'Stormy Weather', for example, reveals Cab Calloway definitely to be Tin Tan's model, with his circus humour, the labial exaggeration that 'swallows' and ironically re-creates his songs, and the architectonic suit that makes all preambles unnecessary ('Let my clothes introduce me so that I can just get on with it'). To this Tin Tan adds his experience of the circus and music hall, his use of the cinematographic scene (the sketch), his ability to improvise and his enormous confidence: apart from the spectators, no one else is looking.

On 5 November 1943 Tin Tan makes his début in the Iris Theatre in Mexico City with a salary of 40 pesos. Cantinflas was the star of the show; Tin Tan was only moderately successful. Which is not surprising: only gradually would the dynamism, the fun and the offensiveness associated with Tin Tan be understood. His sidekick ('carnal') Marcelo was an old-fashioned comic, the interlocutor who takes all the jokes or offers his physique up for ritual derision (in his case, fatness and baldness; while in the complementary case of the dwarf José René Ruiz 'Tun Tun', closeness to the ground). While we must acknowledge the very real differences, Marcelo is to Tin Tan what Margaret Dumont is to Groucho Marx: the ideal victim of jokes and humorous situations. The receiver of blows aimed originally at the comic, he represented offended respectability, his face swollen by the surprise of gratuitous verbal or physical attack.

Tin Tan and Marcelo are contracted to work in the Follies Theatre, The

Patio – a fashionable night club – and to do a weekly radio programme on the station XEW. Tin Tan is also given a part in René Cardona's film *Hotel de verano* ['Summer Hotel']: 'They paid me 350 pesos for a number, which was nothing, but what the hell, I was still very green as far as film was concerned!' In fact, Tin Tan's first films were not very good. He is not a humorist, either, although he resorts to North American vaudeville humour when he is on the offensive and improvising. He has no graded repertoire of jokes, nor has he timed the rhythm of his punch lines, but he does have other allies: ferocity of gesture, verbal aggression, an enthusiasm for chaos, sentimentalism dissolved by irony, and a lack of respect for solemnity and its sense of propriety (property). From such a balancing act, and the continuous sense of impending catastrophe that accompanies it, he mocks decorum without demolishing everything that surrounds him (unlike the Marx Brothers, because of a hatred for institutions), nor does he call for universal ruin (like Buster Keaton). The results are, nevertheless, equally apocalyptic. Tin Tan passes by and nothing remains standing, no one escapes the chaos.

From the series of films made by Humberto Gómez Landero – *El hijo desobediente* ['Disobedient Son', 1945], *Hay muertos que no hacen ruido* ['The Noiseless Dead', 1946], *Con la música por dentro* ['Music Inside', 1946], *El niño perdido* ['The Lost Child', 1947] and *Músico, poeta y loco* ['Music, Poet, Madman', 1947] – Tin Tan's character possesses the characteristics (despite the director's lack of imagination) that he will then go on to hone endlessly: impudence, cynicism, amorous frivolity, and an ineptitude balanced by destructive efficiency. Tin Tan's verve leaves an immediate impression: he acts as if he had transposed the audience itself right into the screen.

¡Qué mené, carnalita, qué mené!

Tin Tan leaves no word in peace – he twists words, stretches them, discovering their sonorous interrelations. He emancipates urban speech. In Gómez Landero's films the story and dialogue credits go to Guz Aguila (Guzmán Aguilera). But Guz Aguila, an able scriptwriter in the Frivolous Theatre for two decades, is inadequate when it comes to the linguistic vitality of Tin Tan. In a dialogue in *Músico, poeta y loco* Tin Tan, working in a shop that sells windows, says to a client:

'Orejas, sabe que estaba chompeta [ear] me falla un poquetín. . . . Y su guaifo [husband] ¿cómo está por ahí? . . . [Looking at his suit] Usa muy buena garra.

Fijón. ¡Qué mené, carnalita, qué mené! [Fantastic!] . . . No, no, no, jainita [honey] . . .'

['Ere, my earhole's not working. . . . And how's yer hubbie, what's he up to? He's looking great. Wow babe! . . . No, no, no, honey . . .']

And Marcelo responds: 'Se me hace que le pusiste de a feo a la yesca y te anda girando la chompeta.' [It seems to me you did the dirty, and she's pulling your tube.'] And so on. Tin Tan 'jazzes' up speech; he improvises, contriving neologisms on the move.

In 1948 Tin Tan begins his collaboration with Gilberto Martínez Solares (director) and Juan García 'el Peralvillo' (scriptwriter). In an interview published in *Cuadernos de la Cineteca (4)*, Martínez Solares says, somewhat contemptuously:

Tin Tan was an extraordinary comedian. At first, I didn't have much confidence in him. I didn't feel like working with him either. He was a bit common, both in the characters he portrayed and in the places he worked, right? Tents, theatres. . . . I wrote stories, although I've never been good at street talk, especially neighbourhood talk, which was my collaborator Juan García's strength.

Calabacitas tiernas ['Tender Little Pumpkins'], the film that begins the collaboration between Tin Tan, Martínez Solares and Juan García, is enjoyable today for its energy, despite breakdowns in plot. Tin Tan sings, dances, seduces, pretends to be what he isn't, doubts being who he is, and confronts himself in the mirror like Harpo Marx in *Duck Soup*. Audaciously performing on the tightrope that separates the theatre from film, he walks to the rhythm of the city suburbs, from the *danzón* to the swing. In *Calabacitas tiernas* the modern urban comic appears, largely emancipated from sentimentalism, installing the logic of survival into the domain of fun ('relajo'), while acknowledging that he is condemned to fail. Without his Pachuco clothing, and that touch of contemporaneity provided by Anglo words, Tin Tan is as irreverently up-to-date as times permit. He improvises, entrances the camera, speaks to the audience ('the Lord of One Thousand Brains'), gets obviously bored with old-fashioned dignity, refuses to protect his honour, pays no tribute whatsoever to linguistic serfdom and, furthermore, does not care if he offends the audience.

Listen, Marcelino, play one that makes me cry from here to the next song

Inevitably, Tin Tan's real environment is the picaresque – which I define here quickly as the gift of taking advantage of all circumstances except the really advantageous ones. He is a good-for-nothing who has no room for either justice or injustice; he is no one's fool and everybody's fool. His character perfectly combines extremes: adulation and lechery, sentimentalism and daylight robbery, solidarity and plunder. And in this coming and going from heroism to antiheroism (from radical failure to fleeting victory), Tin Tan displays a modernity which – loyal to the circular resignation of the circus – other comedians like Cantinflas, Palillo, Monolín and Shilinsky, Polo Ortín, El Chaflán, El Chicote and even Resortes (who is modern only when he dances) never knew.

The Tin Tan who matters, and who speaks to us now, is the product of fifteen years of filming and recording between 1945 and 1959. What follows this period is almost unbearable: the sadness that comes from watching a great but wasted comic actor, a comic who is misunderstood and abandoned by an industry that exploited him without recognizing his brilliance. But from *El hijo desobediente* ['Disobedient Son'] to *El Violetero* ['Violets for Sale', 1959], Tin Tan is that extraordinary figure who marks a generation (in ways that were understood only much later), transcends the lamentable scripts, redeems through improvisation the badly planned scenes, democratizes relations with the public, and opens the door to a modern humour that will influence not only a whole generation of television comedians (Héctor Suárez, The Polivoces, Alejandro Suárez and, of course, the Loco Valdés) but also, through the mythical evocation of his figure in the trade, recent ones like Andrés Bustamente, Ausencio Cruz and Víctor Trujillo.

Tin Tan never completely distances himself from the Frivolous Theatre. He is a film comedian – no doubt – with a gift for speedy repartee and a facility for acrobatics, dance, extreme facial plasticity, and the insult as a form of relationship. He is also a creature of the sketch (to which he resorts whenever he feels lost). In his terrific hullabaloos, amid the destruction of a house or a shop, it may suddenly appear:

'Now, yes, Marcelino, you're going to have to work with UNESCO.'
'With UNESCO?'
'Yes, with a broom.'*

---

* 'Un esco' + 'Ba' = 'un escoba' = a broom! [Translator's note.]

For years Cantinflas's strategy of appearing in only one film a year was praised. During the 1950s, on the other hand, Tin Tan limited himself by filming every two or three months. Now, however, the majority of Cantinflas's films are almost unwatchable – except, in my view, *Aguila o sol* ['Heads or Tails'], *El signo de la muerte* ['The Sign of Death'], *Ahí está el detalle* ['That's the Point!'], *El gendarme desconocido* ['The Unknown Policeman'] and *Ni sangre ni arena* ['Neither Blood nor Sand']. But even the worst of Tin Tan's films contain memorable scenes, songs, and jokes. His vitality enables him to overcome the limitations imposed on his character by the industry, the mediocrity of the screenplays (when they exist), the idea that film is defined by speed and forgetfulness, and the alarming ineptitude of the young 'starlets' (with one exception: Sylvia Pinal in *El rey del barrio* ['King of the Neighbourhood']). The scorn of the critics hardly matters. The partial incomprehension of the public that celebrates him, however, without knowing the contemporaneity of his lack of inhibition, is overwhelming. Tin Tan's inhibition has only tenuous support: the freedom to improvise, from Martínez Solares (who on seeing him, according to Wolf Ruvinskis, laughed and just carried on filming); a popular register, provided by Juan García 'el Peravillo'; not to mention the discretion and efficiency of his sidekick, Marcelo.

And his successes are not meagre. In the 'Golden Age of Mexican Cinema', only one other actor breaks down the rigid barriers of convention: Joaquín Pardavé preserves and transmits the accumulated knowledge of actors in the tradition of Frivolous Theatre – whose ceremonial and measured diction acts as the architecture of irony, and whose voices are, almost literally, 'decorated with the epoch'. On saying this I am not forgetting the contributions of Resortes, Mantequilla, El Chaflán, El Chicote, Oscar Pulido, Amelia Wilhelmy and Delia Magaña, but none of these managed satisfactorily to transcend the inertia of screenwriters and the haste of directors. While Pardavé achieves his success thanks to his complete understanding of traditional sensibility, Tin Tan does so through his lack of inhibitions – Germán does not bow before the camera; rather, he makes it his accomplice, his witness, his immediate applause, part of his own environment.

I believe that *El rey del barrio* ['King of the Neighbourhood', 1949] is Tin Tan's best film. In saying this I am not forgetting *Simbad el Mareado* ['Seasick Sinbad'], *El revoltoso* ['Rebel'], *El Ceniciento* ['Cindarello'], *Ay amor . . . cómo me has puesto* ['Oh Darling! Look What You've Done!'], or *El sultán descalzo* ['Barefoot Sultan']. In *El rey del barrio* Tin Tan reaches his apogee: he is flexible, ironic, sentimental and destructive, and his character, fruit of both the astuteness of the industry and his own biography, is perfect, as defenceless as a catastrophe, and with the eloquence of someone who has nothing to lose. Tin Tan is the most joyous product of urban neighbourhoods, someone who explains himself in the light of the devastation he disseminates. He is, at one and the same time, contemporary in attitude and as anachronistic as the neighbourhoods that will soon be demolished, the pool hall crooks, and the methods used for injecting the past with actuality and a night at the movies with dance-hall rhythm. *El rey del barrio* contains some of Tin Tan's best sequences: the humiliation of detective Marcelo in the house they are painting, the fabulous duet with Vitola (in a 'cirivivirí' that pursues the grotesque by celebrating the ridiculous), and the bolero 'Contigo' [With You] which Tin Tan, drunk and in love, sings while taking charge of the block he lives in, transforming it into a set from *Romeo and Juliet*.

When he sings – be it rancheras or boleros – Tin Tan's humour is extremely effective. His style is naturally exaggerated. Nevertheless, he successfully manages to distort neither the meaning of the joke nor the virtues of romance. When he dances, Tin Tan is the Pachuco who adds spice to the choreographic fun. He is the neighbourhood dandy, and when it comes to the bolero, he celebrates the 'pick-up', and falls 'madly in love' – which is the invasion of *machismo* by lyricism – without a hint of vocal pretension. His style thus provides an alternative outlet for the transcultural tang that censorship pursued in his speech. Tin Tan is the crooner and the bolero singer, impregnated with the onomatopoeia of boogie-woogie. He sings with his whole mouth ('my drooling snout'). And if he cannot be solemn like Juan Arvizu or Emilio Tuero, nor sensual like Frank Sinatra, Tin Tan does manage both to parody a variety of styles and to unify them into his own ironic and openly affected ('cursi') one. As a singer, Tin Tan is, unusually, parodic and orthodox at the same time.

Chaos within chaos

How do you put a Tin Tan film together? For the most part, they are dismal distortions of classics or of contemporary successes. Their names bear the mark of the immediacy of the joke: *The Mark of the Fox* ['La marca del zorrillo'], *The 3½ Musketeers* ['Los tres mosqueteros y medio'], *Cindarello* ['El Ceniciento'], *Seasick Sinbad* ['Simbad el Mareado'], *Sleeping Beau* ['El Bello Durmiente'], *The Viscount of Monte Cristo* ['El Vizconde de Montecristo'], *The Blue Beard* ['El Barba Azul'], *Look What Happened to Samson!* ['Lo que le pasó a Sansón'], *Rebel Without a Home* ['Rebelde sin casa'], *Puss-without-Boots* ['El gato sin botas'], *The Phantom of the Operetta* ['El fantasma de la opereta']. Even *El Violetero* is, in part, a caricature of *María Candelaria*, a humorous bow on Tin Tan's part, happy to imitate the 'Indio' Fernándezque way of speaking Castilian in Xochimilco (and then immediately to move on to Spanglish).

To the weakness of the plots and the irresponsibility of the producers, convinced that cinema is the art of the immediate recovery of their investments, Tin Tan opposes his obsession for parody and hatred of boredom. From this point of view, improvisation is the only way to escape memorizing the script – the film industry's equivalent to the prisonhouse of boredom. The task of 'nationalizing' the delirium then falls to folklore, and there is plenty of it; while reality becomes whatever happens before or after each comic scene. In such a cinema, parody involves much more than the transformation of situations that are already grotesque or ridiculous in themselves. Parody is the continuous, knockabout invention of the world just as it should be, where satire is the mistress of ceremonies for those historical times-gone-by, melodrama, passionate affairs, incomprehensible plots. Nothing is serious, except death – but that occurs only in the film showing next door.

Tin Tan is, in the main, the product of his youthful energy dramatized in dance, leaping about, irreverence, and frenetic escapes. Tin Tan sings mambo and cha-cha-cha, shouts, knocks over and destroys whatever is within reach, sings serenades, fails as if his life depended on it, and sets everything around him going. With the passing of years, he concentrates on verbal humour. But without a competent team in his later films, and impotent and disenchanted when it came to routine (although there are always magnificent moments: see *El Quelito*, for example), Tin Tan looks as if he has had enough. People admire his charm, he is honoured and always working, but no one thinks he will last. He is as he is, and it is best not to dedicate another minute to the subject: he is, or was, a Pachuco embattled by linguistic censorship; he is, or was, a product of neighbourhood and small-town vaudeville; he is, or was, a comic who refused to allow himself to be intimidated by the cinema. From our own privileged perspective today, there is no real sense in quarrelling with the stupidity of the Mexican film industry, which also wasted Resortes and Mantequilla, and buried Pardavé, Pedro Armendáriz, Fernando and Andrés Soler, David Silva, Tito Junco, Roberto Cañedo and other excellent actors in abominable melodramas. Tin Tan was used and abused by a booming industry, but thanks to this very situation he was also able to work free from the intimidation suffered by the established and 'sacred' stars. He did what he wanted as often as he could, and became, for the generations that followed, the emblem of a kind of urban vitality which still, when it's time for fun ('relajo'), moves us today.

9

The Boy Fidencio and
the Roads to Ecstasy

A miracle is the innocent and naive explanation of the real mystery that inhabits man, of the power that hides in him. (Pier Paolo Pasolini)

What are the limits of the sacred in contexts of extreme deprivation? Not centuries of Christianity nor of Enlightenment, nor of official *Guadalupismo* — that is, religion as both pedagogic instrument of formation and standard-bearer of capital – nor even years of intense secularization, have put a stop to millions of Mexicans believing in spirits and faith healers, conceiving of the coming of the new Millennium in anything but the most portentous terms, and thus offering themselves up to the most unlikely beliefs, becoming members of cults that are like huge extended families, and acquiring the verve of rural and suburban proselytizers (although, one must immediately add, it is possible to find such believers in the middle and upper classes too!). In Mexico and Latin America the universe of myths, rituals, centres of worship, of socially uncontrolled emotions and annual pilgrimages to the most inconceivable of sacred places, of marvellous tales, charismatic heroes and stories of saints whose names are not even included in the calendar of days, are all reproduced as dense cultural formations. This millenarian nation of popular religion is, however, marginalized as 'superstition' and denied the prerogatives of 'real' secular Nationhood and 'high' administered religion.

Illuminated by the Lord

One extraordinary example of murky messianism and faith healing: the miracle-worker known as the Boy Fidencio. José Fidencio de Jesús Constantino Síntora was one of twenty-five children born to Socorro Constantino and Mari del Tránsito Síntora. Although he celebrated his birthday on 17 October, according to his birth certificate Fidencio was born on 13 November 1898 on the Las Cuevas ranch in the municipality of Iránuco, state of Guanajuato. He died in Espinazo, state of Nuevo León, in 1938. From early childhood he distinguished himself by his devotion to Catholic ritual and his surprising gifts. The solitary and melancholic young altar boy, whose only friend was the local priest, reads his classmates' minds and tells them their futures, and in return receives insults and blows. (Today, Fidencio would be a highly paid 'psychic'.)

Orphaned as a child, Fidencio finishes his third year of primary school and works as a waiter and cook for the family of an ex-colonel in Pancho Villa's army who manages ranches. According to Mr López de la Fuente, Fidencio 'liked to work in the kitchen, but above all he liked to help the midwives, washing the clothes of women who had just given birth'. With the López de la Fuentes he experiences the 'benefits' of family life: he is regularly beaten and economically exploited. In 1921 the family moves to Espinazo, a railroad town, taking Fidencio with them.

By 1927, the twenty-nine-year-old Boy (synonym of 'pure soul') is the faith healer of the region, legitimized by many a testimonial of gratitude: he heals miners after a cave-in; varicose veins – 'which could not even have been cured in New York' – disappear; he extracts tumours, cares for mothers who have just given birth, and attends lepers. The young man with the effeminate voice is soon the centre of Espinazo town life. 'One market day,' remembers Marcelino Fraire Arreola, from nearby state capital Hidalgo,

> it was announced that the Boy Fidencio would make an appearance. And he was brought as if he were Christ! When the public function came to an end we were told that if we wanted to touch him we would have to go to a room in the Municipal Palace. Fidencio drank and sang five or six songs. He was good at singing, he had the voice of a soprano. Two young women held him, giving him beer to drink and lighting his cigarettes.

An unrecognized messianism

It is curious that the Fidencio legend blurs the central issue: the Boy as the Christ-of-our-times. Eager to see his image reproduced, Fidencio adopts a series of poses that evoke the divine – be it in the place of the Virgin of Guadalupe blessing converts, or as the Sacred Heart of Jesus, or dressed in linen carrying the cross, or praying next to a patient as in a painting of old, or vanquishing the devil. When he dies, however, he receives the blessings of the Church, which refuses to see him as the founder of a new religion, preferring instead the image of a Catholic saint.

This apparent contradiction is strengthened by the humility of Fidencio, who constantly professes his ignorance, saying he is no more than 'an instrument in the hands of the Lord'. He testifies to a popular religion that is both innovative and heterodox, and fuses Aztec gods and Christian saints, spiritualism and Marianism, revolutionary messianism and Father Rispalda's catechism, the Saint of Cabora and the legend of Saint Felipe de Jesús. Nothing is foreign to this endless mix, so the Catholic hierarchy, however much it hates faith healers and country messiahs, rarely opposes it openly. For this reason, neither the 'blasphemous' character of his photos nor the notorious irregularity of his procedures brings Fidencio into conflict with a religious hierarchy that feigns ignorance of this leader of pilgrimages, who even has his own nuns ('the Boy's slaves') and priests.

The circle and the corral

Fidencio begins his treatment of the ill at dawn, having chosen those who deserve it the night before. Each day is allocated according to those who are sick 'of the eyes, the skin, those who are mad, those who need operating on . . .', and the treatment is carried out in different places. There is a sign above the entrance to the patio:

> THE POOR ARE NOT POOR
> THE RICH ARE NOT RICH
> ONLY THOSE WHO SUFFER PAIN
> ARE POOR.

Fidencio is the object of an exasperated devotion, and often paraded on people's shoulders as if he were an icon canopy. Week after week trains full of the wounded, women about to give birth, those suffering from cancer or leprosy, those with no hope of recovery, come to Espinazo, to the 'Miracle Circle', the corral, and to the 'Colony of Hope' for lepers. Thousands watch the Boy as he heals the sick on the roof of a house, in an empty train wagon, on a hill, even in a bathtub. The boy is a full-time faith healer, insisting that he attends the sick even when he is asleep. He is tireless, refusing to take food for up to forty-eight or even seventy-two hours: 'Everyone followed him, and whoever was nearest was cured'. And, possessed by a mysticism that leaves no room for reflection, he laboured on in this fashion for twelve years, concentrating fully on carrying out his duty, responding thus to the expressions of gratitude and admiration. He is chaste ('a virgin like Christ') and disinterested: he will lose 'the gift of healing' if he ever succumbs to fornication or charges for his miraculous intervention. (If anyone wanted to make a donation, it was used to tend the sick.)

A collective composed of the sick awaits the promise of good health. Suffering is the key to the Fidencio cult, and to classic messianism as well. 'I was born to suffer,' repeats the Boy, and the tens of thousands of *unhealed* still loyal to him tell the other side of this story: the transformation, thanks to faith, of *imposed* suffering into *joyful* suffering. Even the failed acts of healing do not produce anger against the 'con man', because in such cases happiness annuls or neutral-izes indifference before the facts, and 'cosmic emotion' assumes the form of enthusiasm and freedom (see William James's *The Varieties of Religious Experience*).

The methods of the Boy Saint

Fidencio uses an array of faith-healing methods. They include:

- *Hydrotherapy*: the Boy bathes those who are ill with syphilis, blindness or lep-rosy for days. Those suffering from scabies are sent to bathe in the sulphurous waters of Puerto Blanco, while the mad are woken at dawn and beaten, then bathed by the Boy in the River Charco. (Pilgrims still bathe in the 'sacred Charco' today.) The water used by Fidencio for bathing is called 'Boy's Water': the liquid, through saintly contamination, is considered to have medicinal properties;
- *Telepathy*: the Boy makes his diagnosis by simply looking at the patient, without consultation or the use of X-rays;
- *Logotherapy*: a 'primitive psychoanalysis' – the patient reveals his values and goals;
- *Psychosomatic medicines*: the ill had to pray before therapy, since for Fidencio illness and sin were contiguous. On eliminating the latter, health might reimpose itself;
- *Melotherapy*: Fidencio sings as he cures (and cries when moved. His favourite songs are: 'La hija del penal', 'Las cuatro milpas', 'La Norteña', and 'La rielera');

- *Laying on of hands and feet:* he used to line up a number of people and walk across their stomachs;
- *Impactotherapy:* the Boy, standing on a roof, hill or other high point, would throw the fruit and eggs given to him at the people who gathered, believing that if the projectiles hit the sick or injured parts of their bodies they would be cured; being hit with a tomato, a guayaba or an apple thrown by the Boy was the same as being blessed. 'For hours on end, we had to bring him boxes and boxes of tomatoes, oranges, apples and eggs. . . .' Fidencio also produced psychological shocks in patients by leaving them in a cage with a puma (without teeth or claws). According to witnesses, this therapy never failed with the deaf and dumb. To the above add surgery, and the use of plants and medicines from popular tradition.

The visit of President Plutarco Elías Calles

The rituals and hopes of the faithful are consolidated by the faith of a feverish and ascetic man moved by 'divine impulse', and lacking any great sense of reality; but governed by a strong code of purity, and with an acute need to serve and obey. Such a model was indeed replicated in the years that followed, but none of the village or regional saints (including the Sorcerer Leonardo Alcalá in Mexico City during the 1940s) ever had Fidencio's power of attraction, which was based first on a happy combination of personal qualities (his appearance, voice and generosity), second on his ability to influence women, and third on his numerous apparent successes in healing. The barren landscape of Espinazo also helped to consolidate the mood, as did the devotional hunger that had overtaken the town.

What most characterizes the mystic is a strong link between religious exaltation and social marginalization. Fidencio says:

> For man has to suffer hunger, thirst, and the heat of the sun, experience his own hunger and poverty, and the tiredness and sweat of his brothers in order to reach God; for God does not make his presence felt in the well-perfumed palaces of luxury, nor does he approach those who in their vanity and arrogance take meticulous care of their clothes and bodies. (see Manuel Terán Lira's book *El Niño Fidencio*)

The culminating point of the legend: the President of the Republic, Plutarco Elías Calles, visits the Boy. Eager to rid himself of a painful illness, on 8 February 1928 Calles comes to Espinazo accompanied by General Juan Andrew Almazán,

Governor of the state of Nuevo León, Aarón Saénz, and the mayor of Mina, Dámaso Cárdenas. On arriving the President is greeted with the National Anthem, followed by the hymn of Fidencio's followers, 'La hija del penal' ['Prison Daughter']:

> Oh! Virgin of our Consolation, come!
> Since my suffering is my pain
> help me keep my goodness.
>
> Oh! Little Virgin, save him!
> I want to be his love,
> the eternal prisoner of his love.

The rabidly anticlerical Calles meets the altar boy Fidencio. The Boy gives the President 'special treatment', a rose-leaf tea with honey, rubs him with a tomato and soap pomade, and wraps him in bandages. According to witnesses, Calles says to Fidencio: 'You're the only one who tells me the truth about my illness.' Then the President puts on one of the Boy's tunics, and goes out to the town square.

Calles's visit ratifies the then palpably close relation between 'scientific' and popular belief: in 1928 General Calles, at war with religious fanaticism and struggling to impose a monopoly over the nation's system of education, confides in an almost illiterate faith healer. There is no great contradiction here, however, since one can be a spiritualist and still support agrarian reform. Indeed, whole sectors of the population believe in such alternatives, accepting divine healing without sharing the faith.

This that we do, oh Lord

If the figure of the Boy Fidencio persists, refusing to be lost among the many other more local legends, it is first because of his authenticity, and second because the 'self-sufficient healing' he represents so irritated the Catholic hierarchy. The Boy found his strength in self-negation. The moment helps too: in an extraordinary anticlimax, after the brutal secularization that was the Revolution, an unarmed saint without doctrinal apparatus, solely interested in providing Divine Well-Being, triumphs. He sees himself, typically, as a messenger from up-on-high, as the transmitter of the ungraspable forces of nature that God controls. He, José de Jesús Fidencio Síntora, is no one, except when he is possessed by extraterrestrial powers. Then the gift of health appears, as does the right to demand the humiliation of his followers, which will be rewarded with the alle-viation of their pain – this is a power that does not differentiate between a leper and President Calles. If, according to medieval classification, he is one of 'God's fools', a 'sacred fool', the earthly bearer of supreme innocence, in his own eyes he is simply and gloriously an instrument of the Lord. He lives amid pain and poverty because this is his mission on Earth. This is what confuses Dr Francisco Vela González, a Harvard graduate, vice-president of the state of Nuevo León's Health Council and Federal Sanitation officer, who visits Espinazo in 1930. He reacts by writing a series of condemnatory articles in which he points out the unsanitary conditions in the camp, the high mortality rate (over two thousand dead in two years – the seriously ill go there to die) and concludes:

> Fidencio is innocent, and without knowing it suffers from a mental condition which consists in thinking he has been blessed with the task of curing the sick. Those around him, however, are not innocent children, and have taken advan-tage of the credulity of the ignorant masses, including some who are not so ignorant. Espinazo has been and still is an embarrassment to Nuevo León and the Nation as a whole. When will it all end?

The miracle worker dies in 1938, and for three days a crowd stands guard over his coffin awaiting his resurrection. Since then, the Boy Fidencio has been the supreme symbol of a kind of popular religiosity that is self-sacrificing, violent in its self-flagellation, incapable of despair and discouragement, and born again in every cult or ritual.

The history of the Boy Fidencio is a question of that extreme vision of the vanquished whose sickness is poverty.

'You suffer to know that in some way you are alive'

Who documents? In a most pitiful but systematic way, only the yellow press pay any attention to this dimension of popular culture. Let us turn, for example, to the magazine *Alarma*, dated 4 July 1984. The headline reads: 'Con man! He says he is the Son of the Virgin Mary! He Cheats and Runs! He claims he can cure all sickness!' And the text continues:

> From Chiapas. They say he has been chosen by God, that he is the son of Mary, the protector of the heavenly skies, and whoever has faith in him, and his little animals, would be healed by simply passing branches over their body to purify their soul. People naively follow him everywhere, thinking that the

'Master' will cure them of their ills. Some authorities, however, have insisted that he and his 'helpers' leave the municipality. But they turn up elsewhere, and rumours immediately attract a public to the cleansing, where the 'Master' blesses the newly cut branches that will later be passed over the bodies of the donkeys and the sick. When it is all over, people ask: 'How much?' The Master's secretary answers: 'Nothing, brother, because God sent the Master to alleviate the pain on Earth, but if you want to leave a little something for the dead, you may deposit it here.'

By foregrounding the secular, fashion likens 'the sacred' to 'the unknown'. But if the Boy Fidencio's powers are the gifts of God, the faith healer Pachita, in contrast, however Catholic she may be, founds her credibility on her psychic powers. In this regard, it helps to remember that between 1928 and today scientific knowledge has been disseminated on a mass scale, while the mass media have become all-pervasive – now, the Boy Fidencio would have become a mass spectacle within weeks, and be so harassed by the press and media that his cause would probably disintegrate.

This has not been the case, however, for his disciples and followers. There is nothing less glamorous than the world recorded in Nicolás Echevarría's extraordinary film *El Niño Fidencio*, about the Fidencio cult in the 1980s. The camera registers the details of faith in this film: the damaged bodies burdened with pain; faces on which is registered only one emotion; the stubborn, recalcitrant expressions, hardened by monomania; immersions in mud; songs, prayers, prematurely aged women; invalids, people suffering from polio, cancer; the Boy's 'slaves' and priests. And in fact, all this is irrecoverable, even by scandalmongering press and TV programmes hyping the bizarre. So you who simply suffer, unable to attract the attention of high technology, move over!

Exploiters and believers, con men and miracle-workers, the distortion of ignorance and acts of clairvoyance which rework fragments of the New Testament. It is there for everyone to see, the metamorphosis of the Christian doctrine and its methods of teaching in Mexico. For millions of people, the promises of human salvation that are evoked by 'the Kingdom of God' and the Millennium inherited from the Jewish messianic tradition constitute the space in which they simultaneously find peace of mind, a sense of belonging, and a feeling of singularity.

But such messianisms are rarely taken into account culturally. Their most frequent image may be found in Juan Rulfo's short story 'Anacleto Morones', with its old daughters-of-the-devil 'dressed in black, sweating like mules under the mere light of the sun', victims of the abusive sorcerer, the Boy Anacleto. This image is only a caricature. Today, however, now that the belief in the cult of progress has been seriously dented, it may be possible to begin to understand such popular phenomena. The coiner of the aphorism 'People will not believe in God absolutely if they are not allowed to believe in Him incorrectly' may be right after all.

Marginal mysticism

A new tradition of syncretism combines Catholicism as a mass social practice, with pilgrimage as an end in itself (the road to the sacred place is always the most rewarding), faith healing, Marianist spiritualism, and those charismatic personalities who, whether they attempt to found a religion or not, use themselves as a filter for religious experience. What is to be understood by 'marginal mysticism'? To begin with, here are some of its most representative figures: Teresa Urrea, the Saint of Cabora, the Boy Fidencio, Pachita the faith healer born in the Zone of Silence, the Sorcerer Leonardo Alcalá from Mexico City, in some ways María Sabina, the shaman of Huautla, and more recently, the case of Nueva Jerusalem, the millenarian community in Michoacán, with its leader Papá Nabor. In each of these phenomena one finds the following characteristics:

- the verbal compliance of the orthodox Catholic hierarchy, although in practice everything is heterodox. In response the Church chooses either confrontation (for example, in Cabora) or apparent indifference (Fidencio);
- faith in the unbreakable bond between everyday life and the liturgical representation of the beyond. Everything (Heaven, Hell, Limbo, virgins, apparitions, miracles, satanic and seraphic possession) is natural, because the secular world does not exist and history happens only at a distance;
- the appropriation of only those values which distance faith from individualism. Life is lived to accomplish essential goals, those in which the will to sacrifice is a form of transfiguration. In this case, mysticism is the abandonment of self, the renunciation of possessions, the battle for primordial ideals (the model of Saint Joan of Arc for the Saint of Cabora, the model of Christ for the Boy Fidencio, the model of Saint Paul for Papá Nabor), the pronouncement of prophecies, the embodiment of nature (Pachita's operations and cleansing, the portentous songs of María Sabina), and the presumption of living as God commanded.

Neither this mysticism of the cultural and social margins nor the marginalized themselves are affected by prestige or social visibility. Rather, they are stimulated by the intimacy of a life that blooms in poverty and misery, by a community's passion for asceticism, and the renunciation of suffering through expiation. Offering oneself up to the abject is proof of the renunciation of the worldly.

Marginalized mysticisms are also enclaves of psychic resistance: whoever follows the 'chosen ones' has no real understanding of some of the central ideas of dominant culture: 'fanaticism', 'superstition', 'heresy', 'irrationality'. Such words of condemnation fail to touch them, for the simple reason that they do not live the language that rejects them. This is the advantage of their marginality: to have no idea of how they are considered and judged. They do not know, for example, that according to a hypothesis held by the North American philosopher William James, miracles can also be the most supreme attempts at self-persuasion. In this context, the story of Fidencio and his followers belongs to the most extreme condition of the vanquished: illness in poverty, that slow, continuous bad luck that shelters acts of self-sacrifice which are violent in their self-flagellation, reluctant to despair, avid for the resurrection of souls and bodies.

The Boy Fidencio's litany begins in that place beyond despair.

10

Millenarianisms in Mexico: From Cabora to Chiapas

Behold, the tabernacle of God is with men, and he shall dwell with them and they shall be his peoples, and God himself shall be with them, and be their God: And he shall wipe away every tear from their eyes; and death shall be no more; neither shall there be mourning, nor crying, nor pain, any more: the first things are passed away. (Revelation 21: 3–4)

Millenarianism: faith in the thunder at the end of all time, a form of belief that delegates the meaning of all life to an ever-approaching universal end. In Mexico, a Catholic country, millenarianism is the place where Indian beliefs, which have never been uprooted, come into contact with the cultural effects of The Book of Revelation, whose call to the chosen who are to survive the Last Judgement is the most interpreted and least assimilated in the history of Christianity. The promise of an eternal light-to-come is made by prophets who create micro-religions out of groups of chosen ones, putting themselves forward as the instruments of expiation and grandeur, and organizing a system of disciples that is, for the most part, made up of women. Through these messianic prophets, millenarianism penetrates significant sectors of the population, revealing to them a 'changing sense of life' that religion no longer offers them (or, perhaps, never has). From this point of view, *Guadalupismo* (whose beginnings may be studied in Jacques Lafaye's book *Quetzalcóatl and Guadalupe*) may be thought of as constituting the 'orthodox' Mexican millenarianism. Alongside it, however, there also exists a heterodox millenarianism that has hardly been studied at all, which has emerged from cultural syncretism and been made possible by the persuasive powers of vigorous personalities from the popular classes who have 'seen the Light'. The context is provided by unwritten law. In societies in which the lives of the majority are subject to misery and ignominy, consolation from suffering and frustration is sought in religious practices – and a pact with extraterrestrial forces impregnates native cultures at all levels: economic, social, political and philosophic.

During the colonial period, the discontent of the Indians, anxious to reject the intruders who have taken their land, generates religious cults which, in their own way, express defiance. Hidden away or in semi-clandestinity, taking what interests them from Catholicism and linking it to their old beliefs, the Indians resist racial and economic segregation. The possibilities for such resistance are few, since the Inquisition is alert to such transgression, and a number of 'returns to paganism' are severely – mortally – punished. Because of this ferocious repression, cults that are so numerous elsewhere – for example, the nativist religions of African countries, or the armed prophets of Brazil – take time to make themselves *visible* in Mexico. Personalities with the charisma of Antonio Conselheiro (eternalized by Euclides da Cunha in *Rebellion in the Backlands*), whose intransigent and heroic fanaticism affirms the link between history and cosmogony, emerge only rarely in Mexico.

The Saint of Cabora

In 1880 there is a case of millenarianism in Mexico that quickly moves on to a war footing. Transported by mystic images which, like those of Joan of Arc, set her soul alight, the young Teresa Urrea urges her village to rebel. Very schematically, the story is as follows: in Cabora, state of Sonora, the adolescent Teresa suffers an epileptic fit. When she regains consciousness it is believed that she has risen from the dead, so she is declared a saint. She founds a messianic movement that spreads among Indians and whites living in the villages in the hills of the states of Sonora and Chihuahua. The cult of the Saint of Cabora eventually reaches the Tarahumara village of Tomóchic. In a pilgrimage of villagers to Cabora, the Saint says to one of their elders that he is 'just like Saint Joseph'. On his return, Mr José Carranza is taken for his celestial namesake, and the extension of Christian and pagan rituals rapidly enters a new phase. The village leader, Cruz Chávez, becomes a patriarch and expels the local priest. This aggravates an already difficult situation: on an earlier visit to Tomóchic, the Governor of Chihuahua had been fascinated by the images of Saint Anne and Saint Joaquim painted on an enormous canvas in the church. Having ordered that they be cut down, he takes them to Chihuahua. Angered, the Tomochicans protest and force the Governor to return the images.

Now in conflict with both civil and ecclesiastical authorities, the people of Tomóchic become the objects of a policy of extermination. In 1892 the Fifth Infantry Battalion is sent to force the villagers to submit, but the soldiers are routed. The Ninth Battalion is then sent in. It levels the village, killing all its inhabitants – who die, weapons held aloft, shouting: 'Long live Father Cruz! . . . Long live our Lord! . . . Death to the sons of the devil!'; adding: 'Long live the power of God! Long live the Virgin Mary! Long live the Saint of Cabora!'

The young lieutenant Heriberto Frías tells the story in his novelized chronicle *Tomóchic*, and asks himself through the character of Miguel Mercado, his *alter ego*:

> The Saint of Cabora . . .! Could it have been that little Teresa Urrea – a humble daughter of Northern Sinaloa, bred and nourished in Sonora, in the shadows of sombre ruins, listening to the cries of war and hate of the rebel Yaquis – who had filled the naive and terrible soul of Tomóchic with the delirium of a mysticism ferociously armed with Winchester rifles, and an armour-plated madness inscribed with the words: '*In the Name of the Power of the Lord*'?

Difficulties in the Kingdom of God

How does Utopia affect the habits, certainties and rational projections of a nation or region? More specifically, how does Utopia affect the Right, whose dreams are so often forgotten because, as recent years have shown, there has been a tendency for socialism to represent Utopia? Theocracy and the desire that 'everything should be like before', have also, however, produced their share of utopian movements.

The most notorious Utopia of the Right in twentieth-century Mexico was represented in the *Cristero War* (1926–29), an effect of clerical anger at the policies of the post-Revolutionary State, whose monopolization of power entailed the secularization of education, and thus an anticlerical offensive. The State put a limit on the number of priests in the country, closed down temples, expelled a good number of Spanish priests and nuns, and defied the authority of the Church hierarchy in a variety of ways. The latter responded in any way it could: with clouds of excommunications, a papal bull calling on the faithful to disobey the heretical government, the boycotting of theatres and cinemas, as if to underline the decision of believers not to enjoy themselves in times of persecution (this measure failed – although groups did introduce themselves into cinemas so as to pray aloud during the decisive moments of a film) and with such peremptory actions as the assassination of President-Elect Alvaro Obregón (the assassin's revolver having been blessed by a priest – perhaps to improve its aim). But all this is relatively minor compared to the uprising, following the clarion call of clerics, of a sector of the peasantry, angry at the treatment of its beliefs and at a history of injustice.

In essence – the level which explains their presence (and very probable sacrifice) on the battlefield – the *Cristeros* almost certainly move within a utopian space, sure of having been chosen by God, who watches over their struggle and praises their fervour and devotion. 'Long live Christ the King!': they intend to reinstate the glory of the Kingdom of God so negated by ungodly regimes. And they are as much His children as Hers: 'The Virgin Mary is our protector/Our redeemer/There is nothing to fear./We are Christians/We are Mexicans,/War, war on Lucifer.'

According to Jean Meyer, during the Cristero War the peasant armies marched as if they were taking part in religious processions, and – this is no exaggeration – went into battle as if on a pilgrimage to the sanctuary at Chalma, celebrating Mass, praying and singing songs as if they were glittering shields. They are, of course, as barbaric as their enemies, and more than able to torture and rape teachers they consider 'atheist', cut off the ears of Communists, and execute prisoners without trial. But with their proclamation of Holy War – an orthodox Utopia – they also claim invulnerability. How else can one explain the scapularies or the images of the Virgin of Guadalupe inscribed with the defiant 'Stop, bullet!'?

The rebellion eventually dies out, while the Church hierarchy comes to an agreement with the State behind the backs of the *Cristeros*.

Sinarquists: The blood of the martyrs

During the 1930s, and influenced both by the Cristero War and Spanish Falangism, the second great utopian moment of the twentieth-century Mexican Right emerges: Sinarquism (meaning the opposite of anarchism: *with* order). It celebrates sacrifice, opposes the atheistic State, and sympathizes with Fascism (although it does later distance itself from Nazism).

The mystique of the crucified Redeemer is very real to the peasant sinarquists. In honour of their belief, they ratify a 'Plebiscite of Martyrs', and resist both government repression and the eventual desertion of their urban leadership. To avoid disintegration many decide, without further ado, to build a utopian community. Led by Salvador Abascal, a few thousand faithful undertake the creation of a Kingdom of God, and in 1942 they travel to Southern Baja California to found the *Santa María Auxiliadora* Colony. The rules and aims are very precise: they will exemplify, for all the world to see, the life of true, pure, stainless Catholics who have left behind all the temptations of the age. The whole enterprise is grounded in a devout madness, but there is something moving about its pathetic failure. Abascal is a mystic who refuses to admit even the slightest deviation. He insists on daily communion and confession, demands a dress code that refuses all temptation – even in the most devastating of temperatures – and preaches endlessly to the converted, making the community pray for hours so that heaven will not punish them for the possible presence of a single adulterer. Unfortunately, their orthodoxy is not synonymous with efficiency. The chosen land is barren, the harvest is late, the heat weighs heavier than sin, the supplies collapse, and eventually there is discontent (a man pisses in front of his family, and on being reprimanded, shouts at the leader – who locks himself away to pray).

The project fails, and the sinarquists of *Santa María Auxiliadora* are saved from disaster only by the territory's Jacobin Governor, Francisco J. Múgica. Abascal returns to Mexico City convinced of the iniquity of the world. The Right's will to forget, meanwhile, is brought into operation. But decades later, towards the end of the 1970s, another such Utopia emerges – not so much the Kingdom of God as the reinstatement of theocracy. A priest, who will eventually call himself Father Nabor, finds fertile terrain among the local families of a village in the state of Michoacán. He begins to convert them. They must abandon what he portrays as a soft impious Catholicism, and practise the Saintly Religion as it should be practised. The bishopric is slightly opposed at first, but Father Nabor does not relent, and the idea returns: to re-create one of those turn-of-the-nineteenth-century villages which Agustín Yáñez describes in his extraordinary novel *Al filo del agua* ['The Edge of the Storm'], and return to a life centred around Mass, confession, spiritual exercises, seclusion, devout flagellation, the persecution of the devil in one's own conduct and in the conduct of others, the elimination of non-procreative sexual activity – not without first regretting that the desires of the flesh are so closely related to the reproduction of the species.

Father Nabor is radical. The village will be called New Jerusalem, and the women will wear special robes – like the ones worn by the contemporaries of Jesus Christ in a movie that Father Nabor saw, probably *El mártir del Gólgota* ['The Martyr of Golgotha']; the regime will be strict, and the rhythms of Mass will punctuate the life of the village. The bishopric of Morelia attempts to negotiate a way back to normality, but is rejected. There is mistrust of strangers who, on occasion, are refused entry to the village – this includes the mass media, who probably come only to mock the Middle Ages anyway. In neighbouring villages, obviously suffering the ills of secularization, the fall of Father Nabor's theocracy is predicted. Some flee, while others join the migratory flow to the United States. In response, a regressive Utopia is imposed: television sets are prohibited, Marianite hymns are all that may be heard in the streets – the village vibrates during Holy Week – drowning out the surrounding mockery. What distinguishes this kind of Utopia is suspicion for the outside, self-enclosure, a form of discipline that completely disallows such contemporary evils as videos, and a devotion that takes from Mass and prayer the weapons with which to resist the Evil One.

As is so often the case, Father Nabor's main support comes from women, who persuade the men of the benefits and advantages of not being up to date, and of completely forgetting the existence of fashion. Revolution and migration have been the most important factors that have destroyed the spiritual resources of the people over the last century, while the failures of the *Cristeros* and *Sinarquistas* demonstrate how impossible islands of purity are in a world trampled underfoot by the cult of Progress, that other 'mark of the Beast'. On the other hand, this is what makes for the novelty of New Jerusalem, so entrenched in the existential remains of peasant tradition: even today, perhaps because it has not been reported on television, it survives crises and desertions. Utopia and messianism: the willingness of the soul, discipline, the regimentation of hope, the link with the sacred established through banners and sermons, the tension whereby the political becomes part of the same prayer as rosary beads.

The proletarian vanguard

During the years of armed conflict the Mexican Revolution possessed a mystique provided mainly by the Zapatista and Villista peasantry. The former was especially important, sustained by a myth – communal property in the land – of a Golden Age, and guided by the utopian temperament of Emiliano Zapata himself, who famously refused to sit in the Presidential Chair (due to a fetishistic fear of temptation?), and coined the now famous slogan 'The land belongs to those who work it'. The Constitution of the Republic of 1917, however, is the great founding text, traversed by what was desired as well as what was possible, by what had been conquered and what was still to be done. Then, in practice, such contradictions were dissolved by the cult of Progress which – at least since the 1940s – has been taken to mean consumer society. And the Mexican Revolution, now a set of institutions and coded memories, occupied centre stage, sub-ordinating all other myths and enthusiasms. In such a context the Communists can do very little, only ever managing to convince a few thousand to sacrifice themselves for their socialist Utopia.

From 1919 – the year of the foundation of the Mexican Communist Party – to 1968, the taking of power never really figures among the genuine ambitions of the Left – a declaration of such an intimate modesty that not even the Cuban Revolution could change. In 1968, the student movement persuades hundreds of thousands of people to support its demand for the end (or at least, a lessen-ing) of authoritarianism, and believe that change is possible. Utopian energies are condensed into one phrase: 'Here a new country is emerging'. There is no demand for a New Man, as in Cuba, but for the total transformation of the country. The repression unleashed by the government of Gustavo Díaz Ordaz, which culminates in the massacre at the *Plaza de las Tres Culturas* ['The Square of Three Cultures' or 'Tlatelolco Square'], cancels out such utopian inklings, however, and displaces and imprisons them in a desperate urban guerrilla war-fare in which hundreds of middle-class youths pretend to blast power away with bank robberies and kidnappings. Che Guevara's prophesied Vietnams do not appear, so the Left desists from its prophetic vocation, swapping it for a grad-ualism which, in the event, allows it neither to advance nor to dissolve.

By the 1980s, neo-liberalism – or whatever you want to call the legitimizing strategy of savage capitalism – proposes a mass dream that imagines territories and peoples free from the stigma of underdevelopment. With the fall of the Berlin Wall and the official end of the Cold War, an attempt is made to infuse the term 'free market' with the properties of a totem presiding over an eternal social system. Apart from its own specific meaning, the idea is now held aloft as if it were the banner of a sovereign ideology, making prehistory of all that has gone before it, and of the links established between production and consump-tion, its reality principle. Simultaneously, neo-liberalism also promotes the bad reputation of utopias (even of the term 'Utopia' itself, which is soon identified, in the best of cases, with *science fiction*).

In Latin America 'enterprise thinking' makes of the lot of the privileged few, the only conceivable future, a new order in which the glories of capitalism fulfil the same function as the Last Judgement. The Right believes itself to have been victorious – indeed, to embody victory itself; and businessmen, once somewhat cautious in their responses to demands for social justice, now extol the credo of monopolistic accumulation with a fervour once reserved for Maoists in the 1960s and 1970s. The electronic media are awash with the ideology of free and unrestricted trade, and a *new faith in change* is promoted: where before there was talk of *equality*, now it is a question of *Christian charity*, where once it was *the interests of the people*, it is now *popular capitalism*, and the verb *to privatize* has superseded *to nationalize*.

The Utopia of this century – that which has been desired above all else, and desired most deeply – has been the modernization of body and soul. This is why, without any deliberation other than that of industrial or post-industrial intent, the ideology of savage capitalism pretends to the rank of a religious cult, replacing the dream of revolution. In their speeches, worshippers of the free market rehearse the intolerance and hatred once associated with Stalinism. Each new political watchword – for example, *Total Quality* – becomes in Mexico a clarion call for spiritual reorganization. And since 1991, the signing of the Free Trade Treaty has unleashed para-religious frenzy among industrialists and bureaucrats: this (they say) is our chance for the Big Change, a Utopia to which *we* have a right. Efficiency and productivity become not only the requirement of industrial survival but a call for the rescue of the new Holy Grail, Growth, now in the hands of the faithless whose major heresy is unproductivity. This story is told in a number of ways: Mexico needs new men, a better attitude, and the goals of *Total Quality* will help to produce them. Once upon a time, the Mexican man slept under an enormous hat next to a cactus and a donkey thinking about Lupita, Juanita, Rosita and Teresita (while the Mexican woman warmed up tortillas by the fire . . . but who cares about this image?). Not any more. Such archaisms have been supplanted by the new Utopia, a present from Japan, of industry as a family. The idea of Mexico belonging to the First World is, without a doubt, the most important Utopia for bourgeois and middle-class sectors. The First World: the great car factory of the soul. In the name of the (evident) failure of socialism, neo-liberals seek to erase all dissidence, and represent what is happening (the cruelties of the concentration of wealth) as what must happen. The businessman Lorenzo Servitje produces a text which, in its own way, is a classic of such arrogance: 'Inequality: An Uncomfortable Point of View', in which he almost sanctifies those who 'have the uncommon ability of increasing our disposable goods'. Servitje says:

> The ability of these people to create and accumulate wealth generates a social and economic inequality that causes resentment among those who do not. There is a feeling of injustice that governments frequently try to correct by taking away from those who have and giving to those who have not. Such redistribution works in the short term. Soon, however, the productive sector that made the existence of surplus resources possible slacken or even suspend

their efforts, and society as a whole suffers. From a Christian or humanistic point of view, it may very well be noble and good that such productive, even wealthy, groups dedicate the fruits of their savings to others and live modestly. But it is very unlikely that in real life this would occur. Historical experience teaches us that the resulting economic inequality is a minor evil with which we must live and, therefore, accept.

Migration: the Utopia without documents

The dream is over. The echoes of Gorbachev's definition resound: 'Socialism is the Utopia imposed by a dictatorial regime.' The invitation to stop dreaming is categorical, and pragmatism, it is suggested, should take its place.

Horror at the future entails the restructuring of Utopia, so that the powers of literary and cinematic prophecy are taken over by visions that are mournful and terminal. Such an elemental operation needs great books and films: if there is no convincing positive Utopia, if what is to come is so devastating, the ability to dream concentrates on what is. And what is, is the certainties of the nuclear family, the planetary enjoyment of credit cards and migration to the new Cities of God or of the Sun. For some time now, but especially in recent years, migration has constituted something like the massive return of utopian-like but prestigeless anxieties in which Asians, Africans, Arabs, and Latin Americans designate North America a comparative paradise, risk the future of their children and grandchildren in the crossing of a frontier, and suffer countless hardships so that, once arrived at their destination, they can suffer countless hardships.

The classic Utopia has two mirrors. In one is reflected the sad, grey, threadbare present in which the person (reader, viewer) contemplates the extermination of all possibility; in the other, resplendent one lies the future in which freedom has become the principle that abundantly satisfies necessity. And its realization is just around the corner. Although it is not expressed in the same words, the significance of the migrant's action possesses the radical qualities of that Utopia. They are not going to hoist the flag of the Kingdom of God, nor are they going to build a workers' paradise, nor eliminate injustice. They will, however, at least shake off the chains of a recognized lack of future, and hand down to their descendants the treasure of social mobility – if they are lucky enough to find it. Travelling in order to put down roots. To plan, extirpating the evil chance that is destiny – not society's, but that of one's own family. The migratory Utopia, individual and collective, familial and regional, conceives of the planet in eternal effervescence – Whitmanian or Nerudian – awaiting the strong arms and agile minds that know just how to adapt to the right place.

Market utopias

Is there a return to religion in Latin America which, unthinkable twenty years ago, includes a new dimension of growing diversification? Protestantism, or the so-called 'sects', especially Pentecostal groups, have grown massively throughout Mexico, Central America, Brazil, Puerto Rico and Venezuela, alarming Catholic hierarchies and disseminating the belief that new millenarianisms have replaced the old utopias.

This growth in popular religion, which finds an echo even among academics, does not include on its agenda anything like total transformation but, rather, a transformation of a well-fenced-off 'spiritual life'. What is also clearly on the increase is the search for individual salvation, through one of the thousands of religious alternatives on offer: esotericism, self-help manuals or supermarket Zen. Never have so many, both individually and collectively, placed their trust in so many beliefs. Today, it would seem, those who have never converted to something have never really believed in anything.

The historical utopias are in their death throes, attempting to survive merely on the strength of their authoritarianism. But the reasons for their existence remain. According to George Steiner, the realities of actually existing socialism were kept in the dark because of a terrible overvaluation of people's capacity for altruism, purity, and philosophical and intellectual thought. This needs qualification. The ideal of 'purity' is fatally associated with the Inquisitorial turn of mind that prosecutes dissidents; but altruism remains alive, as do collective goals that are not subordinated to the free market. In this regard Czeslaw Milosz has written:

> The failure of Marx's dream has created the need for another, not the rejection of all dreams, [but a need to be] concerned for society, civilization and humanity in an age in which the nineteenth-century idea of progress has become exhausted, and another idea associated with it, communist revolution, has disintegrated.

In practice, towards the end of this century, Utopia may be defined as the freedom to dream, in which the stimuli for action and pleasurable fantasy alike occupy the spaces of the oppressive inertia of everyday life. If, in everyday speech, the *utopian* is associated with what is *unrealizable* ('What you are saying is frankly utopian!'), 'Utopia' still signifies the will to create, on the basis of everyday behaviour, images of another reality. In the midst of the declared end of all utopias, the point has been reached where the most voluntaristic of gestures is considered a utopian prefiguration.

In politics, one of the main guarantees of the credibility of a project is making sure that it has no utopian content. Pragmatism is foregrounded, as is a vigilant eye for the concrete, not to mention a healthy distance from the excesses of the past, in which people killed and died for causes that had little to do with their immediate needs – they were simply causes. Patriotisms are extinguished by the suspicion of any will to sacrifice; and cynicism, once a disposition held by a few, now emerges triumphant amid the waves of disenchantment. It is not the most desirable of dispositions, people say, but it is a useful antidote against the previous danger, the search for purity.

Be realistic. Demand the impossible

Where might we find utopian enclaves today? I glimpse them in bursts, instants, in movements that may be found in civil society, in the reactions of public opinion, in the coherence of small groups, in the work of rural and urban collectives, in counter-cultural gestures and critiques. Which are, so to speak, phrases prefiguring a language, actions whose essential meaning is their persistence. They are mainly attitudes that have originated in a need to make room for what can be demanded both socially and ethically. One important break with the past is the rejection of the founding slogan of intolerance: the ends justify the means.

I believe that utopianism lies not in intentions, however praiseworthy, but in the articulation of language. The utopian question is a simple one: what possibilities today lie beyond reality? Each Utopia constitutes a hypothesis about human behaviour that attempts to be objective, and adequate to a reality conceived not as inexorable but, rather, as a concatenation of events.

To safeguard the idea of legitimate causes that entail, in whatever order of things, the transformation of the world. This is the deep rationale of today's utopian language, whose demiurgic strength is modestly concentrated in the mere possibility of its existence. The main achievement of utopians is, in an environment that admits only of the most immediate and the most pragmatic, the continuation of their own thought. If the word 'revolutionary' must now be put in inverted commas, awaiting semantic clarification, the word 'Utopia' is still based on the demand for radical change, and the first of these, towards this end of the twentieth century, is of a political character without sectarian subtexts. Today, a utopian language framed by fanaticism is impossible; and caution and modesty are demanded before the City of God, Erewhon, the phalansteries, Campanella's Taprobana, Francis Bacon's Christianopolis – which, on being realized, became an Isle Barataria or, sadly, a prison camp.

Persuading by example

How do utopians speak today? They insist on the realism and legitimacy of their project, endorsed by the consequences of their actions. It is not a question of changing human beings totally but, rather, of opening up spaces for humanism and social justice. For example: the action of ecological groups, their resistance to the pillaging of ecosystems – decisions that have led dozens of people to chain themselves up in protest against the atrocious extermination of whales and seals. This is also to oppose human degradation at a time when the consequences of such reckless extermination of whole species are very well known. But – and this is the most persuasive aspect of utopian language – the essential meaning of the message lies in the attitude. The witness to such acts must answer the question: What drives people to concern themselves so much, and with such tenacity, with the fate of animals? Simply to ask the question in a society so lacking in moral criteria, not to mention responsibility, is an important first step.

Look, too, at the work of AIDS activists with those who are HIV-positive: the struggle to obtain respect for their basic rights from the repressive social and moral powers-that-be, and the putting into practice of healthcare policies that may help to prevent the spread of the disease. Surrounded by fear and panic, their cause is not popular – to say the least – and the situation is made even more difficult when the fact that most activists are also HIV-positive themselves is taken into account. But they insist, and their actions are utopian because they disprove (so well-proven) pessimistic statements about the behaviour of human beings confronted with imminent death – if not their own, then that of many of their friends. Against such pessimism, these activists, all over the world, oppose the utopian perspective of an extreme altruism made everyday – not an exception, but the norm.

The case of human rights activists, so important recently in Latin America, must be mentioned here too: people whose consciences have been wounded by the brutality of repressive regimes. They are mothers and fathers, religious and professional people, people who feel the need to organize their indignation and respond to that new language that sees in ethical correctness the cornerstone of a civilizing project. Human rights activists have persisted when everything else worked against them; they have investigated and denounced, and endowed their rejection of silence and forgetting with political significance. And in doing so – although this is hardly recognized – they reconstruct the very possibility of Utopia, so damaged in this century by those who have tried to build it on a grand scale, and not only in the countries of actually existing socialism. Why do

I foreground the utopian quality of these actions and thoughts? Because today the desire for happiness, the projection of today into the future, has both expanded and contracted. Outside the space of religion (and even here), the millenarian kingdom is receding. What should follow is that the rejection of injustice becomes a matter for all. Today there is no need for theological explanation; the role of sin has been taken over by impunity.

Outside, I insist, of its religious content – so present in Marxist utopias – there is an ongoing secularization of Utopia, centred on the equal distribution of the right to hope. When everything, even the dead weight of yesterday's utopias, conspires to see the real in the irrational and the irrational in the real (and because, on top of the justified discredit of the myth of Progress, people are ready to discredit reason itself for the monsters it produces in its nightmares), once again the real is in fact rational and the rational is real.

Chiapas and the end of the millennium

What does it mean to talk about the 'end of utopias' from the point of view of the economically marginalized? For millions of people, very distanced from revolutionary preaching, such an 'end' hardly makes sense, for they deposit the creative sense of their verification of the real in survival, in the world of the next twenty-four hours. But that is in the cities. In the countryside, and in the Indian world (which includes eight to ten million people), the situation is different. At dawn on 1 January 1994 a group of almost one thousand guerrillas, the Zapatista National Liberation Army (EZLN), entered the town of San Cristóbal de las Casas, in the state of Chiapas. Some wore balaclavas; all wore a uniform consisting of olive-green trousers, coffee-brown shirt, bright scarf and rubber boots. At the same time, the EZLN occupied three other towns: Ocosingo, Altamirano and Las Margaritas. In their Declaration of War, or *Manifesto from the Lacandon Jungle*, the Zapatistas, classically, invited the population to rise up against the Mexican Army, the 'bastion of dictatorship'. In San Cristóbal the spokesperson of the EZLN, who goes by the name of Subcommander Marcos, justifies the uprising on the basis of the exhaustion of all – by which he means 'very limited' – legal means. The projects to increase productivity, and the National Solidarity Programme (PRONASOL) – President Salinas's scheme to alleviate social inequalities – have failed, he says. He also affirms: 'The decision to rise up in arms today responds to the fact that it is the day the Free Trade Treaty comes into effect, which represents a death sentence for the Indian peoples of Mexico, who are dispensable for the government of Carlos Salinas.' In the square in San Cristóbal, surrounded by tourists, Subcommander Marcos is unequivocal:

> This is a subversive movement. Our objective is the solution of the principal problems facing our country, related necessarily to problems of freedom and democracy. This is why we think that the government of Salinas de Gortari is an illegitimate one that can only call for illegitimate elections. The only solution is a call to all citizens and to the Chamber of Deputies and Senators to fulfil their duty and depose Salinas de Gortari and his cabinet, and form a transitional government. And that such a transitional government then call for elections in equality of circumstances for all parties.

The Zapatistas then launch three attacks on an army barracks, and during the weeks that follow there are a number of ferocious battles, especially in Ocosingo and Las Margaritas, with an indeterminate number of dead and wounded (probably more than three hundred), and actions mounted by the Armed Forces that provoke a series of complaints from human rights organizations. Municipal palaces are destroyed, archives burnt, prisoners freed, and more than 20,000 people flee their villages. . . . In their declarations, the Zapatistas oscillate between new attitudes (they are the first who do not want power, but a transition to democracy) and the cultish revolutionary harangues reminiscent of the 1960s: 'Down with the bourgeois government/End capitalism/Build socialism in Mexico now'. The newspapers and television programmes are full of images of the dead and wounded, of bodies that are not buried for days, of aeroplanes dropping what we all suppose are bombs – which, according to the army, are rockets – of a Zapatista with a wooden rifle, of child guerrillas. (Subcommander Marcos explains: 'In the poor areas of Chiapas, children mature very quickly. They start work very young.')

It is emerging now, bit by bit, that the EZNL was the product of a very complex process indeed. Members of clandestine movements (for example, the *Frente de Liberación Nacional* – the National Liberation Front) come to the region of Las Cañadas from other areas, and gradually make contact with Indian communities whose confidence they gain, thanks to their relationship with catechists from the diocese of San Cristóbal, where Bishop Samuel Ruiz has ceded ecclesiastical power to the communities and supported Liberation Theology. Only a few non-Indians remain in Las Cañadas, slowly preparing the insurrection. On 12 October 1992, while the Quincentenary – not of the Discovery any more, but of the Encounter of Two Worlds – is celebrated, a strange army invades San Cristóbal: five thousand Indians armed with bows and arrows demonstrate, knock down a statue of the conquistador Diego de Mazariegos, pronounce anti-government speeches, and leave.

In 1993 there are a number of clashes between guerrillas and the Armed Forces. The existence of armed groups is reported, but the authorities think they are very weak, and take little notice.

Enough!

Surprise at the existence of the EZNL is total. No one, outside the affected areas, thought the existence of a guerrilla army possible: it represented an alternative that had been liquidated internationally. Although the Zapatista Army denies having a perfectly defined ideology (in the sense of being Communist or Marxist–Leninist), in the first two weeks one idea does prevail among politicians, intellectuals and journalists in Mexico City: that the EZLN is a mixture of ex-Maoists and supporters of Liberation Theology. The government responds with an instantaneous counter-claim: it is a matter of two hundred mainly monolingual (non-Spanish-speaking) 'lawbreakers', whose base of support is the diocese of San Cristóbal. The claims are legalistic and nationalist: 'They are the last remnants of a conspiracy against the army'; 'They are foreigners with guerrilla experience who have tricked a number of Indians'; 'They are leftovers from the wars in Central America'. The sentence is passed: violence breeds violence. On 6 January, in his New Year message to the nation, Salinas de Gortari calls the Zapatistas 'professionals of violence', and to those who are not too involved he offers – not without conditions – a possible pardon.

After the first shock of recognition, a new understanding of the Zapatista phenomenon emerges. One phrase in particular begs attention. On 1 January they say 'Enough!' and the expression, otherwise so common, resonates throughout the nation – not to mention in Chiapas, a state with abundant natural resources and extreme poverty, where welfare and educational programmes do not function.

In Chiapas 15,000 people a year die of curable diseases; it boasts 90 per cent of all cases of trachoma in the whole country (mainly in the municipality of Ocosingo), 50 per cent illiteracy, 34 per cent of the communities have no electricity; there is one doctor per 1,500 people; the State's Penal Code punishes murder with six years of imprisonment and the stealing of a cow with eight. To this must be added the economic collapse of the region due mainly to the fall in coffee prices, the ecological destruction in the Lacandon Jungle, the lowest salaries in the country (if they are in fact paid at all, since many are given alcoholic beverages instead). And, at the centre of all this, a racism so persuasive that it is only since the 1970s that Indians have been allowed to walk on the pavements in San Cristóbal. And racism is evident from the very first days of the conflict. The synonym of Indian is 'monolingual', and their condition, according to the authorities, is of being 'easily tricked'. On 18 January, for example, Mr Eloy Cantú, an important official in the Ministry of Interior, declares: 'The leaders of the Zapatista Army do not aim to satisfy or vindicate the social demands of the population, so it clearly is not an insurgent Indian movement. If it were, they would be armed with machetes. . . .'

The document which most influences new perspectives among the social movements of civil society and public opinion is Subcommander Marcos's communiqué of 18 January 1994. I reproduce it almost in its entirety because it unexpectedly moves huge sectors of the population – including the poet Octavio Paz, who is otherwise very critical of Zapatismo – and because it summarizes the EZLN's indictment of the government:

It is only today, 18 January 1994, that we have heard of the federal government's offer of a formal 'pardon' for our forces. But what do we have to beg pardon for? What are we going to be pardoned for? For not dying of hunger? For not keeping quiet about our poverty? For not accepting with humility the gigantic historical weight of hatred and abandon? For rising up in arms when all other paths have been blocked? For not being bound by the Penal Code of Chiapas, the most absurd and repressive in memory? For showing to the rest of the country and the whole world that human dignity is still alive and is located among the poorest of its population? For having prepared ourselves well and conscientiously at the outset? For carrying guns into battle rather than bows and arrows? For having learnt how to fight before doing so? For being Mexican, all of us? For being mainly Indians? For calling on all Mexicans to fight, in whatever forms possible, for what belongs to us? For fighting for freedom, democracy, and justice? For not following the patterns of previous guerrilla forces? For not surrendering? For not selling out? For not betraying ourselves? Who must ask for pardon, and who is in a position to grant it? Those who, for years, have sat at tables full enough to more than satisfy them while we sat with death, a death so much ours, so everyday, that we were no longer afraid of it? Those who filled our bags and souls with declarations and promises? The dead, our dead, so mortally dead from 'natural' deaths, that is, from measles, influenza, cholera, typhoid, tetanus, pneumonia, malaria and other gastrointestinal and pulmonary pleasantries? Our dead, the majority of dead, so democratically dead from grief because no one lifted a finger, because all the dead, our dead, just went, without anyone taking notice, without anyone saying finally 'ENOUGH!', so as to restore meaning to those deaths, without anyone asking the dead of always, our dead, that they return to die again, but this time so as to live? Those who denied our people the right to govern and govern us? Those who had no respect for our customs, colour or language? Those who treat us like foreigners in our own country and ask for our papers and our obedience to laws of whose existence and justice we have no knowledge? Those who have tortured, imprisoned, murdered and disappeared us for the grave 'crime' of wanting a piece of land – not a big piece, not a small piece, just a piece big enough to get enough out of it to fill our stomachs? Who must ask for pardon? And who is in a position to grant it?

The moral persuasion of the Zapatistas is based on the Indian character of the rebellion, however much the government tries to deny it throughout the whole of January. Five hundred and one years after the Conquest, the Indian question returns forcefully to a society that had thought the issue long buried in the mists of pre-modernity. Suddenly, the general awareness of racism in Mexico, the pride in the Indian within us all, the real or theatrical guilt for the abandonment and marginalization of ten million of the country's people, become one important question: why have we not given any importance to the inequality and brutal exploitation of our familiars? Remember that in Mexico City alone, two million Indians live in very adverse circumstances. There are nearly two million in Chiapas as well.

Finding a language

If the first week of January brings both surprise and recognition, the second brings a consensus across parties and social classes: the Indian rebellion is to be explained by the intolerable conditions in the area, and the fact that towards the end of the century no modernization project could do anything for the sixty million poor in the country. Civil society (an imprecise term which includes non-governmental organizations, feminists, trade unions, intellectual and academic sectors and, very importantly, a number of publications) opposes the policy option of military annihilation and demands political solutions instead. On 7 January a peace demonstration in Mexico City attracts more than 100,000 people. A series of further actions follows across the country, while the sales of trustworthy newspapers increases dramatically (*La Jornada* sells 160,000 a day, the weekly *Proceso* more than 300,000, and there are even queues to buy them).

There is widespread rejection of the biased news provided by *Televisa*, which is accused of manipulating and distorting the facts. And the government gives in: President Salinas orders a unilateral cease-fire and sends an amnesty proposal for those involved in the Chiapas rebellion to the Congress. And a moment of free expression is experienced by all, and no one abstains from expressing their opinion. And a language believed to have disappeared returns, one inspired both by the Christian Old Testament and by the Mayan *Popol Vuh* and *Chilam Bayam of Chumayel* – in the version of Subcommander Marcos, the most outstanding figure of the EZLN. Interviewed continuously, he also sends letters and documents to the newspapers, suddenly becoming one of the most widely read writers in Mexico. Here is one of his texts:

> In our voice shall travel the voice of others, of those who have nothing, those condemned to silence and ignorance, those thrown off their land and from history by the arrogance of the powerful, of all those good men and women who walk these lands of pain and anger, of the children and aged dead of abandonment and solitude, of humiliated women, of little men. Through our voice will speak the dead, our dead, so alone and forgotten, so dead and yet so alive in our voices and in our footsteps. . . . We will demand what, by right and by reason, belongs to all: liberty, justice, democracy. Everything for everyone. Nothing for us. . . . Receive our blood brothers, so that so much death shall not be in vain, and so that truth may return to our lands.

From the start, one term, *millenarian*, is repeated – first as an accusation, then as a description. Towards the end of the century an army of four to ten thousand rises to challenge a regular army of 144,000, demanding the resignation of the President of the Republic and the overthrow of the political system. It then accepts negotiations with Bishop Samuel Ruiz as intermediary, and wages a propaganda war. Curiously – or not so curiously – the homily-like language, not without points of coincidence with that of the Canudos, the deliberately archaic language, the announcement of catastrophes and sadness among the long-lost gods, immediately acquires an audience of millions. Octavio Paz describes this as the 'Victory of literature: thanks to his undeniable rhetorical and theatrical talents, Subcommander Marcos has won the battle for public opinion.'

Between the two extremes of the interpretation of millenarianism, the Zapatistas in their balaclavas, are the voice, in public conscience, both of the past (what was ignored and exploited) and of the future (what is to come in recompense for past forgetting and postponements). As the negotiations at the Cathedral of San Cristóbal begin, Marcos reads a speech that arouses the enthusiasm of many:

When we came down from the mountains carrying our rucksacks, our dead and our history, we came to the town in search of our country [patria]; the country that had forgotten us in the farthest, most solitary, poorest, dirtiest corner of the nation. We came to ask the country, our country, why it had left us there with so many dead and for so many years? And we want, through you [the assembled press], to ask once again why it was necessary to kill and die so that you – and through you, the rest of the world – could listen to Ramona say such terrible things as that Indian women want to live, to study, to have hospitals, justice and dignity? Why was it necessary to kill and die so that Ramona could come and so you could listen to what she has to say? Why is it necessary that Laura, Ana María, Irma, Silvia and so many other Indian women have had to arm themselves, become soldiers, rather than university graduates, doctors, engineers, teachers? We came to the town and found this flag, our flag. . . . And we saw that a country lives under this flag; not the country that is forgotten in books and museums, but the only, painful, hopeful, living country. Why must we sleep with our boots on and with one eye open in order to defend this flag? Why do we climb over mountains and canyons, through valleys and jungles, and along roads and tracks carrying and protecting this flag? Why do we carry it with us as the only hope of democracy, freedom and justice? Why do weapons accompany this flag, our flag, day and night? Why? And we want to ask you whether there is another way to live under this flag, another way of living under this flag with dignity and justice. You have said yes; you have talked to us with honest words, with heartfelt words that say: give peace a chance. We have received your message and we have come here with honest and true intentions. We do not come bringing two hearts, there are no dark forces hidden behind us, nor have we come looking for anything else than to talk and listen without our weapons. . . . If there is another way to the same place, the place where this flag flies over democracy, freedom and justice, show us the way. We shall not risk the blood of our comrades. If it is possible that this flag, our flag, your flag, can be raised with dignity, without blooding the earth in which it is planted, so be it. We will open that door and march with other steps. If it is possible that neither weapons nor armies are necessary any longer, that blood and fire are not necessary to cleanse history, all well and good. But if not, and the doors are closed again? And if words are unable to climb the wall of arrogance and misunderstanding? And if the peace is not a dignified nor real one, who, we ask, will deny us the sacred right to live and die like dignified and true men and women? Who will stop us then from dressing again for war and death so as to walk the road of history? Who?

11

'Red News': The Crime Pages in Mexico

The crime or police information pages, the 'red news', have been endowed with a number of functions in Mexico. They provide the reader with a marvellous opportunity to leaf through pages in which 'normality' is frozen into poses by photos that welcome him or her into a world of death and scandal. The crime story generates a morbidity that is aimed at exorcizing urban violence. It encourages a kind of retrospection that imagines the climactic moments – the day before the wake – when passions were let loose, when madness, greed, jealousy and lechery, a total loss of control, provided the rationale for unexpected desire.

Until recently, crime stories were supposed to transform tragedy into spectacle, spectacle into moralistic warning, warning into fun ('relajo'), and fun into the stories of a collectivity. This is why readers, spectators and gossips all compare their reactions to the latest reports (the crime of the season!), and rejoice in the lack of opportunity that frees them from being carried away by sex, money, or just plain 'evil perversion'. What a relief not to find oneself behind the sumptuous façades portrayed in Agatha Christie novels, where crime is the continuation of the family by other means. What joy! Wealth, for her sincerest readers, produces a labyrinthine impression in which victims and murderers are found to be the forking branches of the same genealogical tree. Or the unexpected threatens: a mentally deranged person may suddenly cross the path of someone just like you; one day a young couple open the door confidently, letting in the evil that will be their downfall – a crime which, on exhibiting their intimacy, will blow it up to enormous, sinful proportions.

Criminal violence has periodically set the limits of the protected city, throwing an adventurous light on the taste for crime stories, conversation pieces which become the joyous proof that the reader or commentator is still alive, free, and more or less intact. Like it or not, the 'red news' constitutes one of Mexico's greatest novels, from which everyone may retain the fragmentary memory that typifies for them an idea of crime, corruption, and plain bad luck.

On the hierarchies and justifications of crime

At the turn of the century, the crime story was not very profitable. How could it compete with the Revolution, with its own repertoire of battles, executions, ambushes, murders – with everything that then went by the name of History? The most important criminal episodes of the period were the activities of the Grey Automobile Mob, an organization which is fascinating mainly because of its links to that other subject of the Mexican Revolution, the military, which simultaneously represented the law and protected the underworld. And whatever the fascination exercised by other events in the crime pages (for example, the ex-Miss Mexico who killed her husband, fed up with abuse; or the murder of the high-society lady Chinta Aznar), they are only a parenthesis in the all-embracing concern to monitor the shifts and changes among the different fractions of the Revolution.

As the post-Revolutionary institutions are strengthened, society turns more and more to the 'red news'. It felt right once more to dramatize the surprise felt at transgression (of Morality, of Decency, of conventional class and family relations). As the threat of peasant armies dissipates, the taste for crime stories, the (perverse) fairy stories that only a few days ago were horrendous crimes, increases. Read all about it:

- On 17 April 1929, Luis Romero Carrasco kills two uncles and their two maids (one of advanced age, the other a mere girl) and the parrot. His defence lawyers allege that the murderer, a heavy marijuana smoker, suffered from manic hallucinations. He is condemned to death, and on his way to the Islas Marías prison he is shot 'while attempting to escape', just as described by José Revueltas in his first novel, *Los muros de agua* ['Walls of Water'];
- On 23 October 1945, a gang led by Fermín Esquerro Farfán breaks into the house of Angel, Miguel and María Villar Lledías. They murder the first two and violently beat María who, at fifty-eight, is the younger sister. The case is not solved in court, so the Attorney General of the Federal District of Mexico City, Francisco Castellanos, anxious to find a guilty party, accuses the survivor. Judge Ferrer MacGregor sentences María for the crime of robbery with violence (thus inaugurating a glorious career: he later sentences Demetrio Vallejo and other Railway Union leaders to thirty years in prison

for 'an attempt against the social order', and in 1980 reaches the summit of his notoriety attempting to bribe Judge Darío Maldonado in Mazatlán to free a heroin dealer working for police chief Arturo Durazo Moreno). From prison, María Villar Lledías offers a reward of 50 thousand pesos to anyone who can supply information about the murderers; the offer sparks the memory of someone who refused to be an accomplice. The case attracted attention mainly for its obsessive characteristics: a family of misers unprotected by a fortune, then calculated at 20 million pesos. The Villar Lledías, in their house at 66 Republic of Salvador, without servants, radio or television, given over to an ascetic discipline, had surrounded themselves with money (stuffed in mattresses or hidden under the floorboards), antique gold and silver coins, pearl necklaces, sapphire earrings, platinum bracelets studded with emeralds. . . . The choice of poverty amid huge accumulated wealth is a fascinating subject, to which is added the inevitable stories about looting by the police;

- The infamous sex-strangler Goyo Cárdenas, the Mixcoac Murderer. On 8 September 1942 the press breaks the news about the crimes of Gregorio Cárdenas Hernández, a twenty-seven-year-old chemistry student. Goyo hanged four women – his girlfriend and three prostitutes – and buried them in the little garden of his house. *Stop press!* The exhumation of the bodies becomes front-page news. Here is the first *serial killer* who kills for the simple pleasure of killing; here, the criminal (of whose intelligence there is no doubt!) is up against the rigour of the law embodied in the criminologist Alfonso Quiroz Cuarón; here is the painful excavation that offers up decomposed bodies to a horrified society; here is the laboratory of the murderous 'alchemist'; and here is his clearly psychoanalysable declaration: 'They were street-walkers . . . and I offered them money, took them home and had my way with them. Then – I don't know what came over me, what I felt. It was horrible! I felt an awful hatred towards these women, towards all women, an inexplicable frenzy. . . . An uncontrollable urge to destroy, to tear, to kill. . . . And I killed them!' Terms which until then had been considered 'esoteric' now abound in both conversation and the press: *psychopathology, trauma, necrophilia* (he violates his dead girlfriend), *extreme misogyny* ('I hate all women; they will all pay for it!'), *crepuscular epilepsy* (a term used by the defence). And from prison Goyo Cárdenas conjures up the monomania of the masses: newspapers abound in 'technical' descriptions of the murders, his sanity or insanity causes endless arguments, and selections from his *Memoirs* (notes marked by the delusion of grandeur) are published. To whoever wants to listen he proffers dreams, nightmares and unexpected feats. For example, he brought one of the victims 'back to life' using adrenalin obtained from the renal glands of another of his victims. And since people listen, the stories continue: one victim who 'returns' from Beyond shows Goyo her long, purple, swollen tongue, and guides him to the threshold of Hell. Psychologists and psychiatrists throw themselves into the interpretative feast. Goyo is the character who brings the 'unconscious' into the crime pages, and *Goyomania* (to use a term that would be applied today) flourishes. The house in which the crimes took place almost becomes a tourist spot, with drink and food stands outside; satirical ballads [*corridos*] are composed, and the neighbours give visitors access to their rooftops (for a price), making it possible for them to see the crime scene. Jokes abound, and the 'real' laces Goyo used in his murders are sold by the thousand, as are his shoes, spectacles and test tubes. *A Mexican Jack the Ripper!* Every week, in newspaper exclusives, the prisoner talks of his repentance and his efforts at rehabilitation, and his 'heartbreaking confessions' are echoed in a macabre fashion: Panzón Soto produces a musical show called *The Tacuba Strangler* with considerable success, people slyly repeating the line from the song '*La feria de las flores*' ['The Flower Market'] – 'I will see her transplanted to the orchard of my house' – and a pornographic film showing Goyo's 'orgies' circulates semi-clandestinely. When it comes to 'red news', Goyo Cárdenas is, it can now be stated, the case of the century;

- Higinio Sobera de la Flor, aka Baldy Sobera: on 11 May 1952, twenty-five-year-old Higinio, from the state of Tabasco, kills three people he does not even know: Captain Armando Lepe Ruiz, in a traffic incident (the captain called him a 'clown' and a 'dick' and was instantly shot several times); the young Hortensia López, whom Sobera wanted to seduce, is followed into her taxi, where he kills her; and the adolescent Pedro Galván Santoyo, whom he shoots for no apparent reason at all. The legend that emerges immediately around Sobera de la Flor matches his looks which are, according to popular thinking, even worse than his crimes: shaved head, enormous cap. His 'Lombrosian' looks and complete lack of sympathy make of him the monster in its purest state;

- Mercedes Cassola and Ycilio Massine: in 1959, Mercedes Cassola, a Catalan loanshark and gambler, and her lover, the Italian Ycilio Massine – an adventurer who sometimes dabbled in male prostitution – are ferociously stabbed to death. The murder includes other grotesque details: the castration of Massine, words written in blood on the walls, and so on. A number of high-society people are detained for questioning (and simultaneous blackmail), including supposed homosexuals. The name of the murderer, an old lover of

Cassola's, is spread among journalists, and it is rumoured that Very Important People helped him to leave the country. A pair of 'unknown hands' push Mercedes Cassola's father, who was about to give evidence, in front of a bus;

- On 28 May 1958, the actor Ramón Gay accompanies his colleague Evangelina Elizondo back home. Evangelina's husband, José Luis Paganoni, is waiting for them, and in a fit of jealousy he insults his wife and tries to hit her. Gay defends her, and Paganoni shoots him dead. The following day, in *La Fuente* cabaret, the retired Captain Oscar Lepe shoots and kills the film actor Agustín de Anda. Lepe justifies himself, saying that with his action he has 'wiped away a stain on his honour' which had been sullied by de Anda, who boasted of having enjoyed his daughter – ex-Miss Mexico and film actress – Ana Berta's first favours. Other versions circulated about the motives for the murder, less related to 'Hispanic honour'. Morbidity is driven by the relation established between crime and spectacle, and consolidated by arrogant, *macho* and intolerant personalities like Paganoni and Lepe, who believe they are 'treated unfairly';

- After a traffic incident on 14 June 1964, General Humberto Mariles, winner of the 1948 Olympic horse-jumping gold medal, shoots an unarmed construction worker in the back, claiming 'self-defence' against all the available evidence. This former example to the youth of the nation is sentenced to twenty years' imprisonment, which are immediately reduced to eight, of which he serves five. In 1969 he travels to Europe as an envoy of the Office of Tourism, and is detained in Marseilles for drug trafficking. He threatens to reveal the names of his employers, and in April 1970 dies in *La Sûreté* prison of 'natural causes'.

The age of organized crime

The Mariles case, like the case of the murderer and drugs dealer David Kaplan – who in 1973, together with the Venezuelan Carlos Contreras Castros, escaped from Santa Martha Acatitla Prison ('The Escape of the Century!') in a helicopter belonging to the Metropolitan Police – was certainly striking. Such cases do not, however, produce the same impassioned interest as before. The mere feats of individuals no longer attract attention. In the light of the statistics of a mass society, however implicit, one or two victims do not add up to much, and no one wants to waste their time finding out about the whims of the jealous man (even if they include hanging an unfaithful wife) or the strange case of the very *macho* man who killed his very *macho* friend because he hadn't put an end quickly enough to his *macho* intentions.

Among relatively small collectivities that are still subject to the totalizing proof of rumour and gossip, the taste for 'red news' is structured by a tradition of open-ended stories in which, although no one hypothesis is convincing, all are persuasive as explanations of the real motives for the crime. But the time and space given over to each macabre episode in the newspapers and magazines are getting smaller, while the increase in crime banalizes the meaning of crime stories with a moral. The mass industrialization of the 'red news', spearheaded by magazines like *Alarma* ['Alarm'] and *Alerta* ['Alert'], furthers the 'secularization' of the genre. The axis around which crime stories will now rotate will no longer be the legendary Lecumberri Prison (where it is clear that 'crime does not pay') but the cynical apologias in which the victims turn out to be the real guilty parties, and criminals the stars of a new fairground attraction. And all that is retained of the murders are the mad anecdotes: she killed her lover and sold his remains in *tamales*; a youngster strangled his grandmother because she refused to support his drug habit; and so on.

It is time for a change, and the crime story becomes yet another branch of industry and the police. The drugs trade seizes the headlines throughout the world, its main characters attaining the notoriety once reserved for politicians, sports personalities and film stars. After the 1960s, when drugs were conceived predominantly as a mystical experience (the literal communion with the universe), the consumption of drugs is massified, and millions of users of marijuana, heroin and cocaine generate extraordinary profits, providing the opportunity for that most supreme of jokes: the offer made by Columbian drug barons to repay the foreign debt. Throughout the 1980s, that vast illegal market which, for example, makes of Columbia a 'mega-Sicily', and of money-laundering a major earner for a number of national economics, is revealed. A new industry emerges complete with up-to-date line-management procedures: local and regional collectors, cocaine-processing plants and laboratories, organized transport on a massive scale, a multitude of small dealers ('mules'), wholesale distributors, expert financiers and very elaborate investment plans.

But in its wake, the drugs trade produces thousands of deaths and destroyed lives, as well as compromising national security and legal systems. The crime pages change, to centre their attention on the new antiheroism of the important traffickers and their extraordinary wealth. In Mexico, the first famous dealer – with the exception of Lola la Chata, so often referred to by William Burroughs – is the Cuban-American Alberto Sicilia Falcón, a figure not very different from the character played by Al Pacino in Brian de Palma's *Scarface*. According to numerous witnesses, Falcón is intelligent and skilful. Thanks to his organizational skills he exports tons of marijuana to the United States, diversifying into cocaine within a few years. In Mexico, Falcón has friends in all the right places, in show business and in the police. He is astute and quickly learns the rules of the game in Mexico – so well, indeed, that in 1975, a few months after being imprisoned in Lecumberri Prison, he organizes the building of a tunnel from his cell through which he then proceeds to escape (only to be apprehended soon afterwards because of a sentimental attachment).

The rulers of the drugs trade are Colombian, and the Medellín Cartel eventually becomes the United States government's (non-political) public enemy number one. With their unlimited fortunes the barons employ small but effective armies, and Carlos Lehder, Pablo Escobar Gaviria, the brothers Jorge Luis, Juan David and Fabio Ochoa, the brothers Gilberto José and Miguel Angel Rodríguez Orejuela and Gonzalo Rodríguez Gacha (who is known as 'El Mexicano' because of his love for ranchero songs) become the main characters in a new series of revelations. All too soon the truth is revealed: the reality of narco-power in Latin America includes judges, ministerial employees at all levels, journalists of all kinds, members of high society, chiefs of police, members of the armed services, pilots, customs officials, bureaucrats and businessmen at all levels. Money-laundering supports a number of local economies, and narco-power disseminates a style of private expenditure that is also quickly made public: the offensive and self-aggrandizing parade of residences, jewels, luxury cars, high-power weaponry, sex slaves and gold watches, anatomically well-endowed starlets, the latest model pick-up trucks, helicopters, private jets – everything that their owners could never have obtained with their limited schooling and family connections. A fair exchange: a shorter life-span and/or an eternity in jail in return for escaping the inexorable fate of peasants and corner-shop employees. They escape desolation, so to speak, only through crime. And crime, having become a spectacle, fascinates and seduces. We are talking about real crimes here, not just the stabbing of an unfaithful wife.

The massification of the drugs trade signals a massification of the crime story. Two, three, five bodies a day, found in remote or abandoned lots; and in the half-empty luxury apartments it is difficult to identify the abruptly slain bodies. In Mexico, one particular place soon becomes notorious: the Tierra Blanca neighbourhood in Culiacán (state of Sonora). The initial recruitment is focused on a number of states: Sinaloa, Jalisco, Guerrero, Baja California, Michoacán. Many are seduced by the traffickers, and thousands of peasants are detained or found dead alongside furrows. Meanwhile, the traffickers buy up hotels and car agencies, provincial bank managers climb aboard the wheel of fortune, women obey their husbands and transport the drugs, and many a businessman comes to know and appreciate the benefits of large amounts of laundered cash.

The drugs trade, as governments begin to find out, corrupts the whole edifice of the legal system, extending the conflict between a section of the police force and society. The River Tula crimes are the first well-known case. The Jaguar Brigade of the Crime Prevention Investigations Division (DIPD), commanded by Francisco Sahagún Baca, a lieutenant under Arturo Durazo Moreno, the infamous Metropolitan Chief of Police, tortures and murders thirteen Colombians and their Mexican chauffeur. The Colombians, housebreakers and rapists, had robbed a bank; the Jaguars hear about it, and typically choose to 'expropriate' them. It appears that when one of the criminals died under torture, it was decided to kill the rest. The corpses were thrown into the drainage system, but reappeared, destroyed, in the River Tula.

The public is moved, and the case is unexpectedly linked to the question of the violation of human rights. The journalist Manuel Buendía is the first to denounce the massacre, and the evidence mounts. When the López Portillo government comes to an end, so does Durazo's impunity. This provides the occasion for the appearance of a book (a melodramatic exposé) which, more than any other, changes the 'red news': *Lo negro del Negro Durazo* ['The Dark Side of Darkie Durazo', Editorial Posada, Mexico City 1983] by José González y González, Durazo's ex-bodyguard. It is a testimony whose credibility is heightened by the cynicism of the protagonist and the writer's own big talk:

> I, Pepe González y González, author of this book, began my life as a professional gunman, killing for the first time when I was twenty-eight years old. I have the lives of more than fifty dead victims on my conscience, and I am grateful for the intervention of many a bureaucrat for making sure I have no criminal record. I admit that I have killed on the orders of people like former President Gustavo Díaz Ordaz, Alfonso Corona del Rosal, and many more. I only followed orders.

Darkie Durazo, the protagonist of González's book, would not look out of place in a *film noir* or a novel by Jim Thompson. He had no more to his credit than being a childhood friend of President López Portillo. Everything about his behaviour was scary, and marked by excess, the most spectacular excess being his appointment as Mexico City's Chief of Police – a veritable jackpot – by a person who knew him very well. González refers to the looting of the city, the degradation of the police force, the devastating extension of impunity, the extortion, fraud, torture, the sale of protection to the underworld, the rise of smuggling, the drug trafficking, the networks of an alternative capitalism. No one has ever contradicted or disagreed with González's account. His testimony, which is that of a confessed murderer, has no moral value, and a lot of what he reveals is well known; but yes, the city had been 'protected' by a ruthless and irritable person who had Pharaonic palaces built for him on the outskirts of the city at Ajusco, and by the beach at Zihuatanejo; who mixed with members of the Supreme Court of Justice as well as with stars, and represented on a large scale the political and economic organization that made him possible.

The credibility of *Lo negro del Negro Durazo* is a function of the personal experience of the one million people who bought the book, and the ten million who read it. The crime stories that emerge after it are totally different from their precursors, focusing their attention now on sporadically illuminating the conspiracies of illegal power structures (so dependent on the legal ones). The privileged space of this new crime story is no longer the Black Palace of Lecumberri Prison (which is closed down on 26 August 1976, to reappear soon afterwards as the National Archive) but the labyrinth made up of luxury offices, exclusive restaurants and neighbourhoods, courtrooms where drug traffickers are given their freedom on bail, clandestine landing strips, specialists in the laundering of money, discotheques where the offspring of the Establishment become allied to the pushers of new sensations – advance guards of the emerging new money. Meanwhile, the traditional crime story has disappeared in the search for cases whose only key is to be found in human passion.

In 1983 Durazo flees Mexico, but the DEA (Drugs Enforcement Agency) discovers him in Rio de Janeiro. They follow him to San Juan, Puerto Rico, where he is detained and sent to Los Angeles. The extradition procedures are slow, while in Mexico he is charged only with minor crimes. In 1984, however, another event forces the crime story on to the front pages. On 30 May, the *Excelsior* columnist Manuel Buendía is shot in the back as he leaves his office. The front cover of *Impacto* is merciless: it shows Buendía's dead body prostrate in the street, covered with his raincoat. This crime – a key moment in the history of freedom of expression in Mexico – is the object of a costly and pointless investigation. Only in 1989 are second-rank guilty parties found – or at least, this is how public opinion, that voice without addressee, registers it.

At the moment of his assassination, Buendía was the most widely read journalist in the country. He was investigating, among other matters, the crimes of the extreme Right in Guadalajara, the business deals of the Oil Workers' Union, arms smuggling, the 'irregularities' of the judicial system, the activities of the

CIA in Mexico and, probably, the drugs trade (although there is no proof of this in his articles, nor in his – presumably looted – archives).

The assault on 'red news'

On 17 February 1985, DEA agent Enrique Camarena ('Kiki') is kidnapped as he leaves the US Consulate in the city of Guadalajara. Hours before, Alfredo Zavala Avelar, a pilot whom the DEA hired to fly special missions, was also kidnapped. The Camarena affair, a great *casus belli* for the Mexican and United States governments, divulges the names of traffickers whose local fame will very quickly become international: the Honduran José Ramón Mata Ballesteros, the Mexicans Rafael Caro Quintero, Ernesto Fonseca 'don Neto', Miguel Angel Félix Gallardo and Pablo Acosta. The facts tell another story, more terrible and complex, about the political underground and the consequences of the drugs trade in spheres already deformed by corruption. While public security remains merely of third-order significance, traffickers and police chiefs fraternize, the Most Honourable Civil Servants (never identified, although frequently identifiable) become partners in crime or negotiate its protection, police officers become members of criminal organizations, and money-laundering becomes one of the seven great business temptations (I chose the number seven to underline the Catholicism of the businessmen).

Months before, on 9 November 1984, the Federal Judicial Police and the army invade the *El Búfalo* ranch – a property owned by Caro Quintero and don Neto, among others – in the municipality of Ciudad Jiménez, state of Chihuahua, burn almost four thousand tons of marijuana and detain more than two thousand peasant workers from Sinaloa, Sonora, Durango, Oaxaca, Michoacán and Guerrero. Five to six thousand people work in *El Búfalo*, where the semi-slave conditions force the majority eventually to flee into the surrounding hills.

According to some, keen to avenge the raid on *El Búfalo*, the angry young drug traffickers kidnap Camarena to find out out how much he knows, torture him, and, drunk with power make the big mistake, failing to realize that their purchase of impunity is a purely local affair. According to the DEA – and this is made clearer than water in two semi-official apologias: *Desesperados*, Elaine Shannon's report of the case, and *Drug Wars*, the television mini-series based on the same book – the kidnapping of Camarena is the biggest provocation (the calculated error) in a plot of vast proportions whose centre is everywhere. For the DEA and the State Department the time has come to destroy narco-power, while simultaneously imposing onerous conditions on the Mexican government. From their point of view, what is at issue – apart from the usual geopolitics – is the pride of the DEA, National Security, and the trustworthiness of the neighbouring state.

The response of the Miguel de la Madrid government is slow in coming, and at times clumsy. At first the Camarena case is confined to the traditional crime pages, and the Attorney General dismisses its political and criminal significance, denying or ignoring many of the charges levelled at the lethargy and complicity of the judicial system by the DEA and John Gavin, the US Ambassador in Mexico. The Mexican authorities were at an enormous disadvantage when they were confronted by the aggressive campaigns of both the Reagan and Bush governments. If the meaning given to their offensive by the latter was essentially false (as exemplified in Panama, 'moral concern' is only US imperialism's latest strategy), it did, however, uncover real evidence and make important revelations. The United States resorts to every tactic in the book: it plants information in the mass media, uses economic and diplomatic pressure, directly (and indirectly) identifying important functionaries in de la Madrid's government (from police officers to the Secretary of Defence, Juan Arévalo Gardoqui) as having close connections with the drugs trade; they even kidnap Mexicans from Mexico for their supposed participation in the Camarena case (René Martín Verdugo and the doctor Humberto Alvarez Machain), and broadcast racist slurs about the 'innate corruption' of Mexicans, ignoring at the same time the illegality of their own actions. On 15 June 1992, the US Supreme Court of Justice contests the repatriation of Alvarez Machain, and ratifies the right of the United States to ignore international law and resort to whatever means necessary in 'applying the law'.

The Mexican authorities respond only very timidly to the intimidation organized by the DEA. Statements of fact very soon turn out to be untrue, while flagrant lies remain unaccounted for even when they are rectified. The silence of the government becomes a sign of complicity, of being cornered, and any actions taken are either very partial or very late in coming. So the accusations become a scandal: there are (many) police officers connected to the drugs trade, a parallel system of impunity before the law exists, for 60 million pesos there are those who will let Caro Quintero escape at Guadalajara Airport, while others 'plant' the bodies of Camarena and Zavala near the *El Mareño* ranch in the state of Michoacán – once its owners, the Bravo family, had been assassinated by officers of the law. And the 'cover-up' included detentions, housebreaking, torture and murder. Caro Quintero and don Neto are arrested, police commanders are suspended and put on trial, and a number of businessmen are investigated. But this is not enough for the US authorities – 1985 is the year when the crime story becomes a part of high politics (or is it the other way round?).

Saint Narco

Peasants are noble people, like me and my friends, and Señor Ernesto [Fonseca Carrillo] and his people. We are all people who help Mexico; we build schools and provide farms with electricity and running water. We do what the government doesn't do. Not because we want to make anything of it, nor to be noticed by everyone, but because it makes us feel good. (Rafael Caro Quintero, in an interview with journalists)

The crime story is socialized and endowed with meaning (which involves the transformation of morality into legend) through a combination of 'unforgettable characters' and anecdotes. In recent years there have been three figures who, in their own ways, are emblematic: two rise on the wave of excess (Rafael Caro Quintero and the 'narco-satanist' Adolfo de Jesús Constanzo), the other is peripheral (Juan Moro Ávila, accused of the murder of the journalist Manuel Buendía). Of the criminal figures in Mexico, these three are the ones most favoured by the press, the publishing industry and collective memory.

Of these, Caro Quintero is, without a doubt, the most famous: the paradigmatic (and the word is inevitable) born loser who, in his own brutal way, nevertheless triumphs. According to information provided by the office of the Attorney General of the Republic, Caro, originally from the Northern state of Sinaloa, leaves primary school in his second year and becomes an agricultural worker. At eighteen he leaves La Noria, where he was born, and takes up a job transporting cattle feed in Culiacán. Soon he begins growing marijuana, selling the two to three hundred kilos he harvests wholesale. At twenty-four his rise seems unstoppable: in Caborca, state of Sonora, he is producing five to six tons a year. He extends his contacts in both Mexico and the United States, and meets two of the most important (that is, visible) crime bosses in the area – Ernesto Fonseca Carrillo and Juan José Esparragoza – with whom he begins harvesting in La Cienaga, also in Sonora. In 1983, Caro is important enough both to know and to bribe commanders of the Federal Judicial Police, who agree not to destroy or fumigate his crops. In 1984, through his brother José Luis, he buys the *El Búfalo*, *El Vaquero* and *Pocitos* ranches in Chihuahua, and for the harvest he contracts thousands of men (here the figures vary from ten to thirty thousand farm hands).

Caro is a figure who emerges from the margins. Through his partners in the hotel and automobile businesses, he socializes with Jalisco's high society and associates with the *sancta sanctorum* of the drugs trade. His huge profits allow him to make friendly 'gifts', like the mythical three hundred luxury cars given to his 'customers and friends' in the press, judiciary and police. He also adds a personal touch to his corporate image: in a Guadalajara discotheque he meets Sara Cosío, niece of the politician Guillermo Cosío Vidaurri, then President of the ruling *Partido Revolucionario Institucional* (PRI – the Institutional Revolutionary Party) in Mexico City. This is as far as the facts take us. What follows is pure legend, the combination of facts, possible facts and fantasy. Caro falls in love with Sara, and asks her to marry him. In November 1984 he 'kidnaps' her and takes her to Sonora. He takes her back home for Christmas, and gives her family numerous presents (which they refuse). From the point of view of the crime pages, it hardly matters if what follows is the work of a fevered imagination or just the eccentricities of narco-power: on 14 February 1985, a week after the kidnapping of Camarena, he orders that five luxurious cars be torched in front of the Cosío family residence. If cars are what are most valuable to him, their flame will burn (and apologies for the metaphor) for ever.

The correspondence between Sara and Caro (true or apocryphal, we may never know), is published very widely. In one letter Sara confesses:

> Rafael:
> Although everything has been so crazy, you behaved yourself really well and the truth is you are really good and only pretend to be bad. You treated me with a lot of respect and care. That's why you'll see that I'll do the right thing, and I want you to take care and behave yourself, OK.
>   Thanks. I'll never forget you.
>   Sara

The two-way (or is it one-way?) romance continues, and the romantic scenes are enthusiastically reconstructed by the yellow press – which has never distinguished between public and private. The investigation following the Camarena case obliges Caro to flee, and to seek out the ideal companion with whom to make his escape. He sends Sara a message: 'You're coming with me because I want you.' César Octavio Cosío Vidaurri, Sara's father, makes the announcement:

> Today, at 3.30 in the morning of 7 March, my daughter, Sara Cristina Cosío Martínez, and her friend Patricia Menier, were kidnapped by gunmen working for Rafael Caro Quintero. The kidnapping happened as my wife Cristina,

my son César and the victims returned from a discotheque where they had dined and danced. As they reached Patricia's house, two Grand Marquis cars, one grey and the other white, blocked their way. They were then approached by eight individuals armed with R-15 machine guns and crowbars, who forced the young girls into their vehicles. Hours later, at approximately five o'clock in the morning, Patricia was freed.

Caro and Sara escape to San José, Costa Rica, in a jet owned by the Cordero Stauffer brothers, one of Guadalajara's Best Families. They stay in a house that had been bought for 800,000 dollars cash on the outskirts of San José with a pool, jacuzzi, guesthouse and cabins. Sara Cosío makes a telephone call to her home, and it is traced. On 4 April an anti-terrorist squad and DEA agents raid the house, arrest the bodyguards, and burst into Sara and Caro's room. The scene is a memorable one. She says to a DEA agent: 'I've been kidnapped.' He asks, pointing at the detainee: 'Who's this, darling?' And she, in a weak voice, answers: 'Rafael Caro Quintero.' He reacts: 'Whore.'

This is just what the crime pages needed. Caro and his gang are welcomed back to Mexico as the most dangerous beings imaginable. The television transmits their arrival at the Attorney General's office at dawn, and on the way to the offices of Interpol, groups of youngsters follow, shouting 'Caro, reveal the corrupt!', 'Unmask them all, Caro!', 'Names, Caro, names!'. Without ever having been anything like a social bandit, he is nevertheless treated like one; *corridos* are composed in his honour (rather than his dishonour), telling the story of his outrages. Afterwards, his stay in prison is just as legendary: the devotion of his jailers, the extensions to his cell, the parties. Caro Quintero gains his place in the 'red news' as the drug dealer who, in exchange for a twenty-two-year prison sentence, lived and experienced in the briefest of periods a series of emotions and sensations which, for a person like him, would otherwise have been impossible.

'I'll give you the details of what didn't happen to me'

As crime stories increasingly focus their attention on the relationship between national security and crime (between impunity and violence), readers are confronted more and more with the rudiments of sociology and political science, rather than with the 'magic of crime'. There have, however, been some notable recent exceptions: the man who kidnapped his own family; the case of Elvira Luz Cruz, sentenced for killing her four children; and the case of Gilberto Flores Alavez, imprisoned for killing his paternal grandparents.

It is at the beginning of the 1960s when the crime story becomes, for the first time, a symbol whose eloquence is such that it erases the episode at its origin and becomes an urban fable. A madman, who wanted more than anything else to – literally – save his wife and three children from reality, shuts them up in the home, where he subjects them to sermons and beatings. The case inspires Sergio Magaña's play *Los motivos del lobo* ['The Wolf's Reasons'], and Arturo Ripstein's film *El castillo de la pureza* ['The Castle of Purity'], with a screenplay by José Emilio Pacheco. Here the story is everything. Can solipsism go any further than the negation of the world? The mad father, who can see only the danger of contamination outside, and hates whatever challenges his dictatorship inside the home, is the ultimate metaphor for an authoritarianism which, from the point of view of 'red news', knows what the people in its care need, and the grotesque representation of the fears of the big-city-dweller convinced of the transformation of 'the Outside' into a pure threat.

Desperation, ignorance and anaemically induced physical and mental weakness cause Elvira Luz Cruz to kill her four children. The inevitable question which remains at the centre of the case emerges: to what extent is an abandoned person with no resources whatsoever, driven mad by the inability to feed her children, responsible for her actions? Elvira is not guilty, Elvira is not innocent, and her awful helplessness becomes of interest to public opinion, especially to feminist groups. How can we stop the violence against children so widespread among the popular classes, without at the same time eradicating extreme poverty and one of its psychological effects, the *machismo* that feeds off the domestic environment? The children's father is not concerned either with their fate or with Elvira's desperation. And in 1981, in a squalid room in a popular neighbourhood, locals find the strangled children and Elvira on the point of dying from a suicide attempt. They bring her back to life, beat her severely, and hand her over to the police. Feminists and traditionalists participate in the debate that ensues, and out of the argument comes Felipe Cazal's docudrama *Los motivos de Luz* ['Luz's Motives'] and Dana Rothberg's documentary *Elvira Luz Cruz*.

In 1978 Gilberto Flores Muñoz, former Secretary of Agriculture for the government of Adolfo Ruiz Cortines, and his wife Asunción Izquierdo (the novelist Ana Mairena), are hacked to death with a machete. The guilty party is located very quickly: their twenty-year-old grandson Gilberto Flores Alavez, a follower of the Legionnaires of Christ, who professed mystic devotion. He is given away by the friend who accompanied him to buy the murderous weapon and the bottle of Valium used to put the couple to sleep. The case is immediately overtaken by the furore proper to any great moment in a crime story, and the readers (who consider themselves the real experts) learn of the family quarrels, of Gilberto's habits and obsessions, of the attempts of his father and the defence lawyer quickly to find other 'guilty parties', of the 'ambiguity' that psychologists from the Attorney General's office detect in a person who declares himself to be a twenty-year-old virgin, of the struggle to save Flores Alavez from his own confession: 'I did it, because of a mental illness!' The case produced three novels: Luis Spota's *Mitad oscura* ['The Dark Side', 1982], Luis Guillermo Piazza's *Los cómplices* ['The Accomplices', 1983], and Vicente Leñero's extraordinary documentary reconstruction *Asesinato* ['Murder', 1985].

The Doors of Hell and the bank accounts

Despite Leñero's example, the 'true crime' genre does not prosper in Mexico. Its popularity in the United States began with Truman Capote's *In Cold Blood*, was confirmed by Norman Mailer's *The Excutioner's Song*, and today is the 'appended legacy' of each famous crime and serial killer from the Manson tribe to the Von Bulow case, including the infinite transformation of the Kennedy assassination into the most important crime story of all time. In 1989 alone the 'narco-satanists' are the subject matter of four books in the United States: *Children of Blood: The Matamoros Cult Killings* by Jim Schutze; *Across the Border* by Gary Provost; *Hell Ranch* by Clifford Linedecker; and *Blood Money* by Edward Himes. Apart from questions of reading habit, other reasons for the nonexistence of 'true crime' are simply the difficulties involved in securing trustworthy information, and the rise of the thriller – the crime literature *par excellence* in countries where there is no trust in the judicial system and where, however colourful the figures of true crime, they could never live up to the legendary attachment of social bandits like Chucho el Roto.

A recent chapter in Mexico's crime annals both exhibits and partially negates new developments in the crime story: the case of the 'narco-satanists', a tragedy framed by *Grand Guignol* that can also be seen to resemble the 'gore' film, with its very own Freddy Krueger, the excessive and barbaric Adolfo de Jesús Constanzo, a young Cuban-American brought up in Miami and Haiti by *santero* parents belonging to the Palo Mayombe cult. Constanza comes to Mexico when he is twenty-three, and right from the start his physical attraction and his ability to manipulate the superstitions of others, as well as his own, enable him both to find the customers he needs and to surround himself with fanatics. Messianic and a true believer in demonic forces, boastful and cruel, he gathers around him a cast that includes figures from the world of spectacle, major and minor drug traffickers, police chiefs whom Constanzo initiates ('marks') into *santería*, and a number of characters (almost stereotypical) from the margins.

In Mexico, according to the few available testimonies, Constanzo is a 'charismatic' individual. He knows how to spend money, and how to compromise those close to him; he knows how to promise, threaten and flatter. He endows a number of police officers – in special ceremonies designed by himself – with 'immunity', with the protection of evil spirits in exchange for some consideration. He convinces his show-business clients of the advantages of keeping the ancient gods happy; he promises the gunman Alvaro de León Valdés, aka 'El Duby,' that he cannot be touched by bullets. He shows his 'high priestess' Sara Aldrete the intensities afforded by money and risk; and he shares his world-view with his lovers Omar Orea Ochoa, a student of political science, and Martín Quintana, a very young drugs dealer (Omar does not participate in the crimes, but is nevertheless an unconditional ally of Constanzo's because he literally resolves his life for him).

The whole group embraces *santería*, in Constanzo's own peculiar version of it, with the credulity and indifference of those who do exactly as Fate dictates (in other words, the opportunities to hand). They know two hierarchies, reverence for authority and the power of money, and this duality governs their lives. And what is most fascinating about this loss of will before crime is its similarity to persuasion in totalitarian societies. People who would never have killed do so – and viciously – because they just happened to be there, that day, in the right place, at the beck and call of Constanzo. Opportunity is the only criterion of evil, and those who in other circumstances could be entirely different attain unthought-of levels of bestiality because, suddenly, someone grants them power over the bodies of others. But Constanzo does not invent this criminal psychology at large in those 'lost' zones in cities like Matamoros or Mexico City, so determined already by the existential vacuum of those who have no – or at least, believe they have no – options, and kill because they attribute no significance whatsoever to their own lives. He merely perfects it for his own use. Values play no real part in the formation of these beings, who do not believe in good or evil because theirs is a world without alternatives.

Constanza cannot act morally. He loves cruelty; moreover, cruelty is necessary for the consolidation of his tyranny. He kills and murders for reasons of the drugs trade and his own madness (he and his group repeatedly view John Schlesinger's film *The Believers*, about a Palo Mayombe satanic cult). And what finally destroys him is bending the bow too far. Nothing happens to him for bru-tally killing transvestites, dopeheads and policemen, but for the kidnapping, torture and murder of the North American student Mark Kilroy. Constanzo thus ignores the most basic of facts: the power he has, whatever its extent, is allowed him only in so far as he does not cause any serious problems. The United States government backs the demands made by the Kilroy family, and Constanzo's impunity ends.

A genuine 'gore' movie: murders, with torture and mutilation; initiation ceremonies attended by the head of Interpol in Mexico at which bodies are cut to pieces and their bones are made into necklaces to ward off bad luck; frenetic journeys and escapes. And finally, the hallucinatory dénouement on 6 May 1989: Constanzo is surrounded by the police in his apartment, from where he shouts at his pursuers in ñañigo or Bantu (impossible to know which), shooting wildly in all directions and throwing hundred-dollar bills out of the window: 'Here, you bastards! Take some, you poor bastards!' (And both policemen and onlookers throw themselves fearlessly at the cash.)

Inside, Constanzo asks 'El Duby' to kill Martín, Omar and himself. At first he refuses, so Constanzo threatens him: 'If you don't, I will come back from hell and punish you.' 'El Duby' agrees. At the last moment, Omar refuses to die, but Constanzo and Martín go into the toilet, where 'El Duby' shoots them both dead with a burst of machine-gun fire.

More elements of sheer horror would be impossible to imagine. But if what happens surpasses anyone's imagination, it must be remembered that the narco-satanists were also part of a far more rational sphere structured by the impunity of the drugs trade. From this point of view, Constanzo is not a 'messenger from Hell' but, rather, a minor gangster whose crimes, however monstrous, corre-spond to the simple logic of trafficking in the semi-clandestinity of Mexico City or the shadows of Matamoros – where Constanzo recruits his followers and practises his first bloody rituals. The immense stupidity of crime is circum-scribed by a zone the key to whose forgetting is the common grave.

12

Bolero: A History

Postmodern prologue: Pedro Almodóvar

In *El Super*, a Cuban-American film by Orlando Jiménez, a fifty-something couple psychologically lost in New York City find momentary refuge in their apartment kitchen. Suddenly, in remembrance of things past, they sing '*Somos*' ['We Are'], a bolero written by the Argentine Mario Clavel: '*Somos un sueño imposible/que busca la noche, para olvidarnos del mundo,/del cielo y de todo . . .*' ['We are an impossible dream/That searches for the night to forget the world/The sky, everything . . .']. The couple's vulnerability and sentimental pride are moving, while the bolero they sing organizes emotions and memories according to very precise dates: '*Así suspirábamos en 1956./Así nos reconcil-iábamos en 1958*' ['This is how we sighed in 1956./This is how we made up in 1958']. From belief in romance to the joint invention of the past.

In the last scene of Pedro Almodóvar's excellent film *Dark Habits*, the Mother Superior of a convent, obsessed by the prostitute who has taken refuge there, goes to look for her in her room and discovers that she has fled. The nun lets out a painful cry, the image freezes, and Lucho Gatica is heard singing '*Encadenados*' ['In Chains']: '*Nos hemos hecho tanto, tanto, daño,/que amor entre nosotros es mar-tirio . . .*' ['We've done ourselves so, so much harm,/That love between us is nothing less than martyrdom . . .']. Having been taken radically out of context, the bolero becomes a wound, a genuine anguished hymn.

In *Law of Desire*, Almodóvar's great melodrama, Chucho Navarro's bolero '*Lo dudo*' ['I Doubt It'] – sung by Los Panchos – establishes a deep relationship between the theatre and film director, and the student: '*Hallarás/mil aventuras sin amor,/pero al fin de todas,/sólo tendrás dolor . . .*' ['You will have/Thousands of loveless adventures,/But in the end,/All you will find is pain . . .']. In the end, pursued by the police to the director's apartment, the student who killed for love has a moment of respite: he puts on a record and helps the director undress so that their passion may be displayed while, below, the police wait: '*Lo dudo, lo dudo, lo dudo,/que halles un amor tan puro,/como el que tienes en mí . . .*' ['I doubt it, I doubt it, I doubt/You will ever find a love/As pure as mine . . .']. The bolero, from appearing to be supremely conventional, is now endowed with new and subversive meanings. In *Women on the Edge of a Nervous Breakdown*, the dramatic, melodramatic and self-parodic voice of La Lupe sings '*Teatro*' ['Theatre'] – '*Lo tuyo es puro teatro*' ['You're just acting'] – and the bolero becomes conscious of itself, and of the pleasures of melodrama: suffering acted out in all seriousness. In *High Heels* the singer returns from Mexico singing Agustín Lara's '*Pienso en ti*' ['Thinking of You'], so that we know immediately: the bolero has become the essence of the past – not of the real past, nor even of the idealized past, but of everything that was before Progress destroyed a sentimentalism ('cursilería') whose origins were literary (the new schmaltz does not come from reading books). The glorious product of a sensibility which refuses orthodox burial because it still believes in resurrection, the bolero is what was once called 'romantic' (when a culture still bothered to produce such labels), but has suddenly become a deposit of the experiences of generations who, for all of three minutes (which you can play again and again), believe themselves to have wrought in words and melody what they sought in love and found in melancholy.

Why did I not die when you were mine, and I your God?

Mexico, 1901. Society shivers with the shock – or at least, Society as it was known then, the Society of Ladies and Gentlemen, Landowners and Opera. This society is bolstered by the dictatorship of Porfirio Díaz (1876–1911), known as 'the Porfiriato', and mythically founds itself on a Shockable Conscience acting as moral alarm. Its members have struggled so hard to live as they do in London and Paris that they are right to be scandalized on hearing '*Perjura*' ['Swear'], the song by Miguel Lerdo de Tejada: '*Con tenue velo tu faz hermosa,/camino al templo te conocí . . .*' ['Veil, keep thy beautiful countenance,/I encountered on the way to the temple . . .']. Priests fulminate from their altars, fathers protect their daughters, and outside the salons the song carries far and wide:

Cuando mis labios en tu albo cuello
con fiebre loca en mi bien posé,
y en los transportes de amor excelso
no sé hasta donde mi alma se fue.
¿Por qué no fueron aquellas horas como soñé?
¿Por qué ¡ay! huyeron y ya no pueden jamás volver?
¿Por qué no he muerto cuando eras mía y yo tu dios?
¿Cómo es que vivo si éramos uno y hoy somos dos?

[When feverishly on your alabaster neck/My lips I did lay;/And in transported love, I know not where/My soul did make its way./Why were those hours not like a dream?/Why, oh why! did they flee, not to return?/Why did I not die when you were mine, and I your God?/How is it I am still alive when we were one and now are two?]

The educated voice of the tenor scatters the vibrant tones, producing a double pleasure, that found in art and in moral transgression. It is not for nothing that beauty in song is the delight that augments the sense of respectability. While the *corrido* and the entr'acte [*tonadilla*] are the music of the lower classes, the opera is the place where the new sensibility reigns supreme. With love all around, sopranos become the vehicles *par excellence* of sublime emotion (Angela Peralta, the 'Mexican Nightingale', is a case in point: so close to heaven, so far from the mud). But the tenors express and codify high sentiment, the sensation of lording over reality and possessing it. Symphonies elevate the spirit, but tenors inebriate the soul (remember Werner Herzog's film *Fitzcarraldo*, and its protagonist driven mad by the superstar Enrico Caruso – there's no one like him for discovering whole continents in the melody of an aria, for dominating nature, and overcoming all female resistance to his whims).

The tenor sings '*Perjura*' [' Swear'], and the guardians of public chastity are immediately on guard. They have defended the virginity of eye-and-ear, stood guard over the cultural scene, while 'decent' musical genres, like the *habanera*, delight family gatherings, inciting the young ladies to virtuoso performances at the piano, in song and declamation, in the embroidery of body and soul.

Towards the end of the nineteenth century '*La Paloma*' ['The Dove'] by Sebastián Yradier and '*La Golondrina*' ['The Swallow'] by Narciso Serradel are all the rage, providing just the right balance of melancholy and good taste. The Hit Parade of 1896 includes the following romantic and *habanera* songs: '*Pegúntale a las estrellas*' ['Ask the Stars'], '*Ilusiones perdidas*' ['Lost Hope'], '*Bonaerges*' (the name of a character from Pérez Escrich's novel *El Mártir del Gólgota* ['The Martyr of Golgotha']), '*Tristezas*' ['Sadness'], '*Horas de luto*' ['Mourning Time'],

'*Corazones de mármol*' ['Hearts of Marble'], '*Guarda esa flor*' ['Keep this Flower'] and, finally, '*Resignación*' ['I am Resigned'], whose words broadcast the benefits of love, a sentiment that at least goes some way to clear the mists of a semi-barbaric country:

> Hoy sin pensar en esperanza alguna
> llorando siempre mi ilusión perdida,
> veo correr mi infortunada vida
> hasta aquel día que acabe mi pensar.
> Desprecios, falsedad y desengaños;
> el mundo en vez de amor me ha prodigado
> ¡Que he de hacer, si esta suerte me ha tocado!
> Sufrirla quiero sin pensarlo ya.

[Today without belief in hope/Crying for my lost illusions,/I see my poor life pass by/Until the day of mourning./No love; all I have received in this world/Has been hatred, lies and pretence./What can I do, if this is my only fortune?/Now I want to suffer alone and without a thought.]

Technology makes its presence felt only timidly in 1897 with the perfection of the gramophone, a savage god to which the masses listen struck with fear and piety. The waltz triumphs in High Society; and spectacles that combine music and poetry in the manner of religious ecstasy – 'melopeas' – are all the rage. On 'entering the home', song accentuates the daring of Romantic poetry and the ambiguity of the modernists ('modernistas'). This is why '*Perjura*' ['Swear'] is such a provocation. How do you slip physical desire into centres of devotion? How do you allude to fornication and lovers in a song that may be listened to by the innocent? How do you make a genre that comes from the literary salons 'indecent'?

> Con tenue velo tu faz hermosa
> camino al templo te conocí,
> al verte ¡oh niña, tan pudorosa
> por primera vez amor sentí!
> ¡Ay! cuántas veces la luz del día nos sorprendió
> ¡Ay! cuántas otras tus juramentos el cielo oyó;
> esos momentos, amada mí, no olvidaré
> cuando en tus brazos y en beso amante mi alma dejé.
> Hoy que te miro pasar radiante
> con otro amante como yo fui,
> siento que mi alma en un infierno
> de amor y celos está por ti.

[Veil, keep thy beautiful countenance/I encountered on the way to the temple,/On seeing you, chaste young girl,/For the first time I felt love! Oh! How many times did the daylight catch us/Oh! How many times did the sky above hear your vows?/Such moments, my love, I can never forget/When in your arms a lover's kiss I left./And today, I watch you pass radiant/With another lover like me before/Now feeling my soul in a hell/Of love and jealousy for you.]

Tearful countenance and broken heart

In 1913, during the government of Victoriano Huerta, the avant-garde musician Manuel M. Ponce compiles old songs and rearranges them for piano. Since the ragged armies were so difficult to ignore at the time, the rediscovery of the popular was encouraged. Ponce recovers '*Abandonado*' ['Abandoned': 'I have three vices, and they're very deep . . .'] and '*A la orilla de un palmar*' ['Next to a Palm Grove': 'Her little coral lips, her little starry eyes . . .'], and in so doing he strengthens a sentimentalism which, rather than contradicting the times – which seemed to be represented best in the *corrido* – in fact expresses them.

During the Revolution, romantic song becomes central to the language of the community, in which Lyric, Love and Metaphor become irrefutable values. To die for love. Die? Yes, die. It was not a question of really dying, like the desperate Romantics of previous generations, but, rather, of popularizing the 'culturescape' of the nineteenth century, the mythologies of passionate frenzy. When you hear this waltz (or *Perjura*), remember me . . . and while you're at it, confirm the justice of a society whose language of love so blatantly contradicts everyday behaviour.

With the peasant armies at the gates, Ponce demands that poetry strengthen the spirit. He says of his '*Estrellita*': '[She] is living nostalgia; a complaint on behalf of a youth that is being lost. She embodies the cobblestoned streets of Aguascalientes and my dreams of walking by moonlight.' In '*Estrellita*' Ponce attempts to bridge the gap between classical and popular music: since 'the science of beauty is still in nappies', let the ear be the supreme judge of music. The sole criterion of quality is psychological response: 'We feel emotion', he says in a note on Debussy, 'without the actual provenance of the work of art, or the details of its structure, really mattering. Just as we feel the kiss of the sun – the distance it has travelled to reach us does not matter either.' So – let the popular be redeemed by the intensity of the emotions it occasions, just like with any work of art.

At first, romantic song – in the form of either the waltz or *habanera* –

confirms the pleasure for lyricism in art, theatre and poetry-and-music evenings. It fine-tunes courting, and – wherever possible – seduction, and allows couples to put a date to their passions. At the same time, rhyming poetry ages and dies, and the masses distance themselves from high poetry, from *modernismo*'s discoveries and licence, from a tradition that thinks melodic style is 'sweet and intimate', and gives of it lavishly in soirées and serenades.

A heart-rending melody with painful words. In essence, the *romantic song* is a literary and cultural definition rather than a state of mind. *Romantic* is the poet who kills himself for love; *romantic* is the dishevelled eagerness that looks to the night as the territory of instinct and creativity, believes that a loved one is the virgin land from which all life energy flows, goes to any lengths just to find the right words, and gives himself up to inspiration, the only vow. *Fin-de-siècle* poetry becomes, almost literally, massified as it is diluted and frozen in song, the last refuge, according to this mythology, of naive purity.

A language can survive the customs that determine it. For this reason, even during the armed phase of the Revolution, public language is either Neoclassical or Romantic, while later, in an epoch of rapid modernization, rhyming poetry still captivates. Isolated, read only in fragmentary form, dispossessed of its context, the public language of the nineteenth century becomes affected ('cursi'), like the songs in which it sought refuge. But in the first decades of the twentieth century the language of rapture clearly dominates. I will resort to very precise testimony here: a book published by the Association of Constituent Deputies, *A Literary Anthology*, which includes the speeches, articles and poems of those who had been made Deputies in 1917. In his poem '*Iras de bronze*' ['Bronze Anger'], for example, Deputy Marcelino Dávalos writes:

> Perfumádme la intensa cabellera
> con esencia de nardos; que procuren
> cuando ya al fin dentro del baño muera
> y mis venas el liquido purpuren
> dar a mi faz sonrisa placentera.
> En el áureo tazón de Calcedonia
> escandiadme licor falermitano . . .
> ¡Qué porvenir el vuestro!
> ¡Deja, divino Apolo,
> que se desborde de mi lira el estro
> y un pálido bosquejo haga tan sólo
> de lo que oculta el porvenir siniestro!

[Perfume my intense head of hair/With essence of tuberose; so that/When at last in the bath I die/And my veins the liquid purple,/They give my counte-nance a pleasing smile./In the Calcedonian golden bowl . . . What a future yours!/Let, divine Apollo,/The inspiration flow from my lyre/That it make a pallid search/For what the sinister future holds!]

Deputy Andrés Magallón, meanwhile, evokes his infancy: 'The song "*La Valentina*" ['Valentina'] brings me the sweet and pleasant memory of the now long-lost days of my childhood; of that night constellated with limpid clouds . . . the cry of the night watchman in our ears; the humid earth shaken up by the herd . . .'. While the admirable Deputy Francisco J. Múgica writes in his poem '*Tristes arpegios*' ['Sad Arpeggio']:

> Piensa, virgen, que he sido toda mi vida
> pobre paria que al cielo nunca ha llegado,
> caminante que mira siempre perdida
> la esperanza de un sueño que no ha tocado.
> Que si al cielo yo quiero tornar mis ojos
> y ese cielo lo busco yo en tus sonrisas,
> tus sonrisas me niegan tus labios rojos
> y se cierra tu boca que es mi delicia.

[Think, virgin, that all my life I have been/A poor pariah who has never reached heaven,/A wanderer that looks at a forever lost/Hope of a dream./If I turn my eyes to that sky/And in that sky find your smiles,/Your smiles would deny me your red lips/And your mouth, that is my delight, closes.]

And Jesús Romero Flores writes poems too – for example, '*Sinfonía*' ['Symphony']:

> . . . Virgen: oculta el sol de oro
> sus ignicentes resplandores,
> y Afrone tiende su negrura
> cual presagiando tempestad;
> con alas de ébano en mi torno
> revolotean los dolores:
> ¡luz con tus ojos, vida mía,
> que sus dulcísimos fulgores
> abran un surco esplendoroso
> dentro de la negra inmensidad

[. . . Virgin: the gold sun hides/Your fiery splendour,/. . . Ebony wings around me/Stirring the pain;/Light with your eyes, my life,/So that their sweet light/Opens a splendid way/In the immense darkness.]

President Álvaro Obregón writes poems; President Plutarco Elías Calles writes poems. The 'modernista' poet Rubén Darío was, therefore, right to ask: 'Who isn't romantic?' And the answer unites social classes and regions, moods and prejudices, real and imagined loves (who cares about the difference?). And the examples are legion. A corollary: romantic song borrows its language from what is available at the time, from love or politics. Taken from their original verbal and melodic contexts, the songs seem corny or, it might be best to say, 'with tearful countenance and broken heart' – because for decades romantic song is one of the main channels of a language that unites composer with trade-union leader, housewife with President of the Republic. And the armed stage of the Revolution does not interrupt this flow: even the most violent of radicals sends messages straight from the heart rather than comradely greetings.

So if we want to understand the history of romantic song, let's accept this one fact: before becoming an industry, it was a matter of collective creation. As they begin to programme popular taste, the early radio stations in Mexico – XEW and RCA Victor – respect the existing musical environment to a large extent – that is, the professional poetic vocabulary and literary music that are the vehicles of exaltation. Although the *corrido* contains a plebeian poetic which moves, it possesses no cultural aura and does not 'elevate' or 'transport' its interpreters and listeners. In contrast, how can one resist transportation when one is caught up in songs that both intensify and affirm sentiment?

The most popular images mask a harsh and voracious system that oppresses women by thinking of them as purely ethereal beings. Such a view, moreover, is sustained through the transformation of metaphors into ways of life: the word is declamation, and declamation is collective rapture. And this is taken into account in 1921 by the Secretary of Public Education, who continues the work of collecting popular songs begun in 1911 by Manuel M. Ponce. José Vasconcelos now charges maestro Joaquín Beristáin with the collection of the 'popular soul', defined then as the codified, and thus most convincing, successes of the middle classes rather than the anonymous – and thus uncodified – popular ones.

The Mexican Revolution carries with it such a strong nationalist impulse that it inevitably reinvents the popular; and what comes out on top is the illusion contained in Ramón López Velarde's poem *'Suave Patria'* ['Gentle Motherland'] *'Patria, te doy de tu dicha la clave/sé siempre igual, fiel a tu espejo diario . . .'*

['Motherland, I give you the key to your fortune/Be always the same, daily faithful to your mirror-image . . .'] – in which the image that dominates is that of a countryside frozen in time. Manuel Fernández Esperón, Marcos Ruis, and Alfonso Esparza Oteo all abide by popular speech (which the *carpa* ['tent'] will codify) and neighbourhood speech (ruled over by the comedians):

> Borrachita, me voy
> para la capital
> a servirle al patrón
> que me mandó llamar
> anteayer.

[Drunk, I'm off/To the big city/To serve the boss/Who sent for me/The day before yesterday.]

Popular song vulgarizes literary language, and gradually distances itself from the emotion of romantic song. The latter, meanwhile, consolidates the home, becoming the means by which the new frankness and audacity proper to the growing capital city are made 'decent'.

The secularization of tears

The song '*Perjura*' ['Swear'] establishes many of the rules structuring Mexican romantic song during the twentieth century:

1. The testimonial and confessional values of the genre – 'romantic song' – are accepted. The name is supposed to reflect the state of mind they intend to provoke in their listeners, and is grounded in a great social myth: an abstract but warmly felt adoration of women. Such an operation vulgarizes the mystical tradition, granting the loved woman what had hitherto been the privilege of the Virgin Mary. In his waltz '*María Elena*' (1925), Lorenzo Barcelata is explicit:

> Tuyo es mi corazón, oh sol de mi querer,
> tuyo es todo mi ser, tuyo es, mujer,
> ya todo el corazón te lo entregué,
> eres mi fe, eres mi Dios, eres mi amor.

[My heart is yours, oh sun of my love/I am yours, all of me is yours, woman/I have already given you my heart,/you are my faith, my God, you are my love.]

Women stand in for God in this ardent metamorphosis. And this exaltation is accompanied by the cinematic discovery of the female face, the proliferation of close-ups and apparitions of the Virgin Mary. The songs find their *raison d'être* in excess, so that if Agustín Lara celebrates a prostitute, it is to show that femininity has its place even at the limits of the permissible, and that the apparent lack of morals does not necessarily get in the way of sacralization:

> Mujer, mujer divina
> tienes el veneno que fascina
> en tu mirar . . .

[Woman, divine woman/You possess the poison that fascinates/In your look . . .]

Could he have used a more grandiloquent adjective? If she is *divine*, whoever loves her is transfigured. The institutions of Church and Family do not take much notice, however, and respond only to the most obvious provocation. So, when Lara uses the following words: '*Aunque no quieras tú,/ni quiera yo,/ni quiera Dios/hasta la eternidad/te seguirá mi amor*' ['Although neither you/Nor I, nor God/Want it, my love/Will be yours for eternity'], ecclesiastical censorship imposes: '*Aunque no quieras tú, ni quira yo/lo quiere Dios*' ['Although neither you/Nor I want it/God does'], which means that God ends up imposing his holy writ on the lovers. And when the Cuban José Antonio Méndez writes: '*Desmiento a Dios porque al tenerte yo en vida/no necesito ir al cielo tisú/porque,/alma mía/la gloria eres tú*' ['Since I have you in life I renounce God/I don't need a lamé heaven/Because,/My soul/You are the glory'], censorship eliminates the impiety, and the verse is purified: '*Bendito Dios, porque al tenerte yo en vida . . .*' ['Blessed Lord, having you in life . . .'], with which God commits the slight theological fault of saving a mortal from having to go to heaven. But these are exceptions. More commonly, the slight trembling in the religious edifice caused by this art of loving goes unopposed.

2. The vocabulary of liturgy is applied to other zones of behaviour. The 'secularization of tears' (Cioran) extends pious sentiment to the 'virgins' of masculine idealization; the language proper to religion opens up and incorporates the emotions on which family homes are built, and gives existence total meaning. And this *religiosity* extends not only to personal relations but to the idealizations of actually existing *machismo*, thus 'democratizing' the impulse of minstrels, poets and impassioned musicians. Finally, nineteenth-century bourgeois notions

become part of popular culture: the sacred character of the loved woman, the mystique of matrimonial love and courtship. The housewife is rewarded for her domestic slavery by being first declared the mistress of matters of the heart.

The songwriters – failed poets in the main – generously provide a multitude of key words: *love, heart, god, oath, betrayal, tenderness, soul, sweetness, candour, moon, love, lie, death, kisses, cry, hope, tears, distance, return, compassion, passion, nostalgia, forget, blame, look, bitter, time, eternity, pain, heaven, world, sorry, faith, life, fear, hate, martyrdom, torment.* The words (and the phrases in which they automatically circulate) work mostly at the level of conditioned reflexes, in order to inhibit distraction: the listener should then listen not to the words of the song but, rather, to the states of mind the words name. Right from the start you know that this is a secure place, it is OK: you have entered a self-sufficient and ephemeral universe of excess and loss of control; you are listening to a romantic song, that compensation for conventionality, that lovers' mandate. . . . In 1905 the young lady who has come of age hears the song '*Guarda esa flor*' ['Keep that Flower'], and feels that the marriage crowning her life has been blessed in heaven.

3. It makes no sense to separate the words from the music in popular song. To do so, even in the archetypical case of Agustín Lara, is to misunderstand the form. From a strictly literary point of view, the words are usually poor and repetitive (quality is the exception), but literary persuasion depends here on the affective power of a phrase or melody, and the alliance between music (memorable because rememberable), words (which, to the popular ear, must sound 'poetic'), the singer's voice (saccharine sweet, very original, or in possession of the prefabricated vigour of tenors of 180 decibels) and instrumental eloquence (the guitar, for example, transmits an integral enveloping atmosphere). The social pact: you listen to me with devotion, and I will change your state of mind. The romantic song vulgarizes the music of the elites, supplying the sensitivity that a reader's education or everyday life may deny them. Its job is to express (and forge) the emotions that listeners do not have the time to imagine for themselves. I will never forget you . . . and the listener is submerged in a 'land of fantasies' – not those of his or her particular life, but an amorous Utopia that is their ideal autobiography. And the symbolic exercise reanimates passions atrophied by the lack of addressee or the excess of married life. The song redraws the features of the girlfriend, lover, wife, to offer up enraptured fated faces (in the case of women, would it be correct to talk of self-idealization?).

4. The function of the romantic song is to disseminate poetic discoveries. The

result is the 'poetic' overvaluation of everyday life. This is related to a specific cultural movement. With the appearance of the poetic avant-garde (López Velarde, Tablada, Pellicer, Novo, the avant-garde *Estridentistas*) the fate of softly rhyming, ostensibly musical, poetry is sealed. It does not lose its public, but from the beginning of the 1930s it ceases to be cultivated as an important poetic activity. A minority reserves for itself a new innovative language, while bolero writers and singers take control of the word and – by imitating Rubén Darío or Amado Nervo – endow literature and intimacy with classical pretensions, abandon, a constitutive lack of self-criticism that presents itself as absolute sincerity. Whosoever listens to this poetry, and is moved, is a poet of sorts, and yearns for the shiver provided by allegory.

I needed to see you real close

The romantic song stands in for a refinement that social development has failed to distribute, and is at the origins of that amorous game which the majority cannot play for lack of personal ability, economic possibility and cultural resources. Be inspired, become ecstatic, be moved, let those tears flow, place yourself in the only alternative at your disposal: everyday unreality. Amid the poverty and overcrowding, the subjugation of women and the hatred of difference, genres of popular music emerge that describe forms of care, tenderness and languor that – generally – exist only in the realm of song. But in what other popular place, outside of song, could someone say '*Blanco diván de tul aguardará/tu exquisito abandono de mujer*' ['White tulle divan awaits/Your exquisite womanly abandon']? In fact, patriarchal authoritarianism cedes only very slowly; in romantic fantasy, selfless and attentive love takes control of the scene to offer sweetness, devotion and understanding.

When is the difference between romantic song and homely intimacy clearly perceived? During the 1920s it is repeated, both here and abroad: at last, Mexico is no longer the land of bandits, the lair of Pancho Villa and his barbaric gunmen; so if nationalism is inevitable, at least refine the models, and teach the village male to court and the woman to feel that she is territory to be conquered. The songs are the logical continuity of elitist high poetry, and of the formalities of the salons of the *porfirista* elites. As the practitioners of rhyming verse dwindle, song begins to disseminate poetry massively in domains where the spectre of affectation ('cursi') is hardly insinuated, or even nonexistent: to fear happiness as the songbirds offer you their trill as song; perfumed nectar becomes a need that cannot be postponed.

I am just a poor singer/But sing to you I must . . .

According to Jaime Rico Salazar – in his excellent *One Hundred Years of Boleros* [*Cien años de boleros*, Centro Editorial de Estudios Musicales, Bogotá 1988] – the bolero arrives in Mexico, via Havana, at the turn of the century, is 'nationalized' in 1919 with Armando Villarreal's '*Morena mía*' ['My Brown Girl'], and achieves its first classic in 1924 with '*Presentimiento*' ['Premonition'], with music by Emilio Pacheco and words by the Spanish novelist and poet Pedro Mata: '*El día en que cruzaste por mi camino,/tuve el presentimiento de algo fatal . . .*' ['The day you crossed my path,/I had the premonition that something fatal would occur . . .']. Next, two bolero institutions or legends emerge: Agustín Lara and Agustín 'Guty' Cárdenas – whose '*Un rayito de sol*' ['Little Ray of Sun'] is released in 1926: '*Mi alma que vive errante y soñadora,/siguiendo en pos de una ilusión lejana,/quiere llegar a ti como la aurora,/como un rayo de sol por tu ventana.*' ['My errant, dreaming soul/Pursues a far-off hope,/It reaches out to you like dawn,/Like a ray of sun through your window.']. Guty dies young, murdered in a stupid bar-room brawl, his repertoire enshrining a cult of bohemian life, celebrating inspiration, traditional poetry, respectful courtship and a passion that is extinguished on kneeling at the altar.

In the post-Revolutionary context of the state of Yucatán, characterized by intense class conflict and political radicalization, Guty Cárdenas and Ricardo Palmerín are the direct consequence of a musical and literary culture that was very closely linked to Havana, but nevertheless in need – because of its relative national isolation – of a bit of spiritual excess. However, women are recognized and evoked in different ways in the state capital of Mérida as they become a little more publicly visible; and, in contrast to poets in the rest of Mexico at the turn of the century, poets in Mérida turn away from the audacities of 'modernismo'. There is no experimentation – nor could the equivalent of stylists like Manuel Gutiérrez Nájera or Manuel José Othón emerge there. On the contrary, the poets of Yucatán want nothing more than to be fine neoclassicists, and its singers of boleros to imbue the people with 'inspiration', the quintessential element of this culture and sensibility (which, in the poets Ricardo López Méndez, Antonio Médiz Bolio and Luis Rosado Vega, found admirable representatives). Who, outside such a context of adoration for words, could have written Médiz Bolio's words for Guty's '*Caminantes del Mayab*' ['Mayab Travellers']:

> Caminante, caminante . . .
> que vas por los caminos,
> por los viejos caminos del Mayab.

Que ves arder de tarde
las alas del Xtacay,
que ves brillar de noche
los ojos del Cocay?

[Traveller, traveller . . ./Of the roads, the old roads of Mayab./In the evening,/You watch the Wings of Xtacay burn/At night,/You watch the eyes of Cocay shine.]

Agustín Lara: only once

During the first stage of his career, Lara was the alternative face of conventional sentimentalism, the brothel pianist on whose face an angry prostitute left the mark – a scar – of vice. He is the romantic or 'modernista' poet who worships marginalized women, the apostle of the 'audacious metaphor' that opens the way for his everyday staging of love (from this point of view, schmaltz ['lo cursi'] is in fact the realist language of the supreme fiction of falling in love). Priests, convinced of his transgression of family values, condemn Lara from their pulpits, and those who think they represent public morality (usually lawyers) make him the object of their complaints – which, however, only make him more famous. For some, Lara is simply the intoner of the weaknesses of the flesh, the apostle of verbosity. For others, he is the dissipated and naturally ephemeral symbol who retires only when the working population of Mexico sets off to work and the more devout go to Church. The composer Carlos Cháves ridicules him in friendly fashion as the bearer of the sentimental message of backwardness, but he is also admired because right from the start his melody and poetry express a transitional sensibility, between the Porfirian mentalité and the 'moral relativism' of post-Revolution. Lara is 'modernismo' for the masses, 'aristocratic' pleasures taken from the image of the closest memory, the apotheosis of what is 'prohibited' and 'desired' in everyday life, as is so well expressed in his classic 'Noche de ronda' ['Night Games']:

Luna que se quiebra sobre la tiniebla
de mi soledad.
¿A dónde va?
Dime si esta noche tu te vas de ronda
como ella se fue
¿Con quién está?
Dile que la quiero, dile que me muero
de tanto esperar

que vuelva ya.
Que las rondas no son buenas,
que hacen daño, que dan penas,
y se acaba por llorar . . .

[A moon that breaks on the mist/Of my loneliness./Where is she going?/Tell
me if you are going/Going to work/As she did before./Who is she with?/Tell
her I love her, that I'm dying/From waiting,/ Tell her to return./Because the
game is no good,/It brings only hurt and pain,/It makes you cry . . .]

Basically, at the beginning of Lara's career, the public wants to balance his con-
servatism with his inclination for 'the romantic'. In his book on Agustín Lara,
David Castañeda reveals the results of a poll taken in 1935 on Lara's best songs,
which are:

'Granada'	1992 votes
'Farolito'	1762
'Mujer'	1098
'Rival'	792
'Rosa'	724
'Enamorada'	576
'Marimba'	443
'Bermellón'	391
'Arráncame la vida'	376
'Murcia'	344
'Oración Caribe'	335

(From D. Castañeda, *Balance de Agustín Lara*, Mexico City 1940)

'*Granada*', the big test for old-fashioned singers, is his most popular song. This
has a lot to do with the resistances of a sensibility that refuses to be displaced,
and for a still – in 1935 – very strong taste for the openly operatic.

Lara's talent is enormous, but his fame really emerges from the fits and starts
with which a modern sensibility transforms traditional sensibility; for he dominates an epoch in which the electronic media (radio, records and film)
complement, rather than contradict, the typically pre-modern extolling of love
as fiery rapture and unfulfilled possession. This is why Lara's repertoire, the
central pillar of the new culture industry, becomes part of the most cherished of
national traditions. In all the above songs, as well as innumerable others, traditional sensibility knows that it is different because it promotes technology.

During the 1930s, Lara has no rivals as a star. The taste for the romantic passes through him, because he defines that wild universe that knows no verbal frontiers, the logic of delirium. His most immediate public belongs to the urban bohemian nightlife, but his most faithful listeners will be the middle class, families anxious for that which combines lyrical elegance with *surrender* (the need to fall in love), for the evocation of the times in which the addressee fell in love (nostalgia for experiences that have not been shared), and the possibility to make use of well-worn schemes in the romance to come. He represents Decency Personified: housewives newly glued to the radio, lawyers whose literary intentions have been lost in the law courts or among the files, bureaucrats who refuse to renounce the idea of freedom outside marriage and work, ladies who put the songs to work as background to their hopes for forbidden loves, youngsters who fall in love with the idea of falling in love! Lara becomes indispensable, and his public, on listening to his songs, endow the sexual event itself, and the process of dating, seduction, engagement, marriage, adultery and divorce, with a vaguely religious spirituality. '*Yo que tuve tus ojos,/y tus manos, y tu boca,/y la blanca tibieza que derramaste en mí . . .*' [I who had your eyes,/Your hands and lips,/And the white warmth that flowed in me . . .].

The last laugh of the cumbancha

Was Lara the writer of the words to his songs, the only one responsible for their magnificent – and much-celebrated – discoveries:

> El hastío es pavorreal que se aburre de luz en la tarde
> es tu pie diminuto como un alfiletero
> Son las redes de plata un encaje tan sutil
> Mujer, mujer divina,
> Tienes el veneno que fascina en tu mirada,
> Escondí, concha nácar mis penas en tí
> Noche que se desmaya sobre la arena,
> Mientras canta la playa su inútil pena
> Azul, como un ojera de mujer
> Rival de mi cariño el viento que te besa.

[Tedium, a peacock bored in the light of the afternoon sun/Your foot as tiny as a pincushion/Subtle silver lace./Woman, divine woman,/the poison that fascinates is in your gaze/In thee, mother-of-pearl shell, my sorrows I hide/Nightfall faints in the sand./as the beach sings its useless sorrow/Blue as a woman's eyes/The rival of my love, the breeze, kisses you.]

It is not clear whether Lara or – as has often been suggested – Chamaco Sandoval (a bohemian devastated by drink in search of inspiration) was actually the real songwriter. What is very clear, however, is an effective use of anachronism. The influence of romantic and 'modernista' poets such as Gutiérrez Nájera, Díaz Mirón, Amado Nervo, Rubén Darío and Leopoldo Lugones is very apparent in Lara's writing, all adapted to his need to bring words and music together, and brought to life by an unforgettable metaphor. The phrases that dazzle and entrance spring forth: '*Y en tus ojeras se ven las palmeras borrachas de sol*' [And in your eyes the palm trees can be seen, drunk with sun.]!

How would whores, pimps and drunks read lines such as these:

> Sueño con la paz de tus ojeras
> hechas con violetas de maldad
> y deja que se duermen mis quimeras
> en tu franciscana soledad.
> Yo quiero beber en tus mejillas
> tu febricitante palidez
> Y he de sorprender en tus pupilas
> todo el secreto de tu languidez.

[I dream of the peace in your eyes/Made from evil violets/And let my dreams sleep/In your Franciscan solitude./I want to drink the pallor/From your cheeks/And surprise in your eyes/The secrets of your languor]?

As important, no doubt, because the words (and the unforgettable melodies) unravel and exhibit our own sense of self-importance.

Different dawns, identical passions

Lara sings to the prostitute ('Make your love expensive . . .'), enthrones women, and makes metaphor the centre of all spirituality ('the poison that fascinates is in your gaze'). He is the height of fashion, even 'sinful'. Everything about him, for a time, is meaningful. Why, for example, does his celebration of the prostitute carry so much resonance? For its audacity, especially at a time when other composers of talent are still paying homage to a long-lost world: the farm, the harvest, typical clothes, the village no one leaves, spiritual innocence. The fervour that once canonized the bride, Lara now focuses on those women who could not even be named, and deposits it at their feet. The horror felt is acute, but not very deep: from his song '*Imposible*' ['Impossible') on, the resonance of his messages to sex workers is enormous. What is the point of condemnation when the nation as a whole has become mythologically entranced by 'women of easy virtue'? While threats of excommunication multiply, many reach for the guitar and melancholically intone:

> Vende caro tu amor, aventurera,
> da el precio del dolor a tu pasado,
> y aquel que de tus labios la miel quiera
> que pague con brillantes tu pecado.

[Make your love expensive, adventuress,/Charge for the pains of your past,/And he who wants the honey from your lips/Let him pay for your sin with jewels.]

Lara wants to be not only the author of his songs but also the composer who lives what he composes, the embodiment of the endless rapture that seduces the beautiful film star María Félix, absolutely faithful to the inspiration provided by absinthe and marijuana, and to schmaltz as the realist language of that supreme fiction of being in love. He projects the following image of himself: bohemian, dissipated, at the disposal of the Muse twenty-four hours a day, deeply in love, marked by ugliness and redeemed by genius. The public imitate his voice, celebrate his relationships, worship his allegories. Once proscribed, Lara becomes the minstrel of the nation's soul.

As a poet, Agustín Lara (the name we shall give to whoever wrote the words to the songs) suddenly discovers the vast adjectival and metaphoric resources of a language. From the point of view of popular culture he constitutes an approximate summing-up of what happens when an isolated culture breaks out into the world. This is why so many of his songs are imprinted with the date when they were written, the product of an epoch when to utter a poem was considered a mystical act, and melodic composition a search for the soul. Lara genuinely felt that he was a visionary, an altar dedicated to the Eternal Woman – which explains the tumultuous crowds who surrounded the theatres in which his songs were sung.

Lara is not important only from a historical point of view. The identification of romantic song with 'bohemia' – that is, a group of poets, painters, sculptors, cartoonists, composers and semi-de luxe whores – culminates in him. He takes advantage of the reputation of bohemians, becomes one of them, and proclaims the truth of his sacred madness. In fact, this has little to do with a romantic bohemian cult of self-destruction. Rather, he is lucky enough to be taken as simultaneously a remnant and a prefiguration. On the one hand, he embodies for the public the two strands of Mexican romanticism, which first delights in marginality (the bohemian lifestyle), and second rejects the surrounding vulgarity (poetic sentiment); on the other, he expresses musical and literary tastes that are radically new in so far as they are communicated to a different public in a different way, and articulate the preferences of rapidly growing cities – the strategy of those who, without distancing themselves too much from a previous generation and their values, are nevertheless conscious of a new mode of life. In this context, Agustín Lara (man and work) represents the transition between a closed society to one characterized by fissures, infiltrations, zones of permissiveness. '*Perjura*' ['Swear'] caused a scandal in 1901 because it celebrated the existence of lovers and sex outside ecclesiastical law. Lara causes a scandal (less for what he says than for the memories he stirs) by worshipping a physical love that is performed under contract.

How could you fall in love with a prostitute? In other words, how do you channel a typically homely feeling, blessed by God, towards someone outside the family circle, towards a non-being like a whore? Lara takes up the impulse at the point where the naturalist novel and a formerly elitist poetry, which has now become popular, converge. The poets Antonio Plaza and Manuel Acuña dedicated their verses to the prostitute, and dignified her, in order to confront all the better a society that despised her. The novelists Federico Gamboa and Mariano Azuela show compassion as she is eaten away by illness and despised. Rubio, a character in Gamboa's novel *Santa* (1903), declares: 'There are no such things as moral categories between women, only social ones. They are all women!' As a reward for such brutal levelling, Gamboa endows Rubio with some lucidity: 'But he suddenly realized that the medicines sold by the brothel were useless, and that Santa couldn't scrape off the accumulated stains left by the caresses and kisses of others, not even with tireless lips of bronze.'

The real problem is revealed: jealousy, a man's right to exclusive possession. For reasons that are much deeper than just being a 'sinner', the prostitute is really condemned because it is in her nature to tolerate neither jealousy nor a single owner. The writer Richard Sennett has observed that central to the structures of belief determining nineteenth-century bourgeois sexuality was the fact that although desire was considered a matter of private sentiment, intimate feelings such as sex were still judged according to public criteria. This was the case in Mexico – so much so that no exceptions were admitted. In his novel *María Luisa* (1907), Mariano Azuela describes the agony of a woman forced into prostitution at the same time as he reinforces the condemnation of society at large:

Then a curtain opened, throwing her life into the shadows. Retrospective horror at sexual pleasure now racked her wasted body; shock at the prostitution brutally imposed by the laws of honourable people; her concentrated hatred for a life dedicated to selling her own body; and the alcohol, the blessed alcohol!, with which she was able to forget her miserable life.

It is easy to understand the unease Lara caused. Equally distant from both artistic suffering and religious obligation, he purloins vocabulary from poets like Darío, Díaz Mirón and Santos Chocano; he frees love from the cloisters of the petty bourgeoisie; he exhibits a melodic sense that vulgarizes the discoveries of elitist music; he takes advantage of the changes in morality and, having put all jealousy to one side, falls idealistically in love with harlots. The poet Ramón López Velarde may be even more audacious – he was certainly a genius – but he had no musical accompaniment. In 1926 Lara sings '*Imposible*' ['Impossible'] in public for the first time:

> Yo sé que es imposible que me quieras,
> que tu amor para mí fue pasajero,
> y que cambias tus besos por dinero,
> envenando así mi corazón.
>
> No creas que tus infamias de perjura
> incitan mi rencor para olvidarte,
> te quiero mucho más en vez de odiarte
> y tu castigo se lo dejo a Dios.

[I know it is impossible for you to love me,/That your love for me was only fleeting,/And that you exchange kisses for money,/Poisoning my heart./Do not ever think that your blasphemous acts/Incite me to forget you in anger,/I only love, not hate, you more/Your punishment I leave to God.]

All this should not be taken too seriously, but it should not be minimized either. In the 1920s and 1930s, feelings escape the confines of the home. Patriarchy may not be questioned, but the lessons of the Revolution, the pleasurable promiscuity of soldiers and *soldaderas*, the appearance of tens of thousands of unmarried mothers, the explosion in the number of female factory workers, the massification of prostitution as a labour market, the new views on poverty in the capital city and the growing hatred of strict moral codes, all determine a new sentimentalism that is now supported by film and song. With the declining influence of the theatre, cinema offers up stars, close-ups, styles and modes of behaviour for worship; while song yields memorable phrases and moods. Cinema's influence is speedy. Song, meanwhile, takes root in collective memory.

The new song is made possible by the concessions forced on a family-centred morality, the expansion of Mexico City and the irruption of the mercantile, cultural and advertising potentials of new technology. Radio produces a revolution of its own in questions of taste, and complements the force of moving images by preserving, and repeating, newly discovered emotions. In 1930, RCA Victor and XEW come to Mexico. The demand from a newly emergent visible – and invisible – public for romantic song – women – meant that recording abroad was no longer an option; it had to be immediate, here and now.

Almost single-handedly Lara – and there is ample proof of this – put an end to the invasion of foreign rhythms, limiting even the influence of the tango, and creating a public for Mexican composers. Compulsively, he sings to women and tells them – without actually saying so – that he is not really a composer but a lover. Thanks to both Lara and the Yucatán songsters, romantic song became the form through which the family could continue to be affirmed while still being – because of the resistance of the most traditional sectors – not totally orthodox. The abstract adoration that the close-up in cinema takes to sacred ecstasy culminates in Lara.

The spell: melody turns its back on literary and musical soirées, while the words underline the fact that only the sensual matters. Lara will sing a variety of songs during his career, paying equal tribute to Hispanism as to adventuresses, and fomenting the mirage of a 'Mexican song' whose sincerity made it different from the rest. Lara, the star, courted schmaltz ('cursilería') to the extent where he would get all dressed up to sing to the Virgin of Guadalupe. His poetry would never, however, surpass his admirable parodies of 'modernismo' (he once referred to his mother's hair along the following lines: 'little ball of tenderness where yonder curl breaks'). Together with José Alfredo Jiménez, he constitutes the limits of romantic song. No one will ever go so far to abolish the distinction between artistic creation and the most intimate of revelations.

Bolero's first dawn

Urban growth, assimilating and extending the lessons of the Revolution (nothing is a better teacher of relativism than proximity to death), produces unthought-of freedoms in a society where rapid secularization is difficult to check. To which must be added: the still-dominant esteem for all that is 'poetic' (who, who is anyone, isn't romantic?), the development of the record and radio industries, the expansion of nightlife, that taste for cabarets and brothels (homes from home). The composers who make it after Lara no longer want to be famous personalities, to embody the frenzy of their song. They are, rather, the new professionals of Mexico, Cuba, Puerto Rico, Columbia, Venezuela and Argentina, and their names are: Oswaldo Farrés, Pedro Flores, Rafael Hernández, Consuelo Velázquez, Gabriel Ruiz, Gonzalo Curiel, Orlando de la Rosa, Abel and Alberto Domínguez, Myrta Silva, Mario Ruiz Armengol, Emma Elena Valdelamar, Juan Bruno Tarraza, Isolina Carrillo. The new creators of taste – to the accompaniment of 'great orchestras' – eliminate all pretensions of spirituality from the bolero while making it evoke 'decent' seduction, the libidinal and sentimental atmosphere of the poorest suburbs.

The genre demands voices that can adapt to different moods. Tenors who want to make each song a vocal *tour de force*, like Tito Schippa, Alfonso Ortiz Tirado and the Columbian José Carlos Ramírez, begin to lose ground: Oh! Let the walls of indifference fall! Encourage the ecstasy of listeners for whom melodic harmony is Pretty! Their place is taken by voices in which personal style (the projection of a burning desire that borders on delirium) is everything, whether it be melancholy, happiness, or sexy exuberance. In two decades, all of the following become well-known: Toña la Negra, Elvira Ríos, María Luisa Landín, Beny Moré, Ana María González, Lupita Palomera, Fernando Fernández, Bienvenido Granda, Celio González, Avelina Landín. They are the torch singers, indifferent to vocal prowess but set on squeezing a meaning from each song. They create the new – sexy, strident, instrumental – voice of the Latin American populace, and the fact that they do not as yet depend entirely on the market allows them to sustain a desire for originality.

The bolero reaches its peak in Latin America between 1930 and 1960. There is, in the main, only one repertoire, and Havana, Mexico City, Quito, Monterrey, Caracas, Bogotá, Guatemala City, the Spanish-speaking neighbourhoods of the United States, all listen to '*Nosotros*' ['We'] by Pedro Junco, '*Besar*' ['To Kiss'] by Juan Bruno Terraza, '*Bésame mucho*' ['Kiss Me Often'] by Consuelo Velázquez, '*Vereda Tropical*' ['Tropical Path'] by Gonzalo Curiel, '*Nocturnal*' by José Sabre Marroquín, '*Amor, amor, amor*' ['Love, Love, Love'] by Gabriel Ruiz, '*Dos gardinias*' ['Two Gardenias'] by Isolina Carrillo, and '*Perdón*' ['Sorry'] by Pedro Flores.

Your kisses, born here on my mouth

Towards the end of the 1940s, the Los Panchos Trio (the Mexicans Chucho Navarro and Alfredo 'el Güero' Gil, and the Puerto Rican Hernando Avilés) impose a fashion that will last a decade and more. There are a number of trios specializing in 'folkloric' and ranchera music, but Los Panchos bring something new – and thoroughly urban – to romantic song: a love celebrated in markets, streets and cabarets. They make it big because of their virtuoso guitar playing, the semblance of being a moving serenade. And their success is enormous. For example, between 1948 and 1949 The America Trio, The Ascencio Trio, The Avileño Trio, The Calaveras Trio, The Cantarrecio Trio, The Durango Trio, The Guadalajara Trio, The Samperiro Brothers Trio, The Janitzio Trio, the Los Caporales Trio, The Captains Trio, the Los Compadres Trio, the Los Costeños Trio, The Aguilillas Trio, The Mixteco Trio, The Moreno Trio, The Northeners Trio, the Los Cuervos Trio, the Los Gavilanes Trio, The Tamaulipan Trio, the Los Mexicanos Trio, the Los Norteños Trio, The Urquiza Trio, all appear in nativist films, singing about the values of rural Mexico. Then, in 1948, the Los Panchos make their first film, *En cada puerto un amor* ['A Love in Every Port'], a cabaret melodrama directed by Ernesto Cortázar.

An avalanche of films follows. If in 1948 The Calaveras Trio make ten films, Los Panchos make sixteen: *El gran campeón* ['The Great Champion'], *No me quieras tanto* ['Don't Love Me So Much'], *Rayito de luna* ['Little Moonbeam'], *El sol sale para todos* ['The Sun Shines for Everyone'], *Cuando el alba llegue* ['When Dawn Comes'], *La Negra Angustias* ['Black Angustias'], *Un milagro de amor* ['A Miracle Of Love'], *Hipócrita* ['Hypocrite'], *Callejera* ['Woman of the Street'], *Una gallega en México* ['A Spanish Lady Comes to Mexico'], *Mujeres en mi vida* ['Women in My Life'], *Yo quiero ser mala* ['Bad Woman'], *Amor de la calle* ['Street Love'], *Perdida* ['Doomed'], *Aventurera* ['Adventuress'], *Si fuera una cualquiera* ['If I Were A Tramp']. The plots and meanings of the films are apparent in their titles, as is the order of the Los Panchos Trio's songs. This is a time when Nightlife almost becomes a citizens' duty, and Los Panchos are an essential part of the traffic that links cabarets, brothels and streets to legendary tales of fleeting love. They sing '*Rayito de luna*' ['Little Moonbeam'], '*Ay amor ya no me quieras tanto*' ['Love! Don't Love Me So Much'], '*Contigo*' ['With You'], '*Amor de la calle*' ['Street Love'], '*Hipócrita*' ['Hypocrite'], '*Callejera*' ['Woman of the Street'] and '*Perdida*' ['Doomed'], and their harmonies provide the background for the sinful stroll that is the preamble to tragedy.

If the Los Panchos Trio never make as many films as in 1949 again, as far as concerts and radio are concerned they monopolize the scene, opening up the way for such romantic trios as The Three Diamonds, The Three Aces, The Three Gentlemen, Los Tecolines (who are four), Johnny Albino's The San Juan Trio, Los Dandys, Los Jaibos: trios that massify the bolero, opening up its legendary cabaret *imaginaire* to tortured young love and the family. The Diamonds sing:

> *Usted es la culpable de todas mis angustias/de todos mis pesares.* [You are to blame for all my anguish/All my sorrows.]

Almost at the same time, what becomes known as *filin* (or 'feeling') appears in Havana, associated with composers like José Antonio Méndez and César Portillo de la Luz, and the singers Olga Guillot, Elena Burke and La Lupe. *Filin* uses elements of jazz, while essentializing sentimentalism (the equivalent to *filin* in Mexico is María Victoria), and extends the melody of the bolero, underlining its condition as hymn. José Antonio Méndez sings:

> Eres mi bien,
> lo que me tiene extasiado.
> ¿Por qué negar que estoy de ti enamorado?
> De tu dulce alma
> que es todo sentimiento.

[You are my love,/That keeps me in ecstasy./Why should I deny that I love you/Your sweet soul/That is all feeling.]

The great period of Latin American romantic song, forged by the lived correspondences between public, composers and singers, culminates with the trios, *filin*, the composers from both brothels and conservatories, and the singers from the poor districts. Everything coincides: the maturity of the composers, the personalities of the singers, the malice and credulity of the listeners, the balance between a histrionic passion and the cynicism of a weakening *machismo*, the definitive images of film, the quality of the orchestras, the heyday of the trios. And in Mexico, social and political stability imposes the enjoyment of everyday life. Since we can't do politics any more, let's listen to radio, sing *a cappella*, go to variety shows, love each other until we can't do it any more.

Film concedes its big emotions to bolero, which becomes crucial in the foregrounding of urban scenarios. Pedro Vargas sings 'Adventuress' while Ninón Sevilla dances (in *Aventurera*); Pedro Infante sings while Blanca Estela Pavón whistles '*Amorcito corazón*' ['Little Love Heart'] in *Nosotros los pobres* ['We the Poor']; Ana María González celebrates the promiscuity of '*Cada noche un amor*' ['A Love Every Night'] while Andre Palma and Pedro Armendáriz dance cheek to cheek (in *Distinto amanecer* ['Another Daybreak']); Tin Tan dances and sings

'With You' as Silvia Pinal listens (in *El rey del barrio* ['King of the Neighbourhood']). Songs fix emotion to the cityscapes that films evoke, as well as providing all too faithful descriptions of tastes and beliefs.

Those who participate in the life that links the growing city to the bolero endow it with mythical qualities. But in the 1940s and 1950s bolero is not an identity nor an alternative culture, only a shared taste that takes root in obsession and, more than anything else, the bridge over which couples make their way to becoming families, and loners provide themselves with company while out on the town.

The consecration of radio

Technology is fundamental to this process. The film, record and radio industries provide songs with landscapes that last. And radio, that most persuasive of media, chooses the voices and styles to be privileged, especially from 1930 onwards, after the establishment of the XEW radio station empire – the voice of Latin America from Mexico – which forges a city-wide taste that will become national. XEW displaces the orator in favour of the announcer, provides uneducated voices with opportunities, discreetly relegates sopranos and tenors and promotes the poor margins of the city [*arrabal*] – the most popular myth of the 1940s.

The needs of radio – songs to order – produce great changes at the levels of format and rhythm of production. They also focus attention on an emerging sector that is crystallizing into an archetype: the housewife, she who possesses the ability to distract and alleviate domestic slavery in modest little homes with growing families. Women listen enraptured to the idolatries that are dedicated to them, full to the brim with *macho* recommendations:

> No le debes tú nunca decir a una mujer
> lo que quieres.
> Pues es muy difícil comprender
> el corazón de las mujeres.
> Y por más que tu amor se desespere
> no se debe asomar porque se muere.
> Si le tienes tú veneración a una mujer
> no se lo digas.
> Y jamás le formes un altar con tu querer
> porque te olvida.
> Mientras más vea que la desprecias,

más te querrá,
y nunca ya te olvidará.

[You should never tell a woman/What you want./Because it is difficult to
understand/The heart of a woman./No matter how desperate your love/Do
not even try, you might die./If you worship a woman/Don't tell her. Don't
make an altar of your love/Because she will forget you./The more she sees that
you despise her/The more she will love you,/And never forget you.]

The last great teachings addressed to women found their refuge in romantic
song. According to Mario Clavel's 'Una mujer' ['A Woman']: 'Una mujer debe
ser/soñadora, coqueta y ardiente;/debe darse al amor/con frenético ardor/para ser una
mujer' ['A woman should be/A dreamer, hot and coquettish;/Give herself over to
love/With frenetic ardour/To be a woman']. Nevertheless – and despite the
clearly masculinist orientation of romantic song, mediated by the myth of the
Housewife – women become its principal audience.

Isolated, relegated and without a lot of choice, hundreds of thousands of
women and young girls suddenly become part of the market – without any help
from the patriarchs. Only slightly free from the yoke, this desiring multitude –
one body, one desire – greatly increases the number of units of feeling and emotion on the market . . . and they buy records. In the nineteenth century women
read novels between sighs, read poetry and sob, go to the theatre and dominate
the techniques of melodrama. Now they hold on to song, resisting its more intimate connotations and proving that as far as the theatricalization of feelings is
concerned, romantic song is no longer the exclusive preserve of men.

The model for such behaviour inevitably comes from the USA, with the
first boom of the record industry. Records retain the 'magic moment', the privileged voices and melodies that first dissolve and then reconfigure the audience.
And here the influence of women is enormous, making of the Housewife an
instrument that tames. Thanks to her it is understood that romantic song will
never damage social institutions: note, for example, the enthusiasm for the virility of charro singers of rancheras, who, in song, transform nationality into an
erotic gift.

In national film and romantic song, what matters is the seriousness of the
attempt, the truthfulness of affection and disaffection, the way in which those
involved discover how the words they find to express their feelings are, more
often than not, the feelings themselves. The desertion of traditional morality
takes place without contradiction, and with all due respect for institutions. It is
no longer possible to carry on living as before; faith in the redemptive quality of

poetry has been lost, and the melodrama of 1908 is very different – appearances to the contrary – from the melodrama of 1934.

A fundamental aspect of romantic song is revealed by the fact that it is listened to either on radios in bleak rented rooms or down at the local cinema, or sung out loud in the neighbourhood, or in one's memory in a smoky cabaret: once its literary ties have been broken, the bolero takes charge of melodrama. It is no longer elegies to lost and found love that are heard, but hidden dark plots, the perfect lover purified by his serenade, the wretch who glorifies the accessible rather than the sublime, the adolescent who chooses love from among all the other possibilities on offer, the mature woman who yearns for the happiness of the afternoon when she heard that tune for the first time, the drunk possessed by an impossible lucidity provided (like a rose) by desperation.

Intuition, premonition, palpitations, heartbeats. The great theatre of the world is compressed into three musical minutes, the (so pre-technological) spontaneity of old evaporates, and a street (and homely) theatricality takes charge. Song adds psychological credibility to cabaret, and through the medium of jukeboxes, collectivities gathered in bars and cafés hear songs that make intimate history a public concern – the autobiography of everyone and no one.

If feelings were once explored, now that singers have become the star actors in the emotions of others, they are signed and co-signed by a witness. Night and day, voices – and their musical accompaniment – have become the background to new ways of belonging to the twentieth century. All these emotions discover their thoroughly mass-urban contents through romantic song, in melodramatic gestures that modify a tradition which dates from nineteenth-century Spanish theatre and silent cinema, and no longer obeys the rules of poetry. What composers, musicians and interpreters want is to set the audience's feelings free, abolish the frontiers between reality and theatricality, translate the consciousness of an epoch into the idea of a secret film in which everyone takes the leading role.

In the transition from a society that is proudly closed to a mass society, melodrama emerges as a new foundation, thanks to an operation classically described by Lionel Trilling in his analysis of the relationship between 'sincerity' and 'authenticity'. If, he maintained, sincerity has lost its importance, if the word itself sounds empty and without meaning, this is due to one fact: the ego is no longer referred to as an end but as a means. The term 'authenticity' suggests at one and the same time the deficiencies of 'sincerity', as well as pointing towards the moral demands on the experiences of the ego. In this light, romantic song is the solemn celebration of such contradictions, favouring 'sincerity' over 'authenticity'. Woman are celebrated in a society that oppresses and belittles them;

extreme emotions that cannot actually exist in practice are ennobled; a traditionally poetic vocabulary is maintained in a context in which traditions come and go; the total dominance of men is ratified in spaces in which the participation of active women is on the rise. And even this does not change with the cynical turn in romantic song.

Rock and bolero

Elvis Presley sings 'Don't be Cruel' or 'Hound Dog' or 'Heartbreak Hotel' or 'Blue Suede Shoes' or 'Jailhouse Rock', and teenagers watch the generation gap emerge and widen. Ever since Bill Haley and His Comets sang 'Rock Around the Clock' in Richard Lester's film *The Blackboard Jungle* (mysteriously renamed 'Seeds of Evil' in Mexico), transforming black rhythm and blues into white rock and roll, the latter has been central to 'youth culture' (a mass phenomenon, a myth, and an industrial product). If the great black singers like Chuck Berry, Fats Domino and Little Richard became very popular, it was Elvis Presley, a white singer, who, assimilating the rhythms of the ghettos, makes of them a worldwide phenomenon. The first characteristic of this new international form to note is that it speaks in English – not because the young Argentines, Indians, Mexicans and Italians who have made rock music their own understand it to perfection, but because Americanization is the only culture with global pretensions whose weight exceeds even the brutal fact of colonialism.

The Beatles consolidate the rock–youth couplet, making one of its great gifts all the more apparent: the predominance of sensation over feeling. While the decibels resound, the 'romantic' aspects of song are subjected to literary experimentation, and schmaltz – which does exist – is smuggled in, protected by more prestigious influences: Dylan Thomas in Bob Dylan and Lewis Carroll in The Beatles. The complicated lyrics express a new culture that mixes drugs, sex, social conflict, political struggle and modern poetry.

The rock phenomenon brings the limitations of commercial music in Latin America to the fore. Anglo-Saxon rock music both follows and transforms the mood of the public, redeeming commonplaces with ironic fervour and musical violence. The Mexican record industry during the 1960s, in contrast, refuses to bring itself up to date, nor does it promote experimentation or words to songs that describe the contemporary scene – this is the function of marginalized bands like Three Souls on My Mind. And the spaces in which the public were able to demand of singers and composers a serious translation of their desires into music and song disappear. So, if rock is modern by antonomasia, and if its existence is so precarious in Mexico, we'll have to be modern through the back door.

Weakened, and now lacking the prestigious stamp of modernity, the bolero finds refuge in the taste of those who, for whatever reasons, are still set on nostalgia and a love that is completely intelligible. In this, they are guided by the talents of composers from another generation, among them Alvaro Carrillo, Roberto Cantoral and Armando Manzanero. Carrillo and Cantoral become well known at the end of the 1950s thanks to the rise of the trios. The Three Gentlemen sing '*La Barca*' ['The Boat'] and '*El Reloj*' ['The Watch'] by Cantoral; The Three Aces sing, '*Amor mío*' ['My Love'] by Carrillo. Cantoral's metaphors are completely over the top: '*Hoy mi playa se viste de amargura/porque tu barca tiene que partir/a cruzar otros mares de locura./Cuida que no naufrague tu vivir*' ['Today my shore is decked in sadness/Because your boat is about to leave/For other seas of madness./Beware of shipwreck . . .'], and a whole generation accompanies him in this farewell to poetry. Carrillo is simpler: '*Amor mío, tu rostro querido/no sabe guardar secretos de amor*' ['My love, your dear face/Knows not how to keep the secrets of love'].

Carrillo was a bohemian; he had been a singer in a brothel, and devoted himself each night to the task of seeking inspiration. One by one, each of his songs was a hit: '*Sabor a mí*' ['My Taste'], '*La Mentira*' ['The Lie'], '*Seguiré mi viaje*' ['I'll Go On'], '*Un poco más*'[A Little More']. It is this countercurrent of the 1950s that forgives bolero its sins, making it still a Latin American need. The contemporary desire for change is against it. For it: the radio, the initiation ceremonies of the popular classes, the difficulties of acquiring the commodities of modernity, the pleasures of evocation, and its status as psychological compensation in a context where what some call *Americanization* others call *liberation*. The fact that for a sector of the young urban middle class the bolero has become antiquated does not put a stop to the triumph of Armando Manzanero's extraordinary melodies and forced rhymes in 1967:

> No, porque ya no extraño como antes tu ausencia
> porque ya disfruto aun sin tu presencia
> ya no queda esencia del amor de ayer.

[No, because I no longer miss your absence as before/Because I still enjoy without your presence/The essence of yesterday's love has gone.]

What happens to those who are not among the hundreds of thousands who owe their reality principle to rock, or dance in the funky dives, or who did not go to the Avándaro rock festival, those desperate to understand the words rather than just feel the good vibrations? They remain in their own historical time, sharing moderately in the crazes of their peers, backing the causes they understand and, in a way, remember (because what isn't verbalized isn't lived). So, for example, hundreds of thousands of adolescent Mexicans, as distant from Janis Joplin as they are from Doña Ortiz de Domínguez, hang on to the 'glories of intimacy', and do not consider themselves marginal because they respond to their own traditions and, in the first and last instance, their own taste. Meanwhile, they become ultranationalists (what else can they do?) in a society that is ridding itself of its stubborn monolingualism. Indeed, many sectors resist Americanization with sentiment; and in such a colonized medium, the national successes of the 1970s – I am thinking of Rigo Tovar and Juan Gabriel on the one hand, and Menudo and Los Parchis on the other – constitute a real sociological and sexological phenomenon.

The bolero has not disappeared, and continues despite the mummified nostalgia of many fans, renewing itself in new contexts. The classics are still played and regularly rereleased, new generations are discovering Lara, Gabriel Ruiz or Alvaro Carrillo, and many narrators and poets use the techniques of the bolero. Cultural perception changes, rapture persists.

Yes, we all know: life is not like that, the meanings of clichés change, and to no one but the unemployed would it occur to live merely for the present. But if the romantic spirit is waning, the passion for the memory of passion remains. In kitchens, at sowing circles, during leisure time (when the television is turned off), in tired postcoital moments, to listen to one's idol is to go from the loss of innocence to the recapture of candour, from the loss of virginity to the reconstruction of the hymen. I may not be a virgin, but I'm still a young girl.

Eternal feelings are rekindled in modern society, and inextinguishable passions are re-educated: in a post-Freudian world, romantic song depends on the suspension of disbelief. I want to believe that I fall in love, I want to believe that thwarted in love I become furiously disenchanted, I want to believe that I am moved by this conjunction of drink and memory, I still want to believe that love is something much more than a means for the continuation of the Couple. The crisis of the family is the crisis of old public sentiment, and the perennial resurrection of the bolero testifies to change and permanence. A little more, and maybe later we'll understand each other.

A New Catechism
for Reluctant Indians

The Indian answered drily: 'No, Mr Priest, I don't like your catechism at all.'

The parish priest thought of informing the Inquisition immediately, but he was in a good mood that day and delayed.

'The catechism was not made to be liked or disliked by barbarous and stubborn Indians, but to teach the sacred commandments and precepts.'

'But not like that, Mr Priest, not with that question-and-answer routine which gives the impression that up in Heaven they think the Indians are more stupid than they really are. It's like a child's game: "Who made Heaven and Hell?" And everyone answers in chorus: "God made them." Wouldn't it be better the other way round? You say: "It was God", and we answer: "Who made the Indians, the Heavens, the fish and the rabbits?"'

'God is not here so that we can remake his doctrine, nor can he be worshipped back to front.'

But nothing could stop him. The Indian persisted in his whim, the parish priest informed whom he had to, the heretic disappeared in the dungeons, and because no one dared to mention him, nothing was heard of him again. But the priest remained perturbed; alone, he would murmur: 'It is the absence of everything.' And then he'd ask the appropriate question: 'What is nothingness?' Then he would reaffirm: 'It is the absence of everything in the sense of matter to work upon rather than an absence of power.' Then he'd ask himself: 'How can something come, even though it be nothing, from such an absence?' And he spent days and nights studying the catechism backwards.

Another priest who heard him became concerned, convinced that he was witness to a most heathen game. Since this priest was very wealthy, he summoned the relevant authorities and, once the back-to-front priest had disappeared, he took his place in the parish.

At least here the catechism was taught as it should have been.

INDEX